UN-AMERICAN

UN-AMERICAN

The Fake Patriotism of Donald J. Trump

John J. Pitney Jr.

ROWMAN & LITTLEFIELD
Lanham • Boulder • New York • London

Published by Rowman & Littlefield
An imprint of The Rowman & Littlefield Publishing Group, Inc.
4501 Forbes Boulevard, Suite 200, Lanham, Maryland 20706
www.rowman.com

6 Tinworth Street, London SE11 5AL

British Library Cataloguing in Publication Information Available

Library of Congress Cataloging-in-Publication Data

Names: Pitney, John J., Jr., 1955-.
Un-American: The fake patriotism of Donald J. Trump / John J. Pitney, Jr.
Lanham : Rowman & Littlefield Publishers, 2020. | Includes bibliographical references and index. | Summary: A scathing indictment of Donald Trump on the eve of the 2020 election. In this book, John J. Pitney Jr., one of America's most incisive conservative commentators, exposes a core irony of Trump's presidency: that a man who is quick to question the patriotism of his critics is himself deeply unpatriotic-- Provided by publisher.
Identifiers: LCCN 2019048493 (print) | LCCN 2019048494 (ebook) | ISBN 9781538129258 (cloth) | ISBN 9781538129265 (epub)
Subjects: LCSH: Trump, Donald, 1946- | Trump, Donald, 1946--Political and social views. | United States--Politics and government--2009-2017. | Presidents--United States--Biography.
Classification: LCC E913 .P58 2020 (print) | LCC E913 (ebook) | DDC 973.933092--dc23
LC record available at https://lccn.loc.gov/2019048493 | LC ebook record available at https://lccn.loc.gov/2019048494

CONTENTS

PREFACE

I spent most of my life as a Republican. As a teenager, I worked for the party by stuffing envelopes, ringing doorbells, and performing other mundane tasks of grassroots politics. On the morning of my 18th birthday, I made a special trip to the county seat to register as a Republican. Later, I spent seven years as a full-time staffer for Republican officials and organizations in Albany, New York, and Washington, DC. In the early 1990s, as I began to do more media commentary, I stopped active participation in party affairs, but I continued to vote for GOP candidates. Although I split my ticket from time to time, I voted for every Republican presidential nominee between 1976 and 2012. When Donald Trump clinched the nomination in 2016, however, I knew that the streak would end. Until the night of the election, I hoped that he would lose so that the party could close this sad, bizarre chapter. When he won, it was obvious that he would take the party with him. As he mounted the stage to claim victory, I took out my laptop and changed my registration to independent (or "no party preference" in California terminology).

Since that night, it has become evident that Trump represents something deeper and darker than a break with GOP traditions. He has broken our country's laws, repudiated its principles, and sided with its adversaries. He is, in a word, un-American. I wrote this book to explain how he has hurt the United States, and alas, how he provided me with new material every day.

I am hardly the first to break GOP ranks, and I am grateful to those who prepared the way in books, articles, and tweets: Max Boot, Amanda Carpenter, Mona Charen, George Conway, Mindy Finn, David French, David Frum, Reed Galen, Michael Gerson, Jonah Goldberg, Jennifer Horn, Bill Kristol, Mike Madrid, Liz Mair, Evan McMullin, Mike Murphy, Ana Navarro, Tom Nichols, Jay Nordlinger, Jennifer Rubin, Steve Schmidt, Stuart Stevens, Charles Sykes, John Weaver, Pete Wehner, George Will, and Rick Wilson—among many others.

In writing, I have benefited from comments by my friends Bill Connelly, John Gardner, Lloyd Green, and Jeremy Shane. They bear no responsibility for my views, and of course, any mistakes are mine alone. This book would not have been possible without the loving forbearance of my wife, Lisa. I thank my daughter, Hannah, and my son, JP, for their patience as I sat mumbling and grumbling at my computer screen.

I

TRUMP AND THE
AMERICAN TRADITION

The title of this book is deliberately provocative. At his rallies, Trump fondles the American flag as the loudspeakers blare "God Bless the USA." His slogans are "America First" and "Make America Great Again." How can anyone say that such a person opposes America? The answer is that Trump's display of patriotism is a reality show—not reality.

In 2019, Trump abused his power for his narrow self-interest, pressuring the government of Ukraine for information about his political opponents. It should have shocked Americans that an American president would seek foreign interference in our elections. But it was not Trump's first such betrayal. Consider what he said in July 2016: "I will tell you this—Russia, if you're listening, I hope you're able to find the 30,000 e-mails that are missing. I think you will probably be rewarded mightily by our press. Let's see if that happens."[1] This invitation was so remarkable that it caught the eye of FBI counterintelligence.[2] And on that very day, as the Special Counsel's office would reveal, the Russians made their first attempt to hack the servers used by Hillary Clinton's personal office.[3] In the words of the Mueller report: "The Russian intelligence service known as the Main Intelligence Directorate of the General Staff of the Russian Army (GRU) carried out these operations."[4]

Think about that: A candidate for president was asking a hostile foreign government to steal the private communications of a former secretary of state. Within hours, *its military* did as he had asked. We do not know, and may never know, whether the timing was coincidental or whether the Russian military was responding to Trump's request. Either way, that request was an act of disloyalty to the United States. Trump later claimed to his supporters that he was joking. That was a lie; he made the remark with a serious tone during a press conference. When reporter Katy Tur asked if he had any qualms about what he had just done, he snapped, "Nope, it gives me no pause."[5]

Then Trump failed to do the things that a patriot would do. In the summer of 2016, the FBI warned Trump that Russia and other foreign adversaries would try to infiltrate his campaign.[6] In an official joint statement on October 7, 2016, the Department of Homeland Security and Office of the Director of National Intelligence said that the Russian government had likely directed the hacking of American political figures and organizations. "These thefts and disclosures are intended to interfere with the US election process."[7] By this point, a candidate who loved this country would have ordered an internal review to see if the Russians had compromised the campaign. A loyal American would have denounced foreign interference and pledged to support the intelligence community's fight against it. Trump did no such things. To the contrary, the Mueller report found that the Trump campaign "expected it would benefit electorally from information stolen and released through Russian efforts."[8]

Trump denied knowledge of Russian involvement. "Maybe there is no hacking," he said shortly afterward in a televised debate. "But they always blame Russia. And the reason they blame Russia [is] because they think they're trying to tarnish me with Russia."[9] Trump went on: "I know nothing about Russia. I know—I know about Russia, but I know nothing about the inner workings of Russia. I don't deal there. I have no businesses there." That was another lie: on October 28, 2015, he had signed a letter of intent to proceed with negotiations for a Trump Tower in Moscow.[10] Those negotiations had continued well into 2016.[11] Love of country would have meant telling the truth about his dealings with a foreign adversary. Instead, he railed against leaks, and even after winning the presidency, he likened the intelligence community to Nazi Germany.[12]

On January 20, 2017, Trump put his hand on a Bible and swore to God "that I will faithfully execute the Office of President of the United States, and will to the best of my ability, preserve, protect and defend the Constitution of the United States." The Constitution sets out the wording of that oath, which is unique to the president: no other federal officials pledge that they will "faithfully execute" their offices. That oath imposes a duty of diligence.[13] If Trump had sworn in good faith, he would have made investigating the Russian attack on our country a top priority of his administration, and he would have rallied Congress and the people to support this effort. He did not. Eventually, the Justice Department did appoint a special counsel, and when Attorney General Jeff Sessions gave Trump the news, his reaction revealed what he cared about. According to the Mueller report, "the President slumped back in his chair and said, 'Oh my God. This is terrible. This is the end of my Presidency. I'm f---ed.' . . . Sessions recalled that the President said to him, 'you were supposed to protect me,' or words to that effect."[14] Trump did not mention the Russian threat to American democracy or his oath to protect the Constitution. He only talked about himself. In the months to come, Trump repeatedly obstructed the investigation, violating the "take care" clause of the Constitution. Among other actions, he fired the FBI director and tried to arrange for the firing of the special counsel, though a subordinate declined to carry out that order.

All the while, the Russians kept up the attack. According to the director of national intelligence, "we are seeing aggressive attempts to manipulate social media and to spread propaganda focused on hot-button issues that are intended to exacerbate socio-political divisions. . . . [T]hese actions are persistent, they are pervasive, and they are meant to undermine America's democracy on a daily basis, regardless of whether it is election time or not."[15] FBI Director Christopher Wray said in April 2019: "That is not just an election-cycle threat; it's pretty much a 365-days-a-year threat. And that has absolutely continued. We saw that, therefore, continue full speed in 2018, in the midterms."[16] Rather than reverse course, Trump kept insulting the intelligence community and praising Vladimir Putin. After the public release of the redacted report, he made a point of calling Putin. "We discussed it," Trump boasted to the press. "He actually sort of smiled when he said something to the effect that it started off as a mountain and it ended up being a mouse." When a reporter asked if he had told Putin to stop meddling in our elections, he said that she was rude. Finally, he acknowledged: "We didn't discuss that. Really, we didn't discuss it."[17]

Even worse, he invited the Russians to do it again. If foreigners offered information about your 2020 opponent to your campaign, George Stephanopoulos asked him in 2019, should they take it or call the FBI? When he said that he would want to hear it, Stephanopoulos followed up: "You want that kind of interference in our elections?" Trump said: "It's not an interference, they have information. I think I'd take it. If I thought there was something wrong, I'd go maybe to the FBI. . . . The FBI doesn't have enough agents to take care of it, but you go and talk honestly to congressmen, they all do it, they always have. And that's the way it is. It's called oppo research."[18] He later said that he would report foreign dirt to the FBI if it were "incorrect or badly stated."[19] Thus he would treat the FBI as a Collusion Product Safety Commission, making sure that foreign adversaries could provide only the most accurate, well-written reports on his opponents.

When the story of his Ukraine pressure became public, he not only rationalized his actions, he extended a similar request to yet another country: "And, by the way, likewise, China should start an investigation into the Bidens, because what happened in China is just about as bad as what happened with—with Ukraine."[20] Imitating his flimsy excuse for inviting Russian interference, his apologists claimed that he was just kidding. His demeanor, however, made clear that he was serious.

One could go on and on with related sins of omission and commission. Just as important, however, is that Trump is un-American in a broader sense. Even as he gaudily proclaims his love of country, he subverts nearly everything it stands for.

AMERICAN CREED

Trump is an American in the way that Tony Soprano was a Catholic. He gained the status at birth, proudly displays the identity, sometimes goes through the ritual motions, but utterly disregards the substance. Devotion to country is not about misleading slogans and empty gestures. Instead, it is about ideas and ideals, and the hope that this nation can serve as an example to the rest of the world. To find America's creed, we can look to the Founding documents and the words of its great public figures. The most important words are in the Declaration of Independence: "We hold these truths to be self-evident, that all men are created equal, that they are endowed by their Creator with certain unalienable Rights, that among these are Life, Liberty and the pursuit of Happiness."

The Founders and their heirs believed in truth—not mere opinions or propaganda, but objective reality available to all who would work to find it.[21] Trump rejects truth. He made thousands of false or misleading claims during his first two years in office.[22] He dismisses any facts he dislikes as "fake news," and he sends his minions out to subtract from the sum total of human knowledge. Right after the inauguration, Kellyanne Conway defended the White House press secretary's falsehoods about crowd size by saying he "gave alternative facts to that."[23] During an interview about the special counsel's investigation, his television lawyer Rudy Giuliani told Chuck Todd, "Truth isn't truth."[24]

As for the other key words of the Declaration, ponder what political scientist Harry Jaffa wrote: "Lincoln believed that moral treason consisted, above all, in denying the proposition that 'all men are created equal' or in denying that this was in fact the foundation of the American constitutional system."[25] In 2005, Trump told the *New York Times*: "When they came up with the wonderful statement, all men are created equal, never has there been a more false statement."[26] As we shall see later on, he has made the comment many times. In his other private and public utterances, he has encouraged all kinds of prejudice. And he has been walking the hateful walk since his earliest days in business, when he discriminated against African Americans in rental housing.

Trump's violations of civil rights bear a close connection to another aspect of his un-Americanism: his contempt for the rule of law. "What is the most sacred duty and the greatest source of our security in a Republic?" said Alexander Hamilton. "The answer would be: An inviolable respect for the Constitution and Laws—the first growing out of the last."[27] Trump could not grasp that sentiment. As a private citizen, he consorted with gangsters, exploited undocumented aliens, swindled customers, and cheated on his taxes—among many other things. As a candidate, he encouraged violence against protesters and bragged that he could get the military to follow illegal orders. As president, he undercut the rule of law in the United States and tried to corrode it overseas. As diplomat George Kent testified:

> I do not believe the U.S. should ask other countries to engage in politically associated investigations and prosecutions. . . . As a general principle, I don't think that as a matter of policy the U.S. should do that period, because I have spent much of my career trying to improve the rule of law. And in countries like Ukraine and Georgia, both of which want to join NATO, both of which have enjoyed billions of dollars of assistance from Congress, there is an outstanding issue about people in office in those countries using selectively politically motivated prosecutions to go after their opponents. And that's wrong for the rule of law regardless of what country that happens.[28]

Obeying the law is not enough. The Declaration concluded: "we mutually pledge to each other our Lives, our Fortunes and our sacred Honor." The signers gave up much for their country, and over the following centuries, more than a million Americans died for it. Most people do not have to lay down their lives in battle, but Americanism does ask a certain level of service and sacrifice. As

John F. Kennedy put it, "ask not what your country can do for you—ask what you can do for your country." Trump is not a fan of the second ask. He bone-spurred his way out of the Vietnam draft, cheated on his taxes, and corruptly used his office to enrich himself. State regulators shut down his "charitable" foundation for being a self-dealing fraud.

Just before Kennedy became president, he quoted Pericles: "We do not imitate—for we are a model to others."[29] For someone who talks so much about American greatness, Trump does not see the United States this way. He has disparaged American exceptionalism and expressed admiration for authoritarian regimes. "I find China, frankly, in many ways to be far more honorable than Cryin' Chuck and Nancy. I really do," he said, referring to the Senate Democratic Leader Charles Schumer, and House Speaker Nancy Pelosi.[30] Before GOP donors in Florida, he praised China's president Xi Jinping: "He's now president for life. President for life. No, he's great. And look, he was able to do that. I think it's great. Maybe we'll have to give that a shot some day." Even if he were joking, why would he be lighthearted about dictatorship? As for the United States, he was not kidding: "I'm telling you, it's a rigged system, folks. I've been saying that for a long time. It's a rigged system. And we don't have the right people in there yet. We have a lot of great people, but certain things, we don't have the right people."[31]

Trump does not want China to be more like the United States. He wants the United States to be more like China.

We know that Trump does not believe in American ideals. So what does he believe in? Trump has never held to a consistent and well-developed set of political principles. He has changed parties more often than he has changed wives and has flip-flopped on abortion, gun control, and other issues.[32] For all his high-decibel talk of defending borders, he put his name on a 2013 article that said: "We will have to leave borders behind and go for global unity when it comes to financial stability."[33]

Nevertheless, it is possible to make out some of his attitudes. One involves his view of justice. For Trump, the word means nothing more than the advantage of the stronger.[34] Tony Schwartz, who did all the writing for Trump's *The Art of the Deal*, put it this way: "There is no right and wrong for Trump. There's winning and losing. And that's very different from right and wrong."[35] He damns his opponents by calling them "losers" or claiming that they are "failing," even when they are not. In his eyes, to be rich, popular, or powerful is to be right. As a candidate, he shrugged off criticisms by citing his "great ratings." When reporters asked about an upcoming meeting with President Rodrigo Duterte of the Philippines, who had slaughtered thousands of people under the cover of a "war on drugs," Trump answered: "He is very popular in the Philippines. He has a very high approval rating in the Philippines."[36] When another reporter challenged his wild claims about various topics, he sneered: "I guess I can't be doing so badly, because I'm President, and you're not."[37]

This attitude clashes with the American tradition. Alexander Hamilton wrote that "the little arts of popularity" were unworthy of the nation's chief executive.[38] Jefferson drew a bright line between popularity and justice. It is a "sacred principle," he said in his first inaugural address, "that though the will of the majority is in all cases to prevail, that will to be rightful must be reasonable."[39] Whereas Trump believes that might makes right, Lincoln said the reverse: "Let us have faith that right makes might, and in that faith, let us, to the end, dare to do our duty as we understand it."[40]

Trump also breaks with American tradition by reducing national greatness to crude material terms. "I want to take everything back from the world that we've given them," he said in 2013, adding that he disliked talk of American exceptionalism because other countries have been "eating our lunch for the last 20 years."[41] At a 2016 rally in Bismarck, North Dakota, he said: "You have to be wealthy in order to be great."[42] The Founders approved of the pursuit of wealth, but they would have condemned the notion that it is all that defines us. When the British tried to buy off American colonies by adjusting the tea tax, Benjamin Franklin said: "They have no idea that any people can act from any other principle but that of interest; and they believe that three pence in a pound of tea . . . is sufficient to overcome all the patriotism of an American."[43] President Reagan promoted economic growth during the 1980s, but at the 1992 Republican Convention, he reminded his fellow Americans that there is much more to their nation: "My fondest hope for each one of you—and especially for the young people here—is that you will love your country, not for her power or wealth, but for her selflessness and her idealism."[44]

Campaigning for president, Trump promised his followers that he could single-handedly solve their problems through his personal willpower. Accepting the Republican nomination, he said: "Nobody knows the system better than me, which is why I alone can fix it."[45] A Trump-bylined article in the *National Enquirer* began: "I am the only one who can make America great again!"[46] And during his 2016 Bismarck speech, he said: "Politicians have used you and stolen your votes. They have given you nothing. I will give you everything. I will give you what you've been looking for for 50 years. I'm the only one."[47] In the first *Federalist* paper, Hamilton warned that "of those men who have overturned the liberties of republics, the greatest number have begun their career by paying an obsequious court to the people; commencing demagogues, and ending tyrants."[48]

Note Trump's use of the first-person singular, suggesting a view of power that is personal, not institutional. For him, the red, white, and blue are merely his gang colors. As president, he treats the government as personal property, giving jobs to unqualified family members and speaking of "my generals and my military."[49] When he talks about loyalty, he means loyalty not to the Constitution but to Donald Trump. Reflecting on Trump's demand for fealty from the director of the FBI, James Comey reflected: "Ethical leaders never ask for loyalty. Those leading through fear—like a Cosa Nostra boss—require personal loyalty."[50]

In Trump's binary view of the world, there are only friends and enemies. Anyone who disagrees with him is disloyal and therefore an enemy. He uses the word openly, often referring to the mainstream media as "an enemy of the people." This frame of mind is profoundly un-American. On the eve of the Civil War, when thousands of Southerners were reaching for their rifles in rebellion, Lincoln refused to use the language of enmity. "We are not enemies, but friends. We must not be enemies. Though passion may have strained it must not break our bonds of affection."[51] Richard Nixon, who privately had subordinates keep lists of his opponents, declined to brand them as "enemies" in public. Barack Obama once let the word slip in a discussion of legislative politics and backtracked after harsh criticism from Republicans.[52]

Where does Trump's mindset come from? In explaining the philosophies of other presidents, one might look to the books that they read. Political scientist Lee Edwards once recalled a 1965 visit to Ronald Reagan's home library, where he found many works of history and economics. The volumes were not just for show but were "underlined, dog-eared, with notations in the margins! This guy had read these books!"[53] Accordingly, a study of the works of free-market thinkers such as Milton Friedman and Friedrich Hayek provides insights into Reagan's economic policies. This approach would not work with Donald Trump. His ghostwriter Tony Schwartz said: "I seriously doubt that Trump has ever read a book straight through in his adult life."[54] When a reporter asked if Trump had read any presidential biographies, he admitted: "I never have. I'm always busy doing a lot."[55] He has sometimes pretended to have read other books. In a 1987 interview, he had this comical exchange when Pat Buchanan asked him to name the best book that he had read besides *The Art of the Deal*:

Trump: I really like Tom Wolfe's last book. And I think he's a great author. He's done a beautiful job—

Buchanan: Which book?

Trump: His current book. He's just current book, is just that.

Buchanan: *Bonfire of the Vanities*.

Trump: Yes. And the man has done a very, very good job. And I really can't hear with this earphone, by the way.[56]

Buchanan's subsequent campaigns and writings anticipated many of the themes that Trump would later adopt, but there is no evidence that Trump ever glanced at any of Buchanan's work. It is more likely that Trump advisers, such as Steve Bannon and Steve Miller, passed along some of Buchanan's phrases and policy proposals. The real key to Trump lies not in the pages of books, but in his upbringing and background.

TRUMP WORLD

Senator Orrin Hatch (R-UT) once tried to excuse Trump's bad behavior by saying that he "comes from a different world." In a way, Hatch was right. C. S. Lewis once wrote: "Think of a country where people were admired for running away in battle, or where a man felt proud of double-crossing all the people who had been kindest to him." Lewis assumed that such a place was imaginary, since people "have always agreed that you ought not to put yourself first."[57] But such a setting does exist: it is the world that produced Donald J. Trump. It is *not* the New York City of heroic first responders and industrious immigrants. Instead, the man in the Oval Office comes from a smaller place within the city, a subculture comprising lechers, bigots, grifters, and gangsters. This subculture celebrated hedonism and mocked honesty. This setting shaped Trump from his childhood in the 1950s to his young adulthood in the 1960s and 1970s—the passage from last days of *Mad Men* through Studio 54 to the Trump-unread *Bonfire of the Vanities*.

Trump's grandfather, Friedrich Trump, emigrated from Germany in 1885. He was 16 years old at the time, and under his grandson's policies, American authorities would have barred him as an unaccompanied alien minor.[58] He was able to enter the United States, though, and he plied a variety of trades, such as running businesses in Seattle and the Klondike that provided accommodations for prostitutes.[59] In 1905, he tried to move back to his native land with his German-born wife and reclaim his citizenship, but officials threw him out because he had failed to fulfill his military obligation.[60]

A few months after returning to the United States and settling in the New York borough of Queens, the Trumps had a son named Fred. Friedrich died when Fred was twelve, and after graduating from high school, the younger Trump went into the homebuilding business. By all accounts, Fred Trump was hardworking, but he also had a dark side. On Memorial Day of 1927, about a thousand members of the Ku Klux Klan took part in a parade in Queens. What the *New York Times* described as a "near-riot" broke out, resulting in seven arrests.[61] According to the story, one of the seven was "Fred Trump of 175-24 Devonshire Road"—an address that matched Trump's residence at the time. According to another news account, all of the arrestees were wearing Klan robes.[62] To be clear, the court discharged him, and there is no further documentation that he belonged to the Klan. It is possible that he was a bystander and that the second news account erred in suggesting that he was wearing Klan regalia. It is also fair to say that there is more evidence for Fred Trump being a Klansman than for Barack Obama being a Kenyan.

What is less disputable is that Fred Trump discriminated against African Americans. During the 1930s and 1940s, he made a fortune in the construction industry. After the Second World War, he focused on developing and operating apartment complexes. In December 1950, singer Woody Guthrie leased a unit in a Trump-run Brooklyn complex named Beach Haven. Although Brooklyn's African American population was growing, the complex was nearly all white. After learning about Trump's rental practices, Guthrie wrote in his notebook: "Old Man Trump knows just how much racial hatred he stirred up."[63] The practices continued. In 1963, a Trump rental agent took an application from an African American nurse. Decades later, the agent recounted a talk with his boss: "I asked him what to do and he says, 'Take the application and put it in a drawer and leave it there.'"[64]

Fred Trump's business methods were problematic in other ways. While building Beach Haven, he took on a limited partner who was very helpful in procuring capital and preventing labor problems. The partner could do these things because of his ties to the Mafia crime families.[65] The federal government subsidized much of

Trump's construction at the time, and a scheme to get massive excess payments from the Federal Housing Administration landed him before a US Senate committee. Trump parried the senators' questions in a way that foreshadowed his son's rhetorical tactics. When Herbert Lehman of New York pointed out that the excess payment was lying in a bank account under his control, he denied that he had pocketed it: "I first have to take it out before I pocket it, Senator, isn't that right?" He even managed to cast himself as a victim of an unfair accusation. "This is, I believe, very wrong and it hurts me. The only thing I am happy about is that it is not true."[66]

Donald Trump was born in 1946. Fred raised him and his siblings to be ruthlessly competitive, repeatedly reminding them, "Be a killer." He endowed them with a sense of entitlement, telling young Donald, "You are a king."[67] Fred backed up this pronouncement by providing a kingly lifestyle and a great deal of money. An investigation by the *New York Times* found that the elder Trump's empire supplied Donald Trump with an annual income of $200,000 a year (2018 dollars) by the time he was three years old. Donald was a millionaire in primary school, and as a teenager, he was part owner of an apartment building.[68]

It was not all luxury. Donald was a wild child, and when Fred found that he had a cache of knives, he sent him to a strict boarding school, the New York Military Academy.[69] Donald fit in well at the school, with its good-looking uniforms and emphasis on athletics over academics. Although its military discipline marginally improved his behavior, it did not deepen any sense of patriotism or desire for military service. On graduating in 1964, he enrolled at Fordham University and got the first of several educational draft deferments, which continued after he transferred to the University of Pennsylvania's Wharton School in 1966. After graduating in 1968, he got a medical deferment. Many years later, his lawyer-fixer Michael Cohen testified that Trump told Cohen to fend off questions about how he avoided the Vietnam-era draft. "Mr. Trump claimed it was because of a bone spur, but when I asked for medical records, he gave me none and said there was no surgery. He told me not to answer the specific questions by reporters but rather offer simply the fact that he received a medical deferment. He finished the conversation with the following comment. 'You think I'm stupid, I wasn't going to Vietnam.'"[70] Reporting in 2018 suggested that the diagnosis had come from a Queens podiatrist, who made it as a favor to Fred Trump.[71]

Trump settled back into New York City, going into business with his father. At the time, the metropolitan area was a cauldron of corruption. In 1965, voters had elected a "reform" mayor, but he was profligate with taxpayer money and ineffectual in cleaning up official misconduct. Crookery stretched from the city's political leadership down to the police on the beat. "Ten percent of the cops in New York City are absolutely corrupt," said whistleblower Frank Serpico, "ten percent are absolutely honest, and the other eighty percent—they wish they were honest."[72] The city was also boiling with street crime and racial tension. Its white working class was increasingly angry and resentful, and a couple of high-profile incidents showed how those feelings could become political fuel for public figures clever enough to exploit them.

One such public figure was mob boss Joe Colombo. Whereas other leaders of organized crime had sought a low profile, Colombo brazenly mounted a public relations offensive that drew on the language and techniques of the civil rights movement. Alleging that the government's fight against the Mafia was an expression of ethnic prejudice, he founded an organization called the Italian American Civil Rights League. The group soon claimed 45,000 members and drew support from prominent New York politicians. Among other activities, it picketed the local FBI headquarters. Anticipating the age of "fake news" and "alternative facts," Colombo explained to the *New York Times*: "Mafia, what's the Mafia? There is not a Mafia. Am I head of a family? Yes. My wife and four sons and daughter. That's my family. They even got that wrong." Expounding on an FBI "conspiracy against Italian Americans," he continued: "What gives the Government the right to label anybody. What are we, in Nazi Germany?"[73] Colombo had some impact. His efforts resulted in the scrubbing of the words "Mafia" and "La Cosa Nostra" from the script of *The Godfather* and some official documents.

Nevertheless, the Mafia was quite real. At a rally soon after the interview, a gunman shot him, probably on orders from a rival boss. He lingered for several more years but was totally disabled. His "civil rights" group soon disappeared.

As a New Yorker, an avid consumer of tabloid news, and the son of a builder who dealt with gangsters, Trump surely took note of Colombo's public relations strategy. Perhaps it is pure coincidence, but in 1988, Trump would make his first name-licensing deal—involving limousine hood ornaments—with a reputed member of the Colombo crime family.[74]

A case of disorganized crime must have also caught Trump's attention. On May 8, 1970, hundreds of construction workers rioted in lower Manhattan, beating up long-haired students who were protesting the Vietnam War. Wearing hard hats, waving American flags, and carrying signs that said "America: Love It or Leave It," the rioters soon became avatars of white working-class America.[75] Instead of denouncing the mob violence, President Nixon promptly welcomed construction union leaders to the White House, and accepted their gift of a ceremonial hard hat labeled "Commander in Chief."

Meanwhile, Donald Trump was assuming more and more responsibility in the family business. On October 16, 1973, he appeared on the front page of the *New York Times* for the first time, under the headline "Major Landlord Accused of Antiblack Bias in City." The story reported that the Department of Justice had sued Trump and his father for violating the Fair Housing Act of 1968 in apartment rentals. Trump said that accusations of bias were "absolutely ridiculous," adding that he and his father "never have discriminated, and we never would."[76] In fact, local government and advocacy groups had sent black and white testers to apply for Trump apartments. Agents would encourage white testers to rent, while turning away black testers or steering them to certain complexes with large numbers of minorities.[77] Trump then countersued, claiming abuse of government power. During a break in the depositions, Trump casually said to a government attorney: "You wouldn't want to live with those people either."[78] Two years later, the Trumps settled, signing a consent order in which they agreed not to engage in racial discrimination. Donald claimed victory, saying that the consent order did not include "any requirement that would compel the Trump organization to accept persons on welfare as tenants unless as qualified as any other tenant."[79] By seeming to equate African Americans and welfare recipients, he confirmed suspicions of racial bias.

Representing Trump in the case was attorney Roy Cohn, who had risen to infamy in the early 1950s as Senator Joseph McCarthy's counsel. Trump had first met Cohn at a members-only Manhattan nightspot whose clientele, wrote journalist Harry Hurt III, included "European and Latin American party lovers, and assorted political fixers and gentleman mobsters."[80] Cohn became Trump's *consigliere*, giving him entrée to his unique set of local connections. Cohn's clients included leading Mafia figures, and he even reportedly hosted meetings of the Mafia commission at his townhouse.[81] These mob ties proved critical to the building of Trump Tower. Though most skyscraper construction relies on steel girders, Trump made the unusual decision to use concrete—and the local concrete business was under mob control. Wayne Barrett quoted FBI sources that Trump "did it through Cohn," adding that Cohn might even have set up a meeting between Trump and "Fat Tony" Salerno, boss of the Genovese crime family.[82] At the time, other New York developers were urging the FBI to loosen the grip of the mob-run concrete cartel.[83] If Trump made any such pleas, or if he had any misgivings about working with organized crime, he kept them well hidden.

Through his father, Trump already had political contacts, but Cohn helped him expand his network. "Roy was very, very connected . . . unbelievably," Trump told writer Timothy O'Brien. "And Roy started introducing me to a lot of people. I got to know everybody."[84] In 1979, for instance, a young New Jersey political operative named Roger Stone was seeking office space for the Reagan campaign, and he went to Cohn's townhouse, where he was meeting with Salerno.[85] Cohn told him to see Trump, who agreed to help. That relationship lasted for decades.

Cohn also introduced Trump to other aspects of life in New York. Among his clients were the owners of Studio 54, a disco notorious for debauchery. Cohn arranged for Trump to be there for opening night, and he became a regular. Trump later remembered "things happening there that I have never seen again. . . . Stuff that couldn't happen today because of problems of death."[86] The mention of "death" was a reference to AIDS and other sexually transmitted diseases. In 1997, Trump would tell shock jock Howard Stern: "I've been so lucky in terms of that whole world. It is a dangerous world out there—it's scary, like Vietnam. Sort of like the Vietnam era. It is my personal Vietnam. I feel like a great and very brave soldier."[87]

AIDS came close to home when Cohn contracted the disease in the 1980s. After he disclosed that he was ill, Trump started withdrawing work from him. "I can't believe he's doing this to me," Cohn said. "Donald pisses ice water."[88]

When Cohn died in 1986—disgraced and disbarred—he had left his mark on Donald Trump. His influence was not so much a matter of teaching Trump new things, but refining and reinforcing the attitudes that he had inherited from his father, especially regarding the law. "I don't want to know what the law is," Cohn famously said. "I want to know who the judge is." Trump associate Louise Sunshine told journalist Michael Kruse of seeing the portrayal of Roy Cohn in the play *Angels in America*: "It took me back to the years when Donald, Roy Cohn and I used to sit at lunches at the 21 Club, time after time after time," she told me. "And it totally brought back all the memories, and it brought back exactly who tutored Donald in ignoring the law, and not caring about the law—it was Roy Cohn. He had total disregard for the law—a disregard for the law which Donald has."[89]

ANSWERING OBJECTIONS

Trump's defenders would disapprove of the whole approach of this book. It is useful to anticipate several of the objections that they might raise.

They would probably start with one of their favorite tactics, "whataboutism." A rhetorical device that derives from the old Soviet Union, whataboutism counters an accusation with a charge against the accusers or people that they admire. Hence, the refrain, "What about Hillary's emails?" Like so many rationalizations, whataboutism starts with a bit of truth: throughout American history, many political leaders have indeed done bad things. Trump himself has made this point. In response to questions about racist supporters of a Robert E. Lee statue, he said: "How about Thomas Jefferson? What do you think of Thomas Jefferson? You like him? Are we going to take down the statue? Because he was a major slave owner. Now, are we going to take down his statue?"[90]

Whataboutism is not new, and neither is its refutation. One hundred and fifty-nine years before Trump talked about slaveholding presidents, Abraham Lincoln dealt with the same kind of argument. In debate, when Stephen A. Douglas mentioned Jefferson's slaves, Lincoln replied: "While Mr. Jefferson was the owner of slaves, as undoubtedly he was, in speaking upon this very subject, he used the strong language that 'he trembled for his country when he remembered that God was just.'"[91] Political scientist Jacob Levy reminds us that "all those presidents put forward a public rhetorical face that was better than their worst acts. . . . And their words were part of the process of persuading each generation of Americans that those were constitutively American ideals."[92]

America stands as an ideal even when Americans fall short of it. In 1980, Ronald Reagan quoted Soviet dissident Andrei Sakharov as calling America a leader toward a pluralist and free society, adding: "He is right. We have strayed off course many times and we have been careless with the machinery of freedom bequeathed to us by the Founding Fathers, but, somehow, it has managed to survive our frailties."[93] Martin Luther King said that the authors of the Constitution and the Declaration were "signing a promissory note to which every American was to fall heir," but that "America has given the Negro people a bad check, a check which has come back marked insufficient funds. But we refuse to believe that the bank of justice is bankrupt." But instead of merely decrying history, he challenged the nation to "rise up and live out the true meaning of its creed: 'We hold these truths to be self-evident: that all men are created equal.'"[94]

Trump's ghostwriters sometimes shoehorn references to American ideals into his public statements in which he recites them with all the sincerity of a Trump University sales pitch. As Daniel Krauthammer has observed, "in Trump's unprepared remarks at rallies, in debate performances, TV interviews, press conferences, tweets, they barely appear. Clearly, they do not preoccupy him. Our ideals and their fulfillment are not, in his view, what made America great."[95]

When he utters words that seem statesmanlike and responsible, he is often winking at his audience. At a campaign rally, he said: "When we have a protester inside, which isn't even very often, I say, 'Be very gentle, please don't hurt him.'"[96] Readers should take those words neither seriously nor literally. That admonition followed a series of incidents in which Trump encouraged violence against demonstrators. In Cedar Rapids, Iowa, he said: "So if you see somebody getting ready to throw a tomato, knock the crap out of them, would you, seriously. Okay, just knock the hell, I promise you, I will pay for the legal fees. I promise, I promise."[97]

With specific regard to Trump's dealings with criminals, his defenders might contend that a New York businessman would have had no choice. This excuse does not stand up to scrutiny. Trump was not a candy store owner paying protection money to the local thugs. He was a powerful tycoon who actively sought opportunities for deals with shady characters, both in the United States and abroad. Either he knew that he was playing in dirt or he engaged in what lawyers call "willful blindness," deliberately averting his eyes from the alleged crimes of his associates. He did have choices. Like most other business leaders, he could have done due diligence and stayed clean. He could have gotten in touch with the authorities if he got wind of criminal activity. Instead, he chose another path. As he put it in 2019, "I've seen a lot of things over my life. I don't think in my whole life I've ever called the FBI. In my whole life. You don't call the FBI."[98]

Trump's choices were not victimless. Organized crime, which brings death and destruction to communities across the country, depends on enablers and collaborators like Trump. As a crusading prosecutor once put it:

> Organized crime cannot flourish and grow in a society where voluntary adherence to the rule of law prevails. It does flourish where it can feed off the illegal tendencies of many people. It flourishes in a society where too many people are looking for breaks above and beyond the law, where the duties of being a citizen of the greatest Nation on Earth—paying taxes, testifying in court, serving on juries—are considered burdens to be avoided and sometimes illegally evaded. The existence of organized crime constitutes an indictment of our entire society because it cannot exist without broad support, tacit and otherwise.[99]

The prosecutor was Rudy Giuliani.

Some of Trump's more sophisticated defenders acknowledge his poor character but argue that it is irrelevant. His bad behavior, they say, is purely a matter of personal style and language, not the conduct of official duties. Among other things, this argument overlooks his conflicts of interest, such as those arising from the corporations, lobbies, and entities linked to foreign governments that pay top dollar to rent rooms at Trump hotels. As for language, words *are* policy. Words matter. As Rush Limbaugh loves to say, words mean things. Presidential statements are especially important in the realm of international affairs, where the chief executive acts as the spokesperson for the entire nation. When the president praises dictators, asks foreign leaders for dirt on domestic political opponents, or fails to condemn abuses of human rights, he is setting national policy.

In immigration, law enforcement, and other areas, those who carry out policy often have broad discretion. Trump's words signal to them how they should exercise it. [100] Between his endorsement of "rough" treatment of suspects and his attacks on undocumented aliens, he seems to be having an effect. One federal judge said that ICE was engaging in tactics "we associate with regimes we revile as unjust, regimes where those who have long lived in a country may be taken without notice from streets, home, and work. And sent away. We are not that country; and woe be the day that we become that country under a fiction that laws allow it." [101]

Trump's malignant sway goes even farther, reaching millions of voters. He was only slightly exaggerating when he said "You know what else they say about my people? The polls, they say I have the most loyal people. Did you ever see that? Where I could stand in the middle of Fifth Avenue and shoot somebody and I wouldn't lose any voters, okay? It's like incredible." [102] The words of our two greatest presidents cast light on the impact of our least pro-American one. In a draft of his first inaugural address, George Washington said that "no wall of words—that no mound of parchment can be so formed as to stand against the sweeping torrent of boundless ambition on the one side, aided by the sapping current of corrupted morals on the other." [103] In their 1858 debates, Abraham Lincoln decried Stephen Douglas's indifference to slavery, saying "he is blowing out the moral lights around us . . . penetrating the human soul and eradicating the light of reason and the love of liberty in this American people." [104]

2

WE HOLD THESE TRUTHS

The Founders were acutely aware of the defects of human nature, and they built government structures to harness ambition and control the power of self-interest. But to an extent that we often forget today, they also knew that American government would depend on American virtues. *Federalist 55* put it clearly: "As there is a degree of depravity in mankind which requires a certain degree of circumspection and distrust, so there are other qualities in human nature which justify a certain portion of esteem and confidence. Republican government presupposes the existence of these qualities in a higher degree than any other form."[1] Among these qualities was honesty.

In his Farewell Address, George Washington mentioned a proverb that Benjamin Franklin had coined: "I hold the maxim no less applicable to public than to private affairs, that honesty is always the best policy."[2] That phrase has become a cliché, but it meant something profound to the people who built this country. Instead of relying on fiats from above, Americans would govern themselves through reflection and choice. There would be constant debate and deliberation, which would only work if people could believe one another. "This I hope will be the age of experiments in government," Thomas Jefferson wrote in 1796, "and that their basis will be founded in principles of honesty, not of mere force."[3] Or as Jefferson wrote another time, "The whole art of government consists in the art of being honest."[4]

Behind the virtue of honesty is a belief in the very existence of truth itself. Trump's attitudes bear a curious relationship to an influential school of thought that denies the very existence of objective truth, even holding that the natural and physical sciences are mere social constructs with no claim to neutrality or universal validity.[5] Like jesting Pilate, they ask "What is truth?" and do not stay for an answer. America's early leaders had a different philosophy, believing that perception and reason could reveal the truths of the physical and moral worlds.[6] Hamilton started *Federalist 31* by writing that in every discussion, "there are certain primary truths, or first principles, upon which all subsequent reasonings must depend. These contain an internal evidence which, antecedent to all reflection or combination, commands the assent of the mind."[7] Lincoln said something similar. "One would start with great confidence that he could convince any sane child that the simpler propositions of Euclid are true; but, nevertheless, he would fail, utterly, with one who should deny the definitions and axioms," he wrote in a letter. "The principles of Jefferson are the definitions and axioms of free society. And yet they are denied and evaded, with no small show of success. One dashingly calls them 'glittering generalities,' another bluntly calls them 'self-evident lies,' and still others insidiously argue that they apply only to 'superior races.'"[8]

American history has hardly been free of falsehood. As Lincoln's letter suggests, too many people have believed in myths, such as the pseudoscience that "proved" African American inferiority. And too many politicians have told too many lies. What sets Donald Trump apart, however, is not just the volume of his untruthfulness, but his relentless assault on truth itself. What Lindsey Graham said of another president applies even more today. "This case is requiring parents and teachers to sit down and explain what lying is all about. This case is creating confusion. This case is hitting America far harder than America knows it has been hit."[9]

DONALD THE LIAR

Maggie Haberman writes in the *New York Times*: "His long career in the New York real estate world convinced Mr. Trump that all people are prone to shading their views according to their own self-interest. Objectivity is not something he expects of people, and he long ago came to believe that 'facts' are really arbitrary."[10] During his early years in the public eye, it was already evident that he lied all the time. When Tony Schwartz was writing Trump's 1987 book *The Art of the Deal*, he realized that he had to spin Trump's dishonesty. "I play to people's fantasies," he wrote in Trump's name. "People want to believe that something is the biggest and the greatest and the most spectacular. I call it truthful hyperbole. It's an innocent form of exaggeration—and it's a very effective form of promotion."[11] Decades later, Schwartz expressed regret to journalist Jane Mayer: "'Deceit,' he told me, is never 'innocent.' He added, 'Truthful hyperbole' is a contradiction in terms. It's a way of saying, 'It's a lie, but who cares?' Trump, he said, loved the phrase."[12] Keeping in character, Trump would lie about the book that rationalized his lies. He called it the best-selling business book of all time (not even close).[13] Announcing his candidacy in 2015, he took personal credit for Schwartz's work: "We need a leader that wrote *The Art of the Deal*."[14] (He just made some marks on Schwartz's manuscript.)

In a 1993 deposition concerning the bankruptcy of the Trump Taj Mahal, one of his attorneys said: "Hey, Trump is a leader in the field of expert—he's an expert at interpreting things. Let's put it that way."[15] The attorney was Patrick T. McGahn, whose nephew Donald McGahn would later serve as Trump's White House counsel.

In 2007, Trump sued journalist Timothy O'Brien for questioning his net worth. O'Brien's attorneys deposed Trump, confronting him with numerous statements that he had made. Thirty times during the two-day deposition, they forced him to admit that what he had said was false.[16] He had this dialogue with attorney Andrew Ceresney:

Ceresney: Mr. Trump, have you always been completely truthful in your public statements about your net worth of properties?

Trump: I try.

Ceresney: Have you ever not been truthful?

Trump: My net worth fluctuates, and it goes up and down with the markets and with attitudes and with feelings, even my own feelings, but I try.

Ceresney: Let me just understand that a little. You said your net worth goes up and down based upon your own feelings?

Trump: Yes, even my own feelings, as to where the world is, where the world is going, and that can change rapidly from day to day . . .

Ceresney: When you publicly state a net worth number, what do you base that number on?

Trump: I would say it's my general attitude at the time that the question may be asked. And as I say, it varies. [17]

Many times, he has overstated the size of his properties, such as by claiming 68 floors for the 58-floor Trump Tower. [18] In 2012, a Trump financial statement said he owned a 2,000-acre vineyard in Virginia. But a *Washington Post* check of land records in Virginia showed the Trump family owned only about 1,200 acres. The Trump winery's website says 1,300 acres. [19] The false claim about the vineyard would have been particularly irksome to George Washington and Abraham Lincoln, both of whom worked as surveyors and built reputations for the accuracy of their work. More important, Trump's multiple lies have exposed his businesses to possible prosecution by state officials. "In this instance, it's a legitimate business (banks that loaned to Trump) that is being defrauded," former New

York attorney general Robert Abrams told NBC News. Decisions are being made against fraudulent information."[20]

Trump does not merely lie—he tries to create an alternative reality where the facts are whatever he wants them to be. When inconvenient information crops up, he just dismisses it as "fake news." As he said in a 2018 speech in Kansas City: "What you're seeing and what you're reading is not what's happening."[21] Before he became president, for instance, he brushed aside statistics showing a drop in unemployment under the Obama administration:

- "So many people can't get jobs. The unemployment number, as you know, is totally fiction."[22]
- "You hear a 5 percent unemployment rate. It's such a phony number. That number was put in for presidents and for politicians so that they look good to the people."[23]
- "Nobody has jobs. I wouldn't have caught on—to be honest— I wouldn't have been catching on if the economy were real. It is not a real economy. It is a phony set of numbers. They cooked the books."[24]

As soon as he became president, however, he started endorsing the data. In June 2017, he tweeted: "Regulations way down. 600,000+ new jobs added. Unemployment down to 4.3%. Business and economic enthusiasm way up—record levels!"[25]

Trump lies about his lies. Throughout his early business career, he would regale reporters with tales of his financial or sexual successes while pretending to be a Trump Organization publicist named "John Miller" or "John Barron."[26] There are recordings, but he nevertheless said on *Today*: "No, I don't know anything about it. You're telling me about it for the first time and it doesn't sound like my voice at all."[27] What made that denial particularly weak was a 1990 deposition at which he admitted using a fake name. After the deposition, he told reporters, "Lots of people use pen names. Ernest Hemingway used one."[28]

A more recent example came in 2018, when he tweeted: "I never said Russia did not meddle in the election."[29] Yes, he said just that.

"I don't believe they interfered," he told *Time* in 2016. "That became a laughing point, not a talking point, a laughing point. Any
time I do something, they say 'oh, Russia interfered.'"[30]

A frequent Trump technique is what conservative journalist
Amanda Carpenter calls "advance and deny"—make a false accusation, attribute it to a third party, and deny responsibility. In 2016, the
National Enquirer published an outlandish story linking Ted Cruz's
father to Kennedy assassin Lee Harvey Oswald. "His father was
with Lee Harvey Oswald prior to Oswald's being, you know, shot. I
mean, the whole thing is ridiculous," Trump told Fox News. "Nobody even brings it up. They don't even talk about that. That was
reported, and nobody talks about it."[31] A year later, when *Time*'s
Michael Scherer pressed him on the accusation, he said: "Well that
was in a newspaper. No, no, I like Ted Cruz, he's a friend of mine.
But that was in the newspaper. I wasn't, I didn't say that. I was
referring to a newspaper. A Ted Cruz article referred to a newspaper
story with, had a picture of Ted Cruz, his father, and Lee Harvey
Oswald, having breakfast."[32] (The *Enquirer* photo showed a fuzzy
image of someone other than Cruz's father standing near Oswald. A
breakfast threesome would have been impossible, since Ted Cruz
was born seven years after Oswald died.)

Trump has said that he is a "very stable genius" with "the
world's greatest memory."[33] But his lies often consist of convenient
memory lapses or professions of ignorance. Patrick McGahn explained that his office policy was to meet with Trump in pairs. "We
tried to do it with Donald always if we could because Donald says
certain things and then has a lack of memory."[34] During a 2013
deposition, a lawyer asked him about his relationship with Felix
Sater, a convicted criminal with reputed ties to the Russian mob.
Trump answered, "If he were sitting in the room right now, I really
wouldn't know what he looked like."[35] Sater had an office in Trump
Tower, on the same floor as Trump himself, and had business cards
identifying himself as a senior advisor to Trump. When CNN's Jake
Tapper asked Trump about his endorsement by white supremacist
David Duke, he said: "I know nothing about David Duke. I know
nothing about white supremacists."[36] After that remark sparked

wide disbelief, he used the excuse that he had used in his 1987 conversation with Pat Buchanan about reading habits: "I was sitting in a house in Florida, with a bad earpiece. I could hardly hear what he's saying."[37] His on-again-off-again memory was especially memorable during a deposition about his Trump University scam. Dozens of times, he answered questions by saying that he could not remember. An attorney reminded him that he had claimed "one of the best memories in the world," Trump said he did not remember saying that: "I don't know. Did I use that expression?"[38]

The Russia investigation triggered the off-switch in Trump's memory. A reporter asked him about the arrest of WikiLeaks founder Julian Assange. He responded with the same words that he had used about David Duke: "I know nothing about WikiLeaks. It's not my thing . . . I know nothing really about him."[39] During the 2016 campaign, Trump had said that he loved WikiLeaks and mentioned the organization at least 141 times at 56 events.[40] The Mueller report said: "We noted, among other things, that the President stated on more than 30 occasions that he 'does not recall' or 'remember' or have an 'independent recollection' of information called for by the questions."[41]

BIRTHERISM

Trump had talked about running for president as early as the 1988 campaign, but his first big political splash came in 2011, when he toyed with a run for the 2012 Republican nomination. It began with a big lie. The heart of this flirtation was his appeal to "birtherism," the crackpot notion that Barack Obama was born in Kenya and thus was not a legitimate president. On its face, the idea made no sense. In Obama's birth year of 1961, his mother was an 18-year-old student at the University of Hawaii. Why would she have made a long, expensive journey to give birth in a third-world country? And if she did, why was there a birth announcement in *The Honolulu Advertiser*?[42]

Nevertheless, Trump raised the issue, starting with vague and unfounded innuendoes. "Let me tell you, I'm a really smart guy," he said on *Good Morning America*. "The reason I have a little doubt—just a little—is because he grew up, and nobody knew him. If ever I got the nomination, if I ever decide to run, you may go back and interview people from my kindergarten. They'll remember me. Nobody ever comes forward. Nobody knows who he is until later in his life. It's very strange."[43] (Among the people who knew Obama's family in his early years was Neil Abercrombie, the governor of Hawaii. And yes, reporters did speak to Obama's kindergarten teacher.)

Trump went in deeper during an interview with Laura Ingraham: "He doesn't have a birth certificate, or if he does, there's something on that certificate that is very bad for him. Now, somebody told me—and I have no idea if this is bad for him or not, but perhaps it would be—that where it says 'religion,' it might have 'Muslim.' And if you're a Muslim, you don't change your religion, by the way."[44] (Hawaii birth certificates do not mention religion.) Those comments were a double-barreled shot of prejudice, suggesting that the first African American president was not American and that he belonged to a religion that many Americans unfairly linked to terrorism.

When President Obama released a short-form birth certificate, Trump said that it was no good. "I have people that actually have been studying it and they cannot believe what they're finding," he said on the *Today* show.[45] President Obama then produced his "long form" birth certificate, which confirmed once again that he was from Honolulu. That document should have ended the story—but it did not. In August 2012, Trump tweeted: "An 'extremely credible source' has called my office and told me that @BarackObama's birth certificate is a fraud."[46] In a 2013 interview, Jonathan Karl of ABC News asked him if he still doubted that Obama was born in the United States. "Well I don't know. Was it a birth certificate? You tell me. Some people say that was not his birth certificate. Maybe it was, maybe it wasn't. I'm saying I don't know. Nobody knows. And you don't know either, Jonathan. You're a smart guy. You don't know either." In the same interview, Karl asked him if he thought he had gone overboard with the birther issue. "Well, I don't think I went overboard," he said. "Actually, I think it made me very popular, if you want to know the truth, OK? So I do think I know what I'm doing."[47] His response was revealing. To Trump, the only thing that mattered about the birther notion is that it had made him more popular. It did not bother him that it was wrong.

A few months later, he issued a tweet hinting that a murderous conspiracy was afoot. "How amazing, the State Health Director who verified copies of Obama's 'birth certificate' died in plane crash today. All others lived."[48] There was no foul play: Loretta Fuddy suffered a cardiac arrhythmia while floating in the water and awaiting rescue.[49] Trump never deleted the tweet or retracted the claim. He just let it hang, cruelly adding to her family's pain.

In September 2016, he gave birtherism a new twist, swapping one lie for two others: "Hillary Clinton and her campaign of 2008 started the birther controversy. I finished it. I finished it. You know what I mean. President Barack Obama was born in the United States, period. Now, we all want to get back to making America strong and great again."[50] The first part was untrue. Although some peripheral Clinton supporters circulated birther material, Clinton and her campaign steered clear of the matter. The second part was equally false. Birtherism continued through the release of Obama's birth certificates and Trump's "disavowal" of the idea.

The birther lie hurt the country by raising baseless doubts about the president's legitimacy. It was the kind of tactic that one would undertake to create or deepen social divisions in the United States. Therefore, it is not surprising that the Russians worked in tandem with Trump. During the 2016 campaign, Russian accounts echoed his claim that Clinton had started the controversy. Others continued to promote the Kenya myth.[51] The Russian account TEN_GOP, which looked as if it came from the Tennessee Republican Party, posted this tweet: "Watch: Barack Obama admits he was born in Kenya. #birtherism."[52]

The movement started to die down when Obama departed the White House, but its legacy lingered like a bad infection. A 2017 survey found that although most American adults did not believe that Obama was born in Kenya, 51 percent of Republicans thought that it was "probably" or "definitely" true.[53]

VOTING AND ELECTIONS

During the 2016 election, Trump won 306 electoral votes, though two GOP electors declined to support him, bringing his total down to 304. Trump called his showing a landslide, and at one press conference said it was "the biggest electoral college win since Ronald Reagan."[54] Wrong: George H. W. Bush (1988), Bill Clinton (1992 and 1996), and Barack Obama (2008 and 2012) all got more electoral votes. Trump's winning share of the electoral vote ranked 46th of 58 presidential elections.

One might shrug off that claim as harmless Trumpian hyperbole, but his bogus assertions about the popular vote were more sinister. In all of American history, no winner in the electoral college had ever *lost* the popular tally by a bigger margin than Trump in 2016: nearly 2.9 million ballots. In November 2016, he tweeted: "In addition to winning the Electoral College in a landslide, I won the popular vote if you deduct the millions of people who voted illegally."[55] There was no basis for that pronouncement. He just made it up. But he repeated the falsehood in his first formal meeting with congressional leaders.[56]

He kept embroidering the voter-fraud myth throughout his term. At a 2018 West Virginia roundtable on tax reform, he veered off topic, claiming that "in many places, like California, the same person votes many times. You probably heard about that. They always like to say, 'Oh, that's a conspiracy theory.' Not a conspiracy theory, folks. Millions and millions of people. And it's very hard because the state guards their records. They don't want to see it."[57] He elaborated in an interview with the *Daily Caller*: "The Republicans don't win and that's because of potentially illegal votes, which is what I've been saying for a long time. I have no doubt about it. And I've seen it, I've had friends talk about it when people get in line that have absolutely no right to vote and they go around in circles. Sometimes they go to their car, put on a different hat, put on a different shirt, come in and vote again."[58] In 2019 he said at a fundraising event: "We're going to watch those vote tallies. You know, I keep hearing about the election and the—the various counting measures that they have. There were a lot of close elections that were—they seemed to, every single one of them went Democrat. If it was close they say, 'The Democrat'—Well, there's something going on—you got to—hey, you got to be a little bit more paranoid than you are."[59]

There is zero evidence of widespread voter fraud. During the George W. Bush administration, the Justice Department told US attorneys to make it a priority. After years of investigation, the department charged just 119 individuals and won convictions of 86.[60] Those numbers were minuscule in light of the hundreds of millions of ballots that Americans had cast during those years—and in most of the cases, a single person had voted or registered improperly, often by mistake. "It's remarkable that all of the U.S. attorneys had a mandate and were given adequate resources to raise this to the top of the pile," one former department attorney told *Politico*. "They all agree we found a handful of cases . . . and that was it."[61] In 2017, Trump appointed a commission to investigate the issue and it disbanded after failing to find the massive fraud that it was seeking. In 2018, Democrats did win close races that seemed to lean Republican at first, but only because they had a long-standing advantage among voters who cast provisional or mail ballots.

The 2018 midterm did produce one significant case of election misconduct, however. North Carolina's bipartisan election commission refused to certify a winner in a race for the US House because of irregularities involving absentee ballots. The situation was so bad that the House did not seat a member and the state had to call a new election. By the way, the election fraud took place on behalf of the Republican candidate.

Trump's phony assertions about voter fraud may have affected public beliefs, at least on the Republican side. A 2017 survey found that 47 percent of Republicans thought that Trump had won the popular vote. About two-thirds said that millions of undocumented immigrants had voted and nearly three-fourths said that voter fraud happens somewhat or very often. One truly ominous result came in response to this question: "If Donald Trump were to say that the 2020 presidential election should be postponed until the country can make sure that only eligible American citizens can vote, would you support or oppose postponing the election?" Fifty-two percent of Republicans supported postponement.[62]

BORDERLINE FALSEHOODS

Trump's dishonesty about voter fraud by undocumented aliens was part of a broader set of lies about immigration. "What can be simpler or more accurately stated?" he said in a 2015 statement to the press. "The Mexican Government is forcing their most unwanted people into the United States. They are, in many cases, criminals, drug dealers, rapists, etc."[63] Immigration does not work that way. More important, the available evidence shows that immigrants tend to be less crime-prone than natives of the United States.[64] And a thorough statistical analysis shows that undocumented immigration does not increase violence.[65]

Throughout his first two years as president, he laid siege to the truth about the issue. He said that the government was already building his wall. (It was not.) He said that Mexico would pay for it. (It would not.) At a 2018 rally in Nevada, he said that Democrats "want to open your borders, let people in, illegally, and then they want to pay for those people for health care, education, they want to give them cars, they want to give them drivers licenses. I said last night, we did a great—we did a great, great rally in Arizona last night, and I—I said last night, what kind of car will they supply them? Will it be a Rolls-Royce?"[66] Some states do provide licenses to undocumented immigrants, but as for free cars, he just made that up. "I don't think we like sanctuary cities up here," he continued. "By the way, a lot of people in California don't want them, either. They're rioting now." NBC's Geoff Bennett asked where the riots were. "You shouldn't have—take a look. They want to get out of sanctuary cities. Many places in California want to get out of sanctuary cities." Bennett followed up: "But that's not rioting, sir, right?" Trump insisted: "Yeah, it is rioting in some cases." When Bennett asked again where the riots were, Trump took a question from another reporter.[67] There were no riots against sanctuary cities, and surveys showed that most Californians supported sanctuary laws.[68]

Trump bared his brutality by caging migrant children. He compounded it by lying about the death of a seven-year-old migrant girl. On March 29, 2019, he told reporters: "Well, I think that it's been very well stated that we've done a fantastic job. One of the children—the father gave the child no water for a long period of time. He actually admitted blame."[69] On the day that Trump spoke, an autopsy report confirmed that Jakelin Caal Maquin had died of a bacterial infection on December 8, shortly after the Border Patrol had apprehended her. Her father had supplied her with food and water, and there was no evidence of dehydration.[70]

Some of his lies were not cruel, just foolish. In January 2019, he tweeted: "There are at least 25,772,342 illegal aliens, not the 11,000,000 that have been reported for years, in our Country. So ridiculous!"[71] Ridiculous indeed: just a few weeks earlier, the Department of Homeland Security had put the figure at 12 million.[72]

Trump has helped make the immigration issue even more difficult and divisive than it was before. Looking for ways to undercut American democracy and social cohesion, the Russians have joined the fray. (Notice a pattern here?) The Oxford Internet Institute's Computational Propaganda Research Project examined how Russia's Internet Research Agency (a.k.a. "the troll farm") used social media to misinform and polarize American voters. The troll farm's most-shared Facebook page was "Stop A.I. (Stop All Immigrants)." In 2016, the report observed, the Russian effort was "geared towards extending the anti-immigrant rhetoric that Trump's campaign frequently made use of."[73]

SCIENCE

Trump's dishonesty extends to science, a subject that was much on the minds of the Founders. Though lacking a college education, Benjamin Franklin became a world-renowned scientist. His discoveries and inventions were so significant that he became the only person in the New World to win election both to the Paris Academie Royale des Sciences and the Royal Society of London.[74] In 1743, he founded the American Philosophical Society to promote useful scientific knowledge. Early members included Washington, Adams, Jefferson, Hamilton, and Madison. Another member was Benjamin Rush, a signer of the Declaration of Independence and America's most eminent physician.

A scientific frame of mind suffused their thinking.[75] Jefferson's *Notes on the State of Virginia* included chapters on geology, demographics, and what a later generation would call "climate science." Madison and Hamilton seeded *The Federalist* with learned analogies to physics, biology, and geometry.[76] Abraham Lincoln carried on this tradition. With scarcely any formal education, he schooled himself in science and math, and dabbled as an inventor. On May 22, 1849, he received Patent No. 6469 for a device to lift boats over shoals. To date, he remains as the only president to hold a patent.

Inventors and scientists must deal with the world as it is. Trump does not recognize that constraint. In 2019, he tweeted that Hurricane Dorian was heading for Alabama. After the Birmingham office of the National Weather Service contradicted his claim, he refused to admit error. He showed reporters a weather map that someone (probably Trump himself) had crudely marked up with a Sharpie to make it look as if Alabama had been in the storm's path. His initial misstatement may have briefly caused concern in the state, but his behavior was otherwise laughable. Climate change is more serious. According to NASA and the National Ocean and Atmosphere Administration, five different sets of temperature records show rapid global warming in the past few decades, and all show the past decade has been the warmest.[77] Trump dislikes those data, so he dismisses them—except when he is denying that he has dismissed them. At a 2016 debate, Hillary Clinton said: "Donald thinks that climate change is a hoax perpetrated by the Chinese. I think it's real." He interrupted: "I did not. I did not. I do not say that."[78] He said it. In 2012, he tweeted: "The concept of global warming was created by and for the Chinese in order to make U.S. manufacturing non-competitive."[79] And two years later: "Snowing in Texas and Louisiana, record setting freezing temperatures throughout the country and beyond. Global warming is an expensive hoax!"[80]

He was no more honest about ozone. According to EPA, "The emission of ozone depleting substances has been damaging the ozone layer."[81] Trump just laughed it off. "If I take hair spray, and if I spray it in my apartment, which is all sealed, you're telling me that affects the ozone layer?" he asked a 2016 campaign rally in West Virginia. "I say, no way, folks. No way, OK? No way."[82] Yes, way: indoor gases eventually get outdoors.

In April 2019, he told a fundraising dinner for the National Republican Congressional Committee: "If you have a windmill anywhere near your house, congratulations, your house just went down 75 percent in value. And they say the noise causes cancer."[83] Although any energy project can be a locally unwanted land use, wind farms do not have that great an effect on property values. And the suggestion that wind turbine noise causes cancer was so preposterous that the White House did not bother to defend it. Trump has also mocked wind energy in general, saying that electricity goes off when the wind does not blow. That claim was just as silly as his quip about ozone. As the Energy Department explains, "all forms of power generation may sometimes not operate when called upon [so] operators use the interconnected power system to access other forms of generation when contingencies occur."[84] Oddly, the White House website contained an article by former Interior Secretary Ryan Zinke: "As we look to the future, wind energy—particularly offshore wind—will play a greater role in sustaining American energy dominance. Offshore wind uniquely leverages the natural resources off of our East Coast, bringing jobs and meeting the region's demand for renewable energy."[85]

Trump's fake science has been especially harmful when it comes to discussions of vaccines. America's Founders were passionate advocates of disease prevention. Benjamin Franklin gathered data on the impact of smallpox inoculation and started a charity to provide free inoculation to the poor. General Washington ordered the inoculation of his soldiers because he was losing more of them to disease than to combat.[86] As president, Thomas Jefferson wrote to Edward Jenner, the British scientist who had pioneered the smallpox vaccine: "Medicine has never before produced any single improvement of such utility."[87] Subsequent presidents supported the science of vaccination. During the 1950s, Dwight Eisenhower met with Jonas Salk and worked with Congress to ensure rapid distribution of the polio vaccine.

Myths have always accompanied vaccines. A new and dangerous turn occurred in 1998 when British physician Andrew Wakefield and a dozen colleagues published an article in *The Lancet* suggesting that the measles, mumps, and rubella (MMR) might cause autism. The study got a great deal of media attention on both sides of the Atlantic, and some parents became reluctant to get immunizations for their children. Research soon raised serious questions about his work. A dozen years later, after it became clear that it was fraudulent, *The Lancet* retracted the article, and British authorities stripped Wakefield of his ability to practice medicine. But he had already done permanent damage. Even though many articles had refuted his findings, many people believed in a link between vaccines and autism. This "antivax" movement gradually became more powerful, especially with the growth of social media in the early 21st century.

Trump's first public comment on the issue came in 2007. "When I was growing up, autism wasn't really a factor. And now all of a sudden, it's an epidemic. Everybody has their theory, and my theory is the shots. They're getting these massive injections at one time. I think it's the vaccinations." He made those comments following a press conference at Mar-a-Lago announcing a fundraising campaign by the advocacy group Autism Speaks. He went on: "When a little baby that weighs 20 pounds and 30 pounds gets pumped with 10 and 20 shots at one time, with one injection that's a giant injection, I personally think that has something to do with it."[88]

The notion that the vaccine schedule overwhelms a child's immune system is nonsense. Dr. Paul Offit, a leading expert on vaccines, puts it this way: "Indeed, children confronted more immunologic challenges by receiving only the smallpox vaccine 100 years ago than they do while receiving 14 different vaccines today."[89] And yet in spite of all the scientific evidence, Trump continued to tweet falsehoods about autism and vaccines.

- "Massive combined inoculations to small children is the cause for big increase in autism."[90]
- "Healthy young child goes to doctor, gets pumped with massive shot of many vaccines, doesn't feel good and changes—AUTISM. Many such cases!"[91]
- "If I were President I would push for proper vaccinations but would not allow one time massive shots that a small child cannot take—AUTISM."[92]

In his most reprehensible tweet, he said: "I am being proven right about massive vaccinations—the doctors lied. Save our children & their future."[93] So besides peddling myths, he was carrying his "fake news" theme into the world of medicine, suggesting that physicians were lying when they said that vaccines do not cause autism. Doctors have long worried that the internet was undercutting sound medical advice. With this tweet, Trump made things worse.

He kept up the misinformation after announcing his candidacy. In a 2015 Republican debate, he said: "Just the other day, two years old, two and a half years old, a child, a beautiful child went to have the vaccine, and came back, and a week later got a tremendous fever, got very, very sick, now is autistic."[94] Curiously, he had used almost the same words three years earlier. "It happened to somebody that worked for me recently," he said on Fox News. "I mean, they had this beautiful child, not a problem in the world, and all of the sudden they go in and they get this monster shot . . . then all of the sudden the child is different a month later."[95]

Vaccination turned out to be a minor campaign issue, but Trump continued to smile upon the antivax cause. In August 2016, he met with key antivaxxers including the discredited Andrew Wakefield.[96] During the transition, he conferred with Robert F. Kennedy Jr., a movement figure who had once likened vaccination to the Holocaust. Kennedy claimed that Trump had asked him to lead a "vaccine safety" commission, though the idea fizzled.

Many believers in the vaccine-autism myth claim that they do not oppose all vaccinations but want parents to space them out. This practice is dangerous. When parents delay immunizations, they are putting children at risk for preventable illnesses such as measles, and increasing the chance that they could spread the diseases to other vulnerable people. Even so, by giving this advice, the antivax activists claim that they are not antivaccine. In 2015, Kennedy insisted to *New York Post* columnist Andrea Peyser that he is "fiercely pro-vaccine." Trump told her something similar: "I'm totally pro-vaccine." Then he immediately repeated his favorite antivax canard: "What I've seen is that you put these massive injections at one time into a 20-pound baby. I've seen children who were 100 percent normal and become totally autistic."[97] In 2019, as measles outbreaks reached a 21st-century high, Trump answered a reporter's question by saying: "The vaccinations are so important."[98] Although some news reports suggested that he had shifted his position, he did not retract his earlier statements about combination vaccines and autism. A few offhand words at a press gaggle did not erase years of fearmongering.

Physicians had once hoped that vaccines had eradicated measles in the United States, but unvaccinated children were now catching measles and spreading it to others. Did Trump bear any blame? It is impossible to prove cause and effect, but there is substantial evidence that Trump's tweets and public comments may have lent heft to the antivax movement. A 2016 survey found that respondents who did not plan to get vaccinations for themselves or their families most often named Donald Trump as a public figure they thought shared their views.[99] A postelection showed that 31 percent of Trump voters—compared with 18 percent of Clinton voters—agreed that "vaccines have been shown to cause autism."[100] One experimental study presented people with both true and false statements that Trump had made. Among the latter was: "Vaccines cause autism." The researchers found that when they attributed such information to Trump, his Republican supporters believed it more than if it had no attribution.[101]

And once again, the Russians were involved. One noteworthy source of online confusion about vaccines was the Internet Research Agency—the same Russian troll farm that helped Trump in the 2016 campaign.[102] A typical Russian tweet read: "Did you know #vaccines caused autism? #VaccinateUS." The Russian trolls put out some nominally pro-vaccine content as well. According to a study of the Russian disinformation campaign: "This is consistent with a strategy of promoting discord across a range of controversial topics—a known tactic employed by Russian troll accounts. Such strategies may undermine the public health: normalizing these debates may lead the public to question long-standing scientific consensus regarding vaccine efficacy."[103] There is no reason to think that Trump knew of the Russian effort, much less that he consciously took part in it. But by spreading falsehoods and tacitly encouraging the divisive and destructive antivax movement, he was surely advancing Russian aims.

RUSSIA

And as for Russia itself, one paragraph in the Mueller report nicely sums up Trump's long battle with reality.

> Trump responded to questions about possible connections to Russia by denying any business involvement in Russia—even though the Trump Organization had pursued a business project in Russia as late as June 2016. Trump also expressed skepticism that Russia had hacked the emails at the same time as he and

other Campaign advisors privately sought information about any further planned WikiLeaks releases. After the election, when questions persisted about possible links between Russia and the Trump Campaign, the President-Elect continued to deny any connections to Russia and privately expressed concerns that reports of Russian election interference might lead the public to question the legitimacy of his election.[104]

A month after the 2016 election, Trump tweeted: "Unless you catch 'hackers' in the act, it is very hard to determine who was doing the hacking. Why wasn't this brought up before election?"[105] It was. Weeks before the election, Representative Michael McCaul (R-TX), then chair of the House Committee on Homeland Security said: "I have personally briefed him on that and told him that in my opinion . . . this was in fact a nation-state attack by Russia."[106]

At a 2017 rally in Alabama, he said: "No, Russia did not help me, that I can tell you, okay? Any Russians in the audience? [Laughter] Are there any Russians in the audience, please? I don't see too many Russians. I didn't see too many Russians in Pennsylvania."[107] For years, he kept repeating variations of that line. In 2019, he told the *New York Times*: "All I did was be a good candidate. Russia didn't help me. Russia did not help me."[108]

Wrong. Although the Mueller report did not find prosecutable evidence of a direct conspiracy between the Trump campaign and Russian intelligence, there is no doubt that Russia did help him. A few weeks before he took office, the intelligence community published its assessment that Putin had ordered an influence campaign in 2016 aimed at the US presidential election. "Russia's goals were to undermine public faith in the US democratic process, denigrate Secretary Clinton, and harm her electability and potential presidency. We further assess Putin and the Russian Government developed a clear preference for President-elect Trump."[109]

As usual, Trump lied about what he had done. At the 2019 Conservative Political Action Conference (CPAC), he complained: "If you tell a joke, if you're sarcastic, if you're having fun with the audience, if you're on live television with millions of people and

25,000 people in an arena, and if you say something like, 'Russia, please, if you can, get us Hillary Clinton's emails.' . . . And then that fake CNN and others say, 'He asked Russia to go get the emails. Horrible.'"[110] As noted in the last chapter, he made the remark at a press conference (not a rally) and told a reporter at the time that the invitation gave him no pause. He meant what he said.

THE AUDACITY OF MENDACITY

"Honesty is of pervasive human importance," wrote William Bennett in *The Book of Virtues*. "'I hate that man like the very Gates of Death who says one thing but hides another in his heart,' cries the anguished Achilles in Homer's *Iliad*. Every social activity, every human enterprise requiring people to act in concert, is impeded when people aren't honest with one another."[111] The effect of dishonesty is especially severe in the case of politics. The practitioners of whataboutism can find plenty of past political falsehoods but it is impossible to think of a president who has lied so blatantly about so many things. Instead of fostering healthy skepticism about political arguments, he is encouraging his followers to believe absurd claims and to reject any information that clashes with his interests and opinions.

People are entitled to their own opinions, but not their own facts. Political conflict can be healthy, provided that it involves debate over commonly accepted information and premises. Strenuous disagreements, even when they get rude at times, can lead to some kind of resolution. Without a shared understanding of reality, however, genuine deliberation is impossible. Instead of talking to each other, opposing sides shout about each other. The great danger is that the losing side will not accept defeat as legitimate. That is what happened when Southern states seceded in reaction to Abraham Lincoln's victory in 1860.

Rex Tillerson, who served as secretary of state and observed Trump's lies up close, spoke in May 2018 about the effects of dishonesty in high places. His words are worth quoting at length:

It is only by a fierce defense of the truth and a common set of facts that we create the conditions for a democratic free society, comprised of richly diverse peoples that those free people can explore and find solutions to the very challenges confronting a complex society of free people. If our leaders seek to conceal the truth or we as people become accepting of alternative realities that are no longer grounded in facts, then we as American citizens are on a pathway to relinquishing our freedom. [112]

3

CREATED EQUAL

The Declaration says that we are all created equal, endowed with unalienable rights, including life, liberty, and the pursuit of happiness. The words are connected. Equality means that nobody can judge better than you whether you are happy. "As judges of our own happiness," writes philosopher Danielle Allen, "we are all equals."[1] Equality also means that nobody is good enough to rule others without their consent. In the last letter that he penned before his death in 1826. Jefferson wrote of "the palpable truth, that the mass of mankind has not been born with saddles on their backs, nor a favored few booted and spurred, ready to ride them legitimately, by the grace of god."[2] Jefferson's ideal of equality was the touchstone of Lincoln's thought. To those who said that whites should rule because they were more intelligent, Lincoln replied: "By this rule, you are to be slave to the first man you meet, with an intellect superior to your own. But, say you, it is a question of interest; and, if you can make it your interest, you have the right to enslave another. Very well. And if he can make it his interest, he has the right to enslave you."[3] In a debate with Stephen A. Douglas, he said of the black man: "in the right to eat the bread without the leave of anybody else which his own hand earns, he is my equal and the equal of Judge Douglas, and the equal of every other man."[4]

Lincoln spoke those words less than three years before the Civil War. A persistent myth asserts that the war was about such things as tariffs. The Russians have helped promote this corrosive falsehood, as a footnote in the Mueller report confirms: "For example, one IRA account tweeted, 'To those people, who hate the Confederate flag. Did you know that the flag and the war wasn't about slavery, it was all about money.' The tweet received over 40,000 responses. @Jenn_Abrams 4/24/17 (2:37 p.m.) Tweet."[5] Contrary to the Russian propaganda, the Civil War was indeed about slavery. Alexander Stephens, the vice president of the Confederacy, freely admitted that the ideas of the Founding "rested upon the assumption of the equality of races." He said that the assumption was wrong. "Our new government is founded upon exactly the opposite idea; its foundations are laid, its corner-stone rests, upon the great truth that the negro is not equal to the white man; that slavery subordination to the superior race is his natural and normal condition."[6] That is what Robert E. Lee and other Confederates were fighting for. Fortunately, they lost.

During the 20th century, another challenge to the Founding arose in the form of the eugenics movement, which was more potent than we care to remember. Its followers preached that genes fated some people to be successful and others to be weak, stupid, or immoral. In other words, they embraced the "boots and saddles" philosophy that Jefferson had denounced. The movement aimed to improve the population's genetic makeup by breeding "superior" groups and discouraging the reproduction of their "inferiors." One popular textbook described multigenerational families full of lowlifes. "Hundreds of families such as those described above exist today, spreading disease, immorality, and crime to all parts of this country. . . . If such people were lower animals; we would probably kill them off to prevent them from spreading."[7] These ideas had a racist tone. The textbook said: "These are the Ethiopian or negro type, originating in Africa; the Malay or brown race, from the islands of the Pacific; the American Indian; the Mongolian or yellow race, including the natives of China, Japan, and the Eskimos; and finally, the highest type of all, the Caucasians, represented by the civilized white inhabitants of Europe and America."[8] Eugenic ideology left an imprint on public policy, providing a rationale for sterilizing people with disabilities and severely restricting immigration.

Eugenics started to fall out of favor as we confronted the Nazis in World War II. Various fringe groups clung to such ideas, however, and today's alt-right white supremacists are the most recent example. Jared Taylor, the editor of a white supremacist online magazine, once wrote that "there is no evidence, either in America or abroad, in the present or in the past, that suggests blacks are as intelligent as other races. All of the evidence points to a significant and durable inequality."[9] Alt-right leader Richard Spencer told Dinesh D'Souza: "The white race is expansive whether in terms of conquering, in terms of exploration of the seas or space, or scholarship and analysis of science. We possess something that's peculiar to us, and it makes us special." D'Souza asked if that "something" was genetic. "It is," Spencer replied. "No question. Everything is in the genes."[10]

The white supremacists move from genetics to a flat denial of the principles of the Declaration. Leaders of the alt-right have said that "nothing is less self-evident to us than the notion that all men are created equal" and that no phrase in history "has done more harm."[11] With an approving citation of Alexander Stephens, Spencer said: "We hold these truths to be self-evident: that all men are created unequal."[12]

THE GENE BELIEVER

Leading white supremacists had warm words for Trump in the 2016 campaign. When the press asked him if he accepted such endorsements, he sometimes muttered grudging disavowals, and at other times, he pleaded ignorance about his racist rooters. These reactions did not seem to bother them. "I love it," David Duke told Lisa Mascaro of the *Los Angeles Times*. "The fact that Donald Trump's doing so well, it proves that I'm winning. I am winning." Richard

Spencer added: "Before Trump, our identity ideas, national ideas, they had no place to go."[13]

It is no wonder why so many white supremacists see Trump as a kindred spirit. He has repeatedly repudiated our country's Founding principle.

- In 1999, he told Maureen Dowd: "But a lot of things play well in words—like 'All men are created equal'—that sounds magnificent and beautiful, but that doesn't necessarily make them so."[14]
- In 2004, he told Wolf Blitzer: "But the phrase that 'all men are created equal' is a wonderful phrase, but unfortunately it doesn't work that way. All men are not created equal. Some are born with a genius and some are born without. Now, you need that. If you don't have that, you can forget it."[15]
- In a 2006 video, he said: "You know they come with this statement 'all men are created equal.' Well, it sounds beautiful, and it was written by some very wonderful people and brilliant people, but it's not true because all people and all men [laughter] aren't created [equal] . . . you have to be born and blessed with something up here [pointing to his head]. On the assumption you are, you can become very rich."[16]
- In a 2009 interview, he told Deborah Solomon: "They say all men are created equal. It's not true. Some people are born very smart, some people are born not so smart."[17]

In an unpublished portion of the last interview, Solomon said that the phrase meant that people are entitled to equal rights under law. Trump acknowledged the point but did not say that he agreed with it. Instead, he complained: "The phrase is used often so much and it's a very confusing phrase to a lot of people."[18] His apologists might contend that he was merely talking about the diversity of abilities and was not really suggesting that people are unequal. Yes, he was suggesting just that. Out of all of the phrases in the Founding documents, "all men are created equal" was the only one that he kept repeating, and kept denying.

In recent years, his presidential speechwriters have gamely tried to get him right with America by sticking the word *equal* into some of his prepared texts. But their effort is like sprinkling cinnamon on arsenic: his attitude is a matter of record, and some new pro forma statements will not make the old, candid ones go away.

In Trump's mind, where does the inequality come from? Like the white supremacists, he sees himself as an *übermensch*, and credits genes for his superiority. "Well, I think I was born with a drive for success," he told CNN's Becky Anderson. "I had a father who was successful. He was a builder in Brooklyn and Queens. And he was successful. And, you know, I have a certain gene. I'm a gene believer. Hey, when you connect two racehorses, you usually end up with a fast horse. And I really was—you know, I had a—a good gene pool from the standpoint of that."[19] Five years later, he told a rally in Mobile, Alabama: "Do we believe in the gene thing? I mean, I do. Right? You know, I do. Like they used to say, Secretariat doesn't produce slow horses."[20] A few months after that speech, he tweeted: "I consider my health, stamina and strength one of my greatest assets. The world has watched me for many years and can so testify—great genes!"[21] Trump has often suggested that his genes had endowed him with a vast array of gifts. "I have a natural ability for land," he boasted to biographer Michael D'Antonio.[22] He told reporters for the Associated Press, "I have a natural instinct for science."[23] A Trump spokesperson even credited "good genes" for his peculiar orange skin tone.[24]

It goes without saying that there is no such thing as a "success gene." For complex activities, success depends on the interaction of the person and the setting. The most important thing that Fred Trump left to Donald was not a set of genes but a pile of money. It is not certain that Trump's dishonesty and shamelessness stem from genetics, but it is clear that he had the good luck to come of age in an environment that rewarded such traits instead of disdaining them. If he had grown up with the same character but in different circumstances—say, as a milkman's son in a small town—he would probably have ended up in poverty or prison.

THE COLOR OF INEQUALITY

Trump's obsession with genetic superiority raises that question of whether he thinks that certain demographic groups are inferior, particularly that they are prone to sloth and crime. The evidence indicates that he believes such things, or at least encourages others to believe them.

Recall from the introductory chapter that he first made the front page of the *New York Times* by blatantly discriminating against African American renters. He did not become more enlightened when he moved into the gambling business. "When Donald and Ivana came to the casino, the bosses would order all the black people off the floor," former casino employee Kip Brown told *The New Yorker*. "It was the eighties, I was a teenager, but I remember it: they put us all in the back."[25] The New Jersey Casino Control Commission hit Trump Plaza with a $200,000 fine for keeping black employees away from a racist, mob-connected high roller.[26] In a review of the penalty, an appeals panel said, "In our view, the transcript fairly reeks of Trump Plaza's guilt."[27] Casino executive John O'Donnell recalls bigoted remarks. At one of his casinos, Trump complained about an influx of African American patrons: "It's looking a little dark in here."[28] He disparaged an African American manager: "And isn't it funny, I've got black accountants at Trump Castle and Trump Plaza. Black guys counting my money! I hate it. The only kind of people I want counting my money are short guys that wear yarmulkes every day." He continued, directly referring to his belief in genetic destiny: "I think the guy is lazy, and it's probably not his fault because laziness is a trait in blacks. It really is. I believe that. It's not anything they can control."[29] (Trump tried to belittle O'Donnell as a disgruntled former employee, but admitted, "The stuff O'Donnell wrote about me is probably true.")[30]

Trump's public remarks were scarcely more guarded. In 1989, a young white woman suffered a brutal assault and rape while jogging in New York's Central Park. After a twelve-day coma stemming from a fractured skull and massive blood loss, she had no memory of the attack. Police arrested five suspects, four African Americans and one Hispanic, using trickery and coercion to obtain confessions. The oldest was just 16 years old. A racial frenzy ensued, with the city's tabloids hyping the idea of "wilding"—random, savage attacks by "wolf packs" of black and brown young men. Trump added to the hysteria. "Mayor Koch has stated that hate and rancor should be removed from our hearts," he said in a full-page newspaper ad. "I do not think so. I want to hate these muggers and murderers."[31] In an interview with Larry King, he pressed the theme: "Of course I hate these people and let's all hate these people because maybe hate is what we need if we're gonna get something done." He denied that he was "pre-judging" the suspects, but merely saying that they should get the death penalty if the victim died and they were found guilty.[32]

Of course, Trump would claim that "these people" specifically meant criminals, but many New Yorkers undoubtedly heard a broader racial message. *The Bonfire of the Vanities*, which captured the city's zeitgeist in the late 1980s, revolved around an affluent white man who panicked after getting lost in a black neighborhood. White New Yorkers linked blacks to violent crime, and black New Yorkers were painfully aware of this attitude. "I knew that this famous person calling for us to die was very serious," recalled Yusef Salaam, one of the five. "We were all afraid. Our families were afraid. Our loved ones were afraid. For us to walk around as if we had a target on our backs, that's how things were."[33]

In 1990, despite meager physical evidence, a jury convicted the teens. Attorney Michael Warren, who would later represent them, said that Trump's advertisements played a part. "He poisoned the minds of many people who lived in New York and who, rightfully, had a natural affinity for the victim," said Warren, adding that the jurors "had to be affected by the inflammatory rhetoric in the ads."[34] The five youths would spend between 6 and 13 years behind bars. In 2002, a prisoner serving a life sentence for another crime confessed that he was the culprit. DNA testing confirmed his guilt and cleared the Central Park Five. They later received large settlements from New York City for their unjust imprisonment. Trump disregarded the facts and still insisted that they were guilty. "My opinion on the settlement of the Central Park Jogger case is that it's a disgrace," said a Trump-bylined op-ed in the *New York Daily News*. "The recipients must be laughing out loud at the stupidity of the city."[35] Yusef Salaam wrote: "It's further proof of Trump's bias, racism and inability to admit that he's wrong."[36]

During the years when he was failing in the casino industry, he found a new target of color: Native Americans. Testifying before a congressional subcommittee about tribal casinos, he questioned the racial bona fides of the owners: "They don't look like Indians to me, and they don't look like Indians to Indians, and a lot of people are laughing at it, and you are telling how tough it is, how rough it is, to get approved. Well, you go up to Connecticut, and you look. Now, they don't look like Indians to me."[37] He said that they were not capable of keeping out organized crime—a statement that was richly ironic in light of his long-standing ties to the Mafia. In 2000, he resumed the effort to smear Native Americans. When New York State was considering expansion of tribal casinos, Trump started a stealth campaign to stir up racial fears. With Trump's money, consultant Roger Stone cooked up a front group called "the New York Institute for Law and Safety," which ran newspaper ads attacking the tribe that proposed to run new casinos. One ad said that "the Mohawk Indians have a long and documented history of criminal activity including drug dealing, cigarette and alcohol smuggling, illegal immigrant trafficking and violence." Another asked: "Are these the new neighbors we want?" Signing off on the latter ad, Trump scrawled: "Roger, this could be good!"[38]

The rise of Barack Obama prompted another turn in Trump's racial innuendo. As we have seen, he helped spread the myth that America's first African American president was African, not American. And Trump was hooked on the idea that Obama was lazy. Dozens of times, he tweeted that Obama was playing golf instead of doing his job.[39] Consider this example from 2011: "@BarackObama played golf yesterday. Now he heads to a 10 day vacation in Martha's Vineyard. Nice work ethic."[40] Trump did not let go even after he became president. Giving visitors a tour of the White House, he pointed to a room and lied about his predecessor: "He just sat in here and watched basketball all day."[41] Trump also suggested that Obama was not very intelligent. "I heard he was a terrible student, terrible. How does a bad student go to Columbia and then to Harvard?" Trump claimed in an interview with the Associated Press. "I'm thinking about it. I'm certainly looking into it. Let him show his records."[42] Obama did his undergraduate work at Occidental and Columbia. Though it is true that he did not release his transcripts, he did graduate *magna cum laude* from Harvard Law School and was the first African American president of the *Harvard Law Review*.

Envy and psychological projection are at work here. Obama is younger, thinner, smarter, and more physically vigorous than his successor. Trump is notorious for his aversion to reading, his habit of binge-watching cable television during "executive time," and his many days at his golf courses. Despite his professed pride in "being, like, really smart," there is no record that he ever achieved any academic distinction. In fact, he ordered his fixer Michael Cohen to threaten administrators at his high school and colleges with civil and criminal charges if they disclosed his records.[43]

Trump has insulted the intelligence of many people, not just Barack Obama. But he does seem to reserve a specific contempt for African Americans. In the 2016 campaign, Cohen testified, "he told me that black people would never vote for him because they were too stupid."[44] At a rally in Utica, New York, he attacked Representative Maxine Waters (D-CA): "Maxine Waters, the new face of the Democrat Party. Maxine Waters, she's a real beauty. Maxine. Boy, oh boy, I watch her. Crazy Maxine. Low-IQ person, low IQ, and this is really what is steering, to a certain extent, the Democrats. I mean, she gets up and she wants people to be violent."[45] In an interview with CNN's Don Lemon, basketball legend LeBron James made a negative comment about Trump. In his Twitter reply, Trump managed to deride two African American men at once: "Lebron James was just interviewed by the dumbest man on television, Don Lemon. He made Lebron look smart, which isn't easy to do."[46]

On Twitter during the presidential race, Trump returned to his 1989 theme of black crime, this time even more directly. In April

2015, after civil unrest in Baltimore, he retweeted a blunt message from an anonymous source: "@circuspony2: @realDonaldTrump Did you see all the whites that were robbed & assaulted during the riots, Mr President? #Trump2016."[47] In November of that year, a day after his supporters beat up an African American protester at one of his rallies, he retweeted a blatantly racist image of a masked black man with a pistol, along with bogus statistics purporting to compare black and white murder rates.[48] The original image soon disappeared from Twitter, but *The Little Green Footballs* blog saved a screenshot and traced it back to a neo-Nazi.[49]

During the spring and summer of 2017, the neo-Nazis came to Charlottesville, Virginia. The city council had voted to remove a statue of Robert E. Lee from a local park. The decision provided an occasion for white supremacists to descend on the city. In May, Richard Spencer led a rally and torchlight parade, where attendees chanted: "You will not replace us," "Russia is our friend," and the Nazi slogan "Blood and soil."[50] In July, a small group of Klansmen held another rally. They were protesting "the ongoing cultural genocide . . . of white Americans," according to one Klan member. "They're trying to erase us out of the history books."[51] The white supremacists planned a bigger rally for August. The rally's organizer acknowledged that the Lee statue was merely a symbol of an "existential crisis" facing his kind: "White people are rapidly becoming a minority in the U.S. and Europe," he said in an interview with Pro Publica. "If we're not able to advocate for ourselves we may go extinct."[52] On the evening of August 11, the event started with another torchlight parade. Among the slogans the marchers chanted was: "Jews will not replace us!" The next morning, white supremacists and counter-protesters started gathering. "We are determined to take our country back," David Duke said in a conversation on the sidelines. "We are going to fulfill the promise of Donald Trump. That's what we believe in. That's why we voted for Donald Trump, because he said he's going to take our country back."[53] Before the rally could begin, however, fights broke out, and the police ordered the crowd to disperse. A couple of hours later, one of the white rallygoers deliberately drove his car into a group of pedestrians, killing counter-protester Heather Heyer.

Speaking at his New Jersey golf club, Trump reacted: "We condemn in the strongest possible terms this egregious display of hatred, bigotry, and violence, on many sides. On many sides. It's been going on for a long time in our country. Not Donald Trump, not Barack Obama. This has been going on for a long, long time."[54] In response to criticism that he was vague, the White House issued a statement that his comment included white supremacist groups. The next day, he recited a similar statement from a teleprompter. At a press availability on the following day, he made his now-infamous remarks equating the white supremacists and the counter-protesters:

> [Y]ou had some very bad people in that group, but you also had people that were very fine people, on both sides. . . . And you had people—and I'm not talking about the neo-Nazis and the White nationalists, because they should be condemned totally— but you had many people in that group other than neo-Nazis and White nationalists. . . . Now, in the other group also, you had some fine people. But you also had troublemakers, and you see them come with the black outfits and with the helmets and with the baseball bats. You had a lot of bad people in the other group.[55]

Trump's "even-handed" approach pleased white supremacists. "Really proud of him," Richard Spencer wrote in a text message. "He bucked the narrative of Alt-Right violence, and made a statement that is fair and down to earth. C'ville could have hosted a peaceful rally—just like our event in May—if the police and mayor had done their jobs. Charlottesville needed to police the streets and police the antifa, whose organizations are dedicated to violence." Jared Taylor said: "It is gratifying that there is at least one political figure who recognizes that not everyone who wants to keep the Lee statue is a neo-Nazi or white supremacist, and that many of the counterdemonstrators were violent thugs."[56] And David Duke tweeted: "Thank you President Trump for your honesty & courage to tell the truth about #Charlottesville & condemn the leftist terrorists in BLM/Antifa."[57]

Senator Lindsey Graham of South Carolina condemned Trump for "suggesting there is moral equivalency between the white supremacist neo-Nazis and KKK members who attended the Charlottesville rally and people like Ms. Heyer. I, along with many others, do not endorse this moral equivalency. Many Republicans do not agree with and will fight back against the idea that the Party of Lincoln has a welcome mat out for the David Dukes of the world."[58] Graham was wrong about the last part. Elected Republicans, cowering in the face of Republican primary voters, ended up acquiescing in Trump's behavior. Graham himself became one of Trump's most servile enablers.

Two years later, Richard Spencer looked back: "There is no question that Charlottesville wouldn't have occurred without Trump. It really was because of his campaign and this new potential for a nationalist candidate who was resonating with the public in a very intense way. The alt-right found something in Trump. He changed the paradigm and made this kind of public presence of the alt-right possible."[59] Trump had no regrets. In 2019, a reporter asked him if he still thought that there were many fine people on both sides. He said: "Oh, I've answered that question. And if you look at what I said, you will see that that question was answered perfectly. And I was talking about people that went because they felt very strongly about the monument to Robert E. Lee, a great general."[60] Trump lied. The real purpose of the rally was not to defend a statue of Robert E. Lee but to desecrate the hometown of Thomas Jefferson.

ALIENS

Trump often disparages dark-skinned immigrants and foreigners. "When Mexico sends its people, they're not sending their best," he said at his 2015 announcement of candidacy. "They're sending people that have lots of problems, and they're bringing those problems with us. They're bringing drugs, they're bringing crime, they're rapists, and some, I assume are good people, but I speak to border guards and they tell us what we're getting."[61] As the previous chapter explained, his attacks on immigrants are just factually wrong. Although some migrants do commit serious offenses, a recent study shows that growth in undocumented immigration does not raise local crime rates.[62] In addition to being deceitful, his ugly language reflects and reinforces ugly prejudices. Echoing old xenophobic themes, Trump depicts his rhetorical targets as dangerous, diseased, and dirty.

At a 2018 White House meeting, he said: "We have people coming into the country, or trying to come in—and we're stopping a lot of them—but we're taking people out of the country. You wouldn't believe how bad these people are. These aren't people. These are animals."[63] When reporters questioned his language, he said that he was responding to a comment about the MS-13 gang and that he was referring only to its members. But one could read the plain language of his remarks as applying broadly to people entering the country illegally—just as his 1989 comments on "these people" sounded as if they went beyond the Central Park Five.

When he dwells on Hispanic crime, his horror stories cross the border between the merely lurid and the downright kinky. Consider just three examples from January 2019. At a press statement on a government shutdown, he said, "you'll have traffickers having three and four women with tape on their mouths and tied up, sitting in the back of a van or a car, and they'll drive that van or the car not through a port of entry, where we have very talented people that look for every little morsel of drugs."[64] Two days later, he repeated the idea: "But it's not just illegals. It's criminals. It's drugs. It's the new phenomena that's been age-old, been going on for thousands of years, but it's never been worse than now because of the Internet. Human trafficking—where they grab women, put tape over their mouth, come through our border, and sell them."[65] And a few days after that, he was still talking about Mexicans "taping them up, wrapping tape around their mouths so they can't shout or scream, tying up their hands behind their back and even their legs and putting them in a backseat of a car or a van—three, four, five, six, seven at a time."[66] Human trafficking is horrible, of course, but reporters could find no basis for the details in Trump's tales, which bear a disturbing likeness to bondage fantasy.

Between the raping and taping that he describes with such strange enthusiasm, Trump depicts outsiders as a sexual threat— something that bigots have done since time out of mind. Meanwhile, he is also repeating the ancient canard that they are bearers of sickness. In a 1903 magazine cartoon, a fat, unkempt immigrant carried a box with a message: "One million immigrants came to the U.S. in twelve months." Beside him stood a health inspector who held a syringe and a sign that warned, "He brings disease."[67] In the same vein, Trump tweeted in 2014, "Our government now imports illegal immigrants and deadly diseases. Our leaders are inept."[68] The next year, he retweeted a follower's rhetorical question: "In addition to the criminals among the illegal aliens what about all the infectious diseases they brought to US."[69] And in 2018, he tweeted that Democrats "want Open Borders for anyone to come in. This brings large scale crime and disease."[70] There is no evidence for such a claim, except in the self-fulfilling sense that foul conditions in immigrant detention facilities often sicken the detainees, particularly children.

From 2014 to 2016, there was an outbreak of the Ebola virus in West Africa. Trump did all that he could to turn concern into hysteria. He warned that unless the United States canceled flights from West Africa, "the plague will start and spread inside our 'borders.'"[71] Instead of halting travel, President Obama sent troops to Liberia to set up healthcare facilities and train medical workers. Obama's decision saved thousands of lives in Liberia, and in the end, there were fewer than a dozen cases in the United States. Nevertheless, Trump tweeted: "Why are we sending thousands of ill-trained soldiers into Ebola infested areas of Africa! Bring the plague back to U.S.? Obama is so stupid."[72]

The word *infest* here is telling because it summons up images of vermin. As if by reflex, Trump often uses it when the topic involves immigration or people of immigrant stock. Democrats, he tweeted, "don't care about crime and want illegal immigrants, no matter how bad they may be, to pour into and infest our Country, like MS-13."[73] He tweeted about California: "Soooo many Sanctuary areas want OUT of this ridiculous, crime infested & breeding concept."[74] He criticized Elijah Cummings, a House Democrat from Baltimore who had questioned administration policies at the border. "As proven last week during a Congressional tour, the Border is clean, efficient & well run, just very crowded," Trump tweeted. "Cumming District [sic] is a disgusting, rat and rodent infested mess."[75] In the summer of 2019, he went after four progressive House Democrats, tweeting that they "originally came from countries whose governments are a complete and total catastrophe."[76] He added: "Why don't they go back and help fix the totally broken and crime infested places from which they came."[77] Three of the four were born in the United States, and the fourth was a naturalized citizen who came to the United States as a child refugee from Somalia. But because they were women of color, Trump assumed that they were all foreign. By the way, the Equal Employment Opportunity Commission cites the phrase "Go back to where you came from" as an example of harassment based on national origin.[78]

Despite widespread criticism of his comments, Trump refused to apologize. Instead, his campaign issued a fundraising email singling out one of the four, Alexandria Ocasio-Cortez of New York. Denouncing her proposal for direct popular election of the president, the email said "this is our country, not theirs."[79]

Trump associates third-world countries with filth and squalor. In a June 2017 meeting on immigration, he complained that Haitian visitors "all have AIDS" and that once Nigerians had seen this country, they would never "go back to their huts."[80] During a January 2018 meeting at the Oval Office, he was even more hostile to black and brown people. As Josh Dawsey reported at the *Washington Post*, Trump got annoyed when lawmakers said that the protection of newcomers from Haiti, El Salvador, and African countries should be part of an agreement on immigration. "Why are we having all these people from shithole countries come here?" He singled out one country: "Why do we need more Haitians? Take them out."[81]

He said that he preferred to bring in people from places such as Norway. Of all the developed countries he could have mentioned, why did he pick that one? In the early decades of the 20th century, "Nordic" was a catch-all term for white ethnic purity.[82] White supremacists such as David Duke, Richard Spencer, and Andrew Anglin took his comments as an endorsement of their views. Said Anglin: "This is encouraging and refreshing, as it indicates Trump is more or less on the same page as us with regards to race and immigration." The racist group Identity Evropa, issued a statement: "Although we might put it differently, Identity Evropa shares President Trump's sensible view that immigrants coming from countries like Norway are preferable to those coming from countries like Haiti."[83]

Perhaps the best-known example of Trump's prejudice is his series of attacks on Judge Gonzalo P. Curiel, who presided over a federal civil suit against the fraudulent Trump University. In February 2016, Trump complained at an Arkansas rally about "a very hostile judge . . . who I believe happens to be Spanish, which is fine." The next day, he told Chris Wallace of Fox News: "Now, he is Hispanic, I believe. He is a very hostile judge to me. I said it loud and clear." In San Diego three months later, he called Judge Curiel "a hater of Donald Trump . . . who happens to be, we believe, Mexican."[84] Video shows the crowd booing loudly at the mention of the judge's name. When the remarks caused controversy, Trump told the *New York Times*: "I'm building the wall, I'm building the wall. I have a Mexican judge. He's of Mexican heritage. He should have recused himself, not only for that, for other things."[85] Judge Curiel was born, raised, and educated in Indiana. If he is a Mexican judge, then Trump is a German president.

At the time, some Republicans could still speak out against Trump's bigotry. House Speaker Paul Ryan (R-WI) said: "Claiming a person can't do their job because of their race is sort of like the textbook definition of a racist comment."[86] Senator Lindsey Graham (R-SC) said on CNN: "I don't think he's racist but he's playing the race card. And in the political process he's putting the race card on the table. I think it's very un-American for a political leader to question whether a person can judge based on his heritage."[87] In remarks to the *New York Times*, Graham drove home the point: "This is the most un-American thing from a politician since Joe McCarthy."[88]

Julius Krein, a conservative intellectual who had once supported Trump, wrote in the summer of 2017 that incidents such as his attack on Judge Curiel or his reluctance to disavow David Duke were not merely campaign gaffes. "It is now clear that we were deluding ourselves. Either Mr. Trump is genuinely sympathetic to the David Duke types, or he is so obtuse as to be utterly incapable of learning from his worst mistakes. Either way, he continues to prove his harshest critics right."[89]

APPEARANCE AND DISABILITY

Trump judges people by external characteristics. His favorite adjective is "beautiful," and his opinions about appearance weigh heavily in his personnel choices. He nominated White House physician Ronny Jackson to head the Department of Veterans Affairs even though he had scant administrative background and little experience with veterans' issues. But in addition to making sycophantic comments about Trump's health, Jackson looked the part in the president's eyes. "He's like central casting," said Trump. "He became a Hollywood star. He's going to leave and go make a movie."[90] Conversely, Trump rejects qualified people because of their looks. He declined to reappoint Janet Yellen to chair the Federal Reserve because he reportedly deemed the distinguished economist to be too short for the job.[91] He turned down Senator Bob Corker (R-TN) for similar reasons and later mocked the five-foot-seven lawmaker as "Liddle Bob Corker."[92] One wonders what he would have thought of five-foot-zero Milton Friedman or five-foot-four James Madison.

The obsession with looks also applies to his political foes. During the Republican primary campaign, he dismissed Carly Fiorina: "Look at that face. Would anybody vote for that? Can you imagine that, the face of our next president?"[93] In 2016, he made this odd criticism of Hillary Clinton: "I just don't believe she has a presidential look, and you need a presidential look."[94] He attacked the chair of the House Intelligence Committee as "Pencil Neck Adam Schiff." He initially referred to the California Democrat as "Liddle Adam Schiff," but perhaps an aide informed him that Schiff is five foot eleven.

His scorn for perceived imperfection is especially toxic in the case of disability. He has little use for people with physical disabilities and other limitations and will not go out of his way to help them, even when they are relatives. Trump and his siblings cut off their nephew's medical coverage after he challenged the will of their father, Fred Trump. The nephew had an infant son with a severe neurological disorder causing seizures and brain damage. When a reporter for the *New York Daily News* asked whether terminating the insurance would seem cold-hearted, given the enormous cost of treating the baby's disability, Trump was dismissive. "I can't help that. It's cold when someone sues my father. Had he come to see me, things could very possibly have been much different for them."[95] The nephew and his wife sued Trump and reached a settlement. Their son now lives with cerebral palsy.

Barbara Res, who was vice president of construction at the Trump Organization, recalled Trump talking to an architect in a Trump Tower residential elevator. He asked the architect about raised dots next to the floor numbers. When the architect explained that they were Braille, Trump ordered the architect to get rid of them. The architect demurred, which triggered a Trump outburst. "Get rid of the [expletive] braille," he said. "No blind people are going to live in Trump Tower. Just do it."[96]

His intolerance for disabled people burst into public view when he mocked *New York Times* investigative reporter Serge Kovaleski for his recollection of a story about Muslims and the 9/11 attacks. Trump made fun of Kovaleski's arthrogryposis, a condition that severely limits the use of his arms. "Now, the poor guy—you've got to see this guy, 'Ah, I don't know what I said! I don't remember!'" Trump said as he thrashed his arms.[97] Trump later denied that he was ridiculing Kovaleski's disability, claiming that he did not even remember the reporter. Yet another lie. Kovaleski, who had covered

Trump's business career, told the *New York Times*: "Donald and I were on a first-name basis for years."[98] Someone like Trump would never forget Kovaleski's appearance, which is why he prefaced his mockery with the words "You've got to see this guy." Columnist Ann Coulter made an absurd attempt to defend Trump, saying that he was not specifically deriding Kovaleski, but merely "doing a standard retard, waving his arms and sounding stupid."[99]

The one bit of truth in Coulter's excuse is that Trump uses the r-word as a term of derision. In September 2008, he tweeted about *Fear*, journalist Bob Woodward's account of the first year of his administration. "The already discredited Woodward book, so many lies and phony sources, has me calling Jeff Sessions 'mentally retarded' and 'a dumb southerner.' I said NEITHER, never used those terms on anyone, including Jeff."[100] In fact, audio recordings prove that he had used the r-word to insult people. In April 2004, he told shock jock Howard Stern: "But you know, I was criticized in one magazine, where the writer was retarded and said, 'Donald Trump put up seven million dollars.' I put up, this put up like, 45 times more money. And then, they criticize me for not putting up more money. I mean these guys are dopes."[101] During a September appearance on the show, he started to use the word again but cut himself off: "I have a golf pro who's mentally ret—I mean he's like, really not a smart guy."[102] And although backstage recordings from *Celebrity Apprentice* have not become public, three sources told *The Daily Beast* that he repeatedly used the term against Marlee Matlin, the Oscar-winning deaf actress who competed on the show.[103] *New York Times* journalist Maureen Dowd reported that he walked out on a prank interview with comic actor Sacha Baron Cohen: "I thought he was seriously retarded. It was a total con job. But my daughter, Ivanka, saw it and thought it was very cool."[104] And in an otherwise favorable book about Trump's public relations, Robert Slater quoted him: "Unless you're retarded, who wants to answer questions all day? I would rather be reading the newspaper or bull-shitting."[105]

In 2017, the Trump White House issued a staff-written statement on Down Syndrome Awareness Month: "Sadly, there remain too many people—both in the United States and throughout the world—that still see Down syndrome as an excuse to ignore or discard human life."[106] Antiabortion conservatives take such statements as a sign that Trump believes in the equal dignity of people with disabilities. Unscripted comments point in another direction. Trump had always been pro-choice until he needed evangelical support for his presidential campaign. He claimed that he switched sides because he knew a family that decided not to abort and that their child had become "a total superstar." In an interview for *The Daily Caller*, Jamie Weinstein asked him if he would have made the change if the child had not been a superstar. If Trump sincerely opposed abortion and believed in human equality, he would have answered that the right to life belongs as much to people who struggle with disabilities as to physically perfect superstars. Here is what he said instead: "I've never thought of it. That's an interesting question. I've never thought of it. Probably not, but I've never thought of it. I would say no, but in this case it was an easy one because he's such an outstanding person."[107]

Even when he feigns respect for people with disabilities, his true feelings slip out. Welcoming Olympic athletes to the White House, he said: "And what happened with the Paralympics was so incredible and so inspiring to me. And I watched—it's a little tough to watch too much, but I watched as much as I could."[108] Some said that Trump was merely referring to limits on his time, which was implausible in light of his appetite for television. Lawyer David Cross, who was born without a left hand, wrote that the remark was offensive. "Many people find it 'tough to watch' those of us with disabilities. . . . This physical shunning provides a regular reminder that we are unlike those around us. And that hurts."[109]

Trump's disdain for the disabled extends to people who acquired their disabilities while serving our country. In 1991, he objected to disabled veterans peddling goods near his property, saying that they were "clogging and seriously downgrading the area."[110] In 2004, he wrote Mayor Michael Bloomberg. He claimed that some of the vendors were merely pretending to be veterans, saying that one had said, "Mr. Trump, I am too smart to fight in a war." But he also wanted to keep the real veterans away, too. "Whether they are veterans or not, they [the vendors] should not be allowed to sell on this most important and prestigious shopping street." He asserted that they were making a mess, and then used a word that would gain a great deal of freight during the 2016 campaign: "I hope you can stop this very deplorable situation before it is too late."[111]

SOWING DISCORD

According to the indictment of the Russians' Internet Research Agency (IRA), a strategic goal of their influence campaign was "to sow discord in the U.S. political system."[112] Conflict over equality offers a potent means to this end. After all, it was the ultimate cause of the Civil War. Although Mueller presented no direct evidence of conspiracy, Trump and the Russian trolls both sowed plenty of discord, with the latter often explicitly supporting the former. NBC obtained a Russian document saying that Trump's election had "deepened conflicts in American society" and suggested a successful influence project would "undermine the country's territorial integrity and military and economic potential."[113] Even if they did not work together, they worked in parallel.

The Mueller team identified dozens of US rallies organized by the IRA. The earliest evidence of their effort was a "confederate rally" in November 2015.[114] The Russians also targeted social media ads at whites and racial minorities in order to pit them against one another. Reporters at *USA Today* analyzed 3,517 IRA Facebook ads released by the House Permanent Select Committee on Intelligence. More than half of them, accounting for 25 million ad impressions, directly mentioned race. The next two most common topics were crime and immigration.[115] After the Charlottesville incident, Russian Twitter trolls backed Trump with thousands of tweets such as "#aleex Uncovered Video DESTROYS Liberal Narrative Trump is a White Supremacist #alexx."[116] The pro-Trump surge stopped abruptly after a few days, apparently because Twitter shut down many Russia-linked accounts.

Nevertheless, the Russian leaders must be pleased. A 2019 Pew survey found that 58 percent of Americans said race relations were bad, and 56 percent thought that Trump had made them worse. About two-thirds said that it had become more common for people to express racist views since Trump took office, and 45 percent said that such expressions had become more acceptable.[117]

There is a historical link to a mid-19th-century political movement that opposed immigration. Its members gained the nickname of "Know-Nothings" because of instructions to answer questions by claiming to know nothing about the group. The Know-Nothings spoke of newcomers much as Trump does today, claiming that they brought crime and disease. They referred to Irish Catholic immigrants as "St. Patrick's vermin." Their official name was "the American Party," which was a cover for their un-American attitudes. One Illinois lawyer was not buying. In an 1855 letter to a friend, Abraham Lincoln wrote that "if the Know-Nothings took over, the Declaration of Independence would read: 'All men are created equal, except negroes, and foreigners, and Catholics.' When it comes to this I should prefer emigrating to some country where they make no pretense of loving liberty—to Russia, for instance, where despotism can be taken pure, and without the base alloy of hypocrisy."[118]

4

THE ADMINISTRATION OF JUSTICE

The American Revolution was a rejection of arbitrary power. The Declaration said: "The history of the present King of Great Britain is a history of repeated injuries and usurpations, all having in direct object the establishment of an absolute Tyranny over these States." It followed with a bill of particulars arguing that the king had trampled on long-standing laws and practices. For instance, it charged that he had "obstructed the Administration of Justice by refusing his Assent to Laws for establishing Judiciary Powers." At the end of the litany, it drew a conclusion: "A Prince, whose character is thus marked by every act which may define a Tyrant, is unfit to be the ruler of a free people."

For the Founders, a central principle of government was the rule of law. John Adams famously wrote that a republic had to be "a government of laws and not of men."[1] Ideally, such a system would keep executive officials and judges from making decisions that merely reflected their own will. Instead, they would act according to the law. Those who wrote the statutes would not have a free hand, either. Like the members of the other branches, they would work within the four corners of the Constitution. An elaborate system of checks and balances would encourage officeholders to police those boundaries. As Hamilton wrote, so would "the sanctity of an oath."[2] The president takes a unique oath to preserve, protect, and defend the Constitution. Article VI says that all other officials at the state and federal levels "shall be bound by Oath or Affirmation, to support this Constitution."

The rule of law also means that all are equal before the law. The history of civil rights in the United States has been a long struggle to follow this principle by eliminating legal distinctions among classes of people. The government should not impose burdens or punishments on specific individuals because officials dislike them, nor should it grant benefits to a favored few. In taking the judicial oath, federal judges swear to "administer justice without respect to persons, and do equal right to the poor and to the rich."[3] As every sentient American adult knows, our political and legal systems do not always work this way. Injustices are all too common. But at least we recognize injustices as breaches of our norms, not as the norms themselves.

The mention of norms leads to a more profound point: the rule of law requires respect for law. Punishing criminals is necessary but not sufficient, because there would not be enough police officers and prison cells to keep order if they were the only things that kept Americans from breaking the law. As for those in power, checks and balances are auxiliary precautions. The system runs aground if officials disregard their oaths of office when nobody is looking. The Founders understood the importance of attitudes, which is why Madison wrote of the "veneration" of our institutions. Decades later, Lincoln vividly reiterated the idea in his 1838 Lyceum Address:

> As the patriots of seventy-six did to the support of the Declaration of Independence, so to the support of the Constitution and Laws, let every American pledge his life, his property, and his sacred honor;—let every man remember that to violate the law, is to trample on the blood of his father, and to tear the character of his own, and his children's liberty. Let reverence for the laws . . . become the political religion of the nation.[4]

In our own time, Rudolph Giuliani told the United Nations in 2001: "Our belief in democracy, the rule of law, and respect for human life—that's how you become an American."[5] The oath of naturalization drives home his point. Each new citizen swears to "support and defend the Constitution and laws of the United States of America against all enemies, foreign and domestic" and to "bear true faith and allegiance to the same."

Veneration of our institutions and respect for the law do not happen automatically. They require deliberate maintenance, hence the importance of civic education. A heavy burden falls on political leaders, who have to articulate our ideals and set an example for everyone else. The rule of law suffers when they break the law, mock the law, or take artful dodges around the law. As Madison wrote, "No government, any more than an individual, will long be respected without being truly respectable."[6]

Trump does not regard the law as worthy of respect or veneration. Early in his administration, he met with Native American tribal leaders at the White House and told them to "just do it" and take whatever they wanted from lands under their control. "Chief, chief," he said to one of the leaders, "what are they going to do? Once you get it out of the ground are they going to make you put it back in there? I mean, once it's out of the ground it can't go back in there." As he put it, the rule of necessity trumped the rule of law. "I feel like we've got no choice; other countries are just doing it. China is not asking questions about all of this stuff. They're just doing it. And guys, we've just got to do it."[7]

As a candidate and president, Trump occasionally claimed to revere the Constitution and laws. "I feel very strongly about our Constitution," he said in January 2016. "I'm proud of it, I love it and I want to go through the Constitution."[8] More often, though, he demonstrated an appalling ignorance and disregard. Campaign adviser Sam Nunberg once tried to teach him about the Constitution. "I got as far as the Fourth Amendment, before his finger is pulling down on his lip and his eyes are rolling back in his head."[9] In December 2015, he said that he would sign an executive order that "anybody killing a police officer, the death penalty."[10] Under Article I, only Congress sets the penalties for federal offenses, and under the Tenth Amendment, only the state governments do the same for state offenses. During a primary debate, Trump said that Ted Cruz had been criticizing his sister, a federal judge, "for signing a certain bill." Trump went on, "You know who else signed that bill? Justice Samuel Alito, a very conservative member of the Supreme Court, with my sister, signed that bill." Judges do not sign bills.[11] During a meeting with House Republicans, Representative Tim Walberg (R-MI) asked him about his understanding of Article I, which spells out congressional powers. "I am a constitutionalist. I am going to abide by the Constitution whether it's number 1, number 2, number 12, number 9." [12] The Constitution has only seven articles.

Early in his administration, some officials took the law seriously and were frustrated that Trump did not. Former Secretary of State Rex Tillerson recalled: "So often, the president would say here's what I want to do and here's how I want to do it and I would have to say to him, Mr. President I understand what you want to do but you can't do it that way. It violates the law."[13] Trump does not recognize any such limits. "It's a thing called Article II," he told reporters in July 2019. "Nobody ever mentions Article II. It gives me all of these rights at a level that nobody has ever seen before."[14] At a speech shortly afterward, he was even more direct: "Then I have an Article II, where I have the right to do whatever I want as President."[15] What Article II really says is that the president "shall take Care that the Laws be faithfully executed." In 2016, House Republican Leader Kevin McCarthy (R-CA) wrote: "The take-care clause is a bulwark against tyranny. It supports the separation of powers stipulated in the Constitution: The legislative branch makes law and the executive branch administers it."[16]

Some blame Trump's disregard for his constitutional duties on his laziness and weak intellect, but it is more a matter of defiance and contempt. When he ignores or misstates the law, Trump is showing that he does not really care about it, notwithstanding his lip service to the Constitution. He does not bother to learn the rules that apply to everyone else, because he does not think that those rules apply to him. At least half a dozen times over the years, he has tweeted his "golden rule" for negotiating: "He who has the gold makes the rules."[17] For anyone else, this attitude would be a defect of character. For the chief executive of the United States, it is a dereliction of duty.

LIMITS AND BORDERS

In *The Federalist*, Hamilton stressed the limits of presidential power by comparing it with the royal power that Americans had recently thrown off. "The President of the United States would be an officer elected by the people for FOUR years; the king of Great Britain is a perpetual and HEREDITARY prince. The one would be amenable to personal punishment and disgrace; the person of the other is sacred and inviolable."[18] He said that the former "is the absolute master of his own conduct in the exercise of his office" whereas in a republic, "every magistrate ought to be personally responsible for his behavior in office."[19] Congress, he wrote, can hold a president personally responsible through the impeachment process. "The subjects of its jurisdiction are those offenses which proceed from the misconduct of public men, or, in other words, from the abuse or violation of some public trust."[20]

If Trump read books, he would dislike *The Federalist*. For him, impeachment is not a vital tool for ensuring responsibility. Rather, "it's a dirty word—the word 'impeach.' It's a dirty, filthy, disgusting word."[21] One word that he does approve is *absolute*. Trying to explain why he blurted out highly classified information during a chat with Russian officials, he tweeted: "As President I wanted to share with Russia (at an openly scheduled W.H. meeting) which I have the absolute right to do, facts pertaining to terrorism and airline flight safety."[22] Despite the president's broad authority to declassify information, such reckless disclosures could put lives at risk and thus fall under the heading of the "misconduct of public men." Trump also claimed a power to shield himself from responsibility for crimes: "And yes, I do have an absolute right to pardon myself."[23] Though some legal scholars think that the Constitution might allow for self-pardon, a Justice Department document says otherwise: "Under the fundamental rule that no one may be a judge in his own case, the President cannot pardon himself."[24]

In an attempt to bypass congressional resistance to a border wall, Trump said: "I have the absolute right to declare a national emergency."[25] A president can sign a document declaring a particular situation to be an "emergency," but the resulting powers are subject to the limits of constitutional and statutory law. When he urged his party's lawmakers to uphold his declaration of a border emergency, he asked them to ignore those limits and put purported necessity ahead of the rule of law: "Senate Republicans are not voting on constitutionality or precedent, they are voting on desperately needed Border Security & the Wall. Our Country is being invaded with Drugs, Human Traffickers, & Criminals of all shapes and sizes. That's what this vote is all about. STAY UNITED!"[26] That tweet was a minor milestone: members of Congress swear an oath to support the Constitution, and the president was telling them to neglect that oath.

During the campaign, Trump called for "a total and complete shutdown of Muslims entering the United States."[27] By disfavoring a particular faith, such a ban would have violated the Establishment Clause of the First Amendment. At the time, Republicans kept their distance. Former Vice President Dick Cheney said to Hugh Hewitt: "Well, I think this whole notion that somehow we can just say no more Muslims, just ban a whole religion, goes against everything we stand for and believe in. I mean, religious freedom has been a very important part of our history and where we came from."[28] South Carolina Governor Nikki Haley, who would become UN ambassador, called the proposal "absolutely un-American" and "unconstitutional," adding: "It defies everything that this country was based on and it's just wrong."[29] When he became president, he backed off the explicit Muslim ban, but his administration issued a limited travel ban that applied to a relatively small number of people from several countries. After three iterations, it survived in the Supreme Court, five to four.

Candidate Trump also talked about summary mass deportation, paying no attention to the legal processes of removing people from the country. On a radio program in 2015, future Trump economic adviser Lawrence Kudlow attacked the idea. "It reminds us of the worst parts of World War II. What the hell is that? That's not America. That's not your America. That's not my America. I'm the—whatever. I am third generation from immigrants. That's not America. No. I mean it's just crazy." Speaking with Stephen Moore on the same program, Kudlow continued. "That is un-American. It's smacks by the way of the worst things that we read about in World War II."[30]

The World War II analogy was hyperbolic, but not by much. A few months later, Trump pointedly declined to condemn the internment of Japanese Americans during the war. "I certainly hate the concept of it," he told *Time*. "But I would have had to be there at the time to give you a proper answer. . . . It's a tough thing. It's tough. But you know war is tough. And winning is tough. We don't win anymore."[31] In an unexpected development, the Supreme Court decision upholding Trump's limited travel ban also repudiated the 1944 decision upholding the internment. The majority opinion by Chief Justice Roberts declared that it "was gravely wrong the day it was decided, has been overruled in the court of history, and—to be clear—'has no place in law under the Constitution.'"[32]

The Supreme Court has long been clear about one aspect of undocumented immigration: "It is true that aliens who have once passed through our gates, even illegally, may be expelled only after proceedings conforming to traditional standards of fairness encompassed in due process of law."[33] Justice Scalia drove the point home: "It is well established that the Fifth Amendment entitles aliens to due process of law in deportation proceedings."[34] Trump has repeatedly disrespected this body of law. On June 24, 2018, he tweeted: "We cannot allow all of these people to invade our Country. When somebody comes in, we must immediately, with no Judges or Court Cases, bring them back from where they came."[35] Nearly a year later, he said that "we have to do something about asylum. And to be honest with you, have to get rid of judges."[36] And two days after that, he added: "We have a stupid system of courts. It's the craziest thing in the world. We could be the only country that has it. If you put a foot on the property, you put a foot into the United States: 'Congratulations. Go get Perry Mason to represent you.' You end up with a court case."[37]

In April 2019, he visited Calexico, California, where he said: "We're full, our system's full, our country's full—can't come in! Our country is full, what can you do? We can't handle any more, our country is full. Can't come in, I'm sorry. It's very simple." Behind the scenes, Trump reportedly told border agents to bar migrants and advised them on what to tell any skeptical judges: "Sorry, judge, I can't do it. We don't have the room." After Trump left, their supervisors told them to follow the law and warned they would face legal trouble if they did what Trump had told them. "At the end of the day," a senior administration official told CNN's Jake Tapper, "the President refuses to understand that the Department of Homeland Security is constrained by the laws."[38] In meetings about border wall construction, some aides warned that some of his orders might be illegal. "Don't worry, I'll pardon you," he reportedly responded.[39]

Ironically, Trump himself has broken immigration law. In 1980, he needed to tear down the Bonwit Teller building on Fifth Avenue to make way for Trump Tower. He hired a crew of 200 undocumented Polish workers who worked long hours in dangerous conditions and low pay.[40] His modeling agency used foreign models who came to the country on tourist visas that did not allow them to work here.[41] More recently, he employed undocumented workers at the Trump National Golf Club in Westchester County, New York and the Trump National Golf Club in Bedminster, New Jersey.

GUNS AND UNIFORMS

One definition of government is a monopoly on the legitimate use of violence. Legal scholars and jurists have long worried about the potential abuse of that monopoly, and have put a great deal of thought into regulating the use of force by law enforcement and the military. Trump has never concerned himself about such things.

In his 1989 newspaper ad on the Central Park attack, he said: "Let our politicians give back our police department's power to keep us safe," he wrote. "Unshackle them from the constant chant of 'police brutality,' which every petty criminal hurls immediately at an officer who has just risked his or her life to save another's."[42] Trump did not specify what the "unshackling" would look like: presumably, it would involve batons and firearms. In his *Larry King Show* interview, he complained about the administration of justice. "The problem we have is we don't have any protection for the policeman. The problem with our society is the victim has absolutely no rights and the criminal has unbelievable rights—unbelievable rights."[43] True, the Bill of Rights does provide protections for criminal defendants, but that is a feature, not a bug. The whole point is to put shackles on the government's power to take away our life and liberty. One obvious reason is that this power can harm the innocent as well as the guilty, as in the case of the Central Park Five.

Over the years, Trump did not gain any more respect for this aspect of our constitutional system. During the 2016 campaign, Chuck Todd asked him about a white police officer who had shot an unarmed black man. Trump showed little interest in the problem of unjustified police shootings. "We have to give strength and power back to the police. And you're always going to have mistakes made. And you're always going to have bad apples. But you can't let that stop the fact that police have to regain some control of this tremendous crime wave and killing wave that's happening in this country."[44] His rationale was dishonest because there was no "tremendous crime wave" to begin with. Rates of violent crime had been dropping for a quarter century. And even if crime had remained at the high levels of the 1980s, the end would still not have justified the means. The Bill of Rights does not switch off when crime goes up.

The president of the United States is responsible for more than 100,000 federal law enforcement officers who can make arrests and carry firearms. The chief executive's comments also carry weight with their counterparts at the state and local level. And so it is disturbing that Trump continued to shrug off police brutality even after he took office. He told police on Long Island: "[W]hen you see these thugs being thrown into the back of a paddy wagon—you just see them thrown in, rough, I said, please don't be too nice. Like when you guys put somebody in the car and you're protecting their head, you know, the way you put their hand over? Like, don't hit their head, and they've just killed somebody—don't hit their head. I said, you can take the hand away, okay?"[45] In a remarkable email, the acting head of the Drug Enforcement Administration said: "The President, in remarks delivered yesterday in New York, condoned police misconduct regarding the treatment of individuals placed under arrest by law enforcement."[46]

Such rebukes hardly bother him. At a 2019 rally in Florida, he lamented that Customs and Border Patrol officers do not fire on migrants. "And don't forget, we don't let them and we can't let them use weapons. We can't. Other countries do. We can't. I would never do that. But how do you stop these people?" At that point, an audience member interjected, "Shoot them!" The crowd laughed, and Trump smiled. "That's only in the Panhandle you can get away with that statement."[47] He actually was not kidding. At a private meeting with officials of the Department of Homeland Security, he proposed slowing migrants down by shooting them in the legs. The departmental officials told him that that would be illegal.[48]

Trump is equally cavalier about abuses of force by the military. He does not care that international law and the US Code forbid the deliberate targeting of civilians. "The other thing with the terrorists is you have to take out their families, when you get these terrorists, you have to take out their families," he said in 2015. "They care about their lives, don't kid yourself. When they say they don't care about their lives, you have to take out their families."[49] At a Fox News debate, Bret Baier asked him what he would do if the military refused orders to torture terrorist suspects or target their families.

Trump: They won't refuse. They're not going to refuse me. Believe me.

Baier: But they're illegal.

Trump: Let me just tell you, you look at the Middle East. . . . Can you imagine—can you imagine these people, these animals over in the Middle East, that chop off heads, sitting around talking and seeing that we're having a hard problem with waterboarding? We should go for waterboarding and we should go tougher than waterboarding. That's my opinion.

Baier: But targeting terrorists' families?

Trump: And—and—and—I'm a leader. I'm a leader. I've always been a leader. I've never had any problem leading people. If I say do it, they're going to do it. That's what leadership is all about. [50]

Under criticism, the Trump campaign issued a statement that seemed to backtrack: "I do, however, understand that the United States is bound by laws and treaties and I will not order our military or other officials to violate those laws and will seek their advice on such matters." [51] The formality of the language suggested that an aide wrote that statement and his comments a few days later made it clear that it did not reflect his views. He told CNN's Anderson Cooper: "Everybody believes in the Geneva Convention until they start losing and then they say oh, let's take out the bomb. OK. When they start losing. We have to play with a tougher set of rules." [52] As president, he watched recorded video of a drone strike which the Central Intelligence Agency delayed firing until the target had left a house that contained his family. Trump asked a CIA official, "Why did you wait?" [53] In 2019, he pardoned an Army lieutenant who had murdered an unarmed Iraqi prisoner, and he expressed sympathy for other alleged war criminals. "This attitude is incredibly dangerous," writes historian and combat veteran Wade Beorn. "It doesn't just undermine the enforcement of military justice; it also sends a message to our armed forces about just what kind of conduct the United States takes seriously." [54]

VIOLENT SUPPORTERS

What about violence by civilians? White House spokesperson Sarah Sanders said in 2017: "The president in no way, form or fashion has ever promoted or encouraged violence. If anything, quite the contrary."[55] That claim was wildly, nay, ridiculously wrong. When protesters acted up during his campaign rallies, he responded with soliloquies about beatings.

- In Las Vegas: "You know what they used to do to guys like that when they were in a place like this? They'd be carried out on a stretcher, folks. . . . Here's a guy, throwing punches [*not true*], nasty as hell, screaming at everything else when we're talking, and he's walking out, and we're not allowed—you know, the guards are very gentle with him, he's walking out, like, big high fives, smiling, laughing—I'd like to punch him in the face, I'll tell you."[56]
- In St. Louis: "You know, part of the problem and part of the reason it takes so long is nobody wants to hurt each other anymore, right?"[57]
- In Fayetteville, North Carolina: "In the good old days this [protesting] doesn't happen because they used to treat them very, very rough. And when they protested once, you know, they would not do it again so easily."[58]

Trump supporters dismissed concerns about such language, saying that he was merely talking tough for the amusement of his audience. This line of argument assumes that we should hold a presidential candidate to a lower standard than a traveler in a TSA line. In any case, his tough talk turned ominous in Wilmington, North Carolina, when he said: "Hillary wants to abolish, essentially abolish, the Second Amendment. By the way, and if she gets to pick—if she gets to pick her judges, nothing you can do, folks. Although the Second Amendment people, maybe there is, I don't know."[59] Many heard those remarks as suggesting that supporters of gun rights could literally take up arms against a Clinton presidency.

The campaign claimed he was only saying that Second Amendment enthusiasts should vote against Clinton—which made little sense, since he was talking about what they could do after she won the election.[60] Moreover, an adviser to the campaign had drawn Secret Service attention for saying that Hillary Clinton "should be put in the firing line and shot for treason." Days before his "Second Amendment" comment, Trump praised the adviser, saying that he had "been so great."[61]

As president, Trump hinted at the prospect of a violent conflict between his supporters and opponents. At a 2018 rally in Springfield, Missouri, he said: "No, I would never suggest this, but I will tell you, I—they're so lucky that we're peaceful. Law enforcement, military, construction workers, Bikers for Trump—how about Bikers for Trump? . . . These are great people. But they're peaceful people, and Antifa and all—they'd better hope they stay that way. I hope they stay that way. I hope that stay that way."[62] In 2019, he told Breitbart: "You know, the left plays a tougher game, it's very funny. I actually think that the people on the right are tougher, but they don't play it tougher. Okay? I can tell you I have the support of the police, the support of the military, the support of the Bikers for Trump—I have the tough people, but they don't play it tough—until they go to a certain point, and then it would be very bad, very bad."[63] In September 2019, he retweeted a message from Pastor Robert Jeffress: "If the Democrats are successful in removing the President from office (which they will never be), it will cause a Civil War like fracture in this Nation from which our Country will never heal."[64]

While denouncing the "fake news media" at rallies, he would point at the press pen so that rallygoers would know where to direct their booing and jeering. At a 2018 Montana rally, he praised Representative Greg Gianforte, who had pleaded guilty to a misdemeanor assault against a journalist.

> But Greg is smart. And by the way, never wrestle him. You understand that? Never. [laughter] Any guy that can do a body slam, he's my kind of. . . . [applause] He was my guy. I

shouldn't say this, because . . . there's nothing to be embarrassed about. So I was in Rome with a lot of the leaders from other countries talking about all sorts of things, and I heard about it. And we endorsed Greg very early, but I had heard that he body-slammed a reporter. [applause] And he was way up. And he was way up. And I said, oh, this was like the day of the election, or just before, and I said, oh, this is terrible, he's going to lose the election. Then I said, well, wait a minute, I know Montana pretty well. I think it might help him. And it did! [applause] No, he's a great guy. Tough cookie.[65]

Trump also took to social media to bash the mainstream media. He tweeted an old video clip of him at a wrestling match, but with a CNN logo superimposed on his opponent's head. In the clip, Trump slams the CNN figure to the ground and hits him with simulated punches. Trump added the hashtags #FraudNewsCNN and #FNN, for "fraud news network."[66] Trump also retweeted a meme of a train smashing into a human embodiment of CNN, with the caption "FAKE NEWS CAN'T STOP THE TRUMP TRAIN."[67] This re-tweet drew fierce criticism since it came after the Charlottesville incident where a white supremacist killed Heather Heyer with his car. Trump soon deleted it.

In the fall of 2018, a disturbed Florida man sent pipe bombs to CNN and Democratic critics of the administration. Luckily, none detonated before his capture. After his guilty plea, the would-be bomber sent a letter to the judge saying "the first thing you here [sic] entering Trump rally is we are not going to take it anymore, the forgotten ones, etc. . . . . It was fun, it became like a new found drug."[68]

FREE SPEECH

Khizr Khan, who lost his son in Iraq, spoke at the 2016 Democratic National Convention criticizing Trump for not understanding the Constitution. Trump angrily stated that Khan had "no right to stand in front of millions of people and claim I have never read the Constitution, (which is false) and say many other inaccurate things."[69] Trump proved Khan's point. The First Amendment secures his right to say nearly anything he wants, even if it is inaccurate—and in this case, it was true. Indeed, if bogus statements were unlawful, Trump would have had to don an orange jumpsuit years ago.

In a tweet, he elaborated on his understanding of the First Amendment: "It is not 'freedom of the press' when newspapers and others are allowed to say and write whatever they want even if it is completely false!"[70] At a press availability, he said: "And it's, frankly, disgusting the way the press is able to write whatever they want to write. And people should look into it."[71] Over and over, he has said that he would somehow "open up" the libel laws so that he and other public figures could more easily sue news organizations. If they don't retract these purportedly false statements, he said, "they should, you know, have a form of a trial."[72] In September 2018, he tweeted: "Isn't it a shame that someone can write an article or book, totally make up stories and form a picture of a person that is literally the exact opposite of the fact, and get away with it without retribution or cost. Don't know why Washington politicians don't change libel laws?"[73] At a South Dakota rally shortly afterward, he returned to the subject, asking the state's US senators to chill critical speech by federalizing libel: "Hey Mike and John, could you do me a favor? Create some libel laws that when people say stuff bad about you, you could sue them."[74]

It was always unlikely that Congress could take up libel statutes, which have always been the province of state legislatures. But federal regulation of the airwaves is different, as he has mentioned in tweets:

- "Network news has become so partisan, distorted and fake that licenses must be challenged and, if appropriate, revoked. Not fair to public!"[75]
- "With all of the Fake News coming out of NBC and the Networks, at what point is it appropriate to challenge their License? Bad for country!"[76]

- "NBC FAKE NEWS, which is under intense scrutiny over their killing the Harvey Weinstein story, is now fumbling around making excuses for their probably highly unethical conduct. I have long criticized NBC and their journalistic standards—worse than even CNN. Look at their license?"[77]

Trump has some support. Ipsos found 29 percent of Americans and 48 percent of Republicans agreeing that "the news media is the enemy of the American people." Even more ominously, 26 percent of Americans overall—*and 43 percent of Republicans*—said that "the president should have the authority to close news outlets engaged in bad behavior."[78]

In the summer of 2017, Trump reportedly ordered Gary Cohn, director of the National Economic Council, to get the Justice Department to intervene against AT&T's acquisition of Time Warner, owner of CNN. Rupert Murdoch opposed the merger because it would strengthen a competitor of Fox News, and Trump disliked anything that could benefit a network that he hated. Trump summoned Cohn and chief of staff John Kelly, saying: "I've been telling Cohn to get this lawsuit filed and nothing's happened! I've mentioned it fifty times. And nothing's happened. I want to make sure it's filed. I want that deal blocked!"[79] These stories recall the worst days of Richard Nixon, who told White House aide Charles Colson that threatening antitrust litigation would be an effective way to keep television networks in line. "If the threat of screwing them is going to help us more with their programming than doing it, then keep the threat," Nixon said in a recorded conversation.[80]

Trump failed to stop the merger, but he kept up the fight by taking the unprecedented step of urging a consumer boycott. "I believe that if people stoped [sic] using or subscribing to @ATT, they would be forced to make big changes at @CNN, which is dying in the ratings anyway. It is so unfair with such bad, Fake News! Why wouldn't they act. When the World watches @CNN, it gets a false picture of USA. Sad!"[81]

ENEMIES AND FRIENDS

The AT&T fight is hardly the only time that Trump has sought to turn the law into a political switchblade. Case in point: his never-ending war on Hillary Clinton. During the campaign, he would smile as rally audiences chanted "Lock her up!" In their second debate, he said: "But if I win, I am going to instruct my attorney general to get a special prosecutor to look into your situation, because there has never been so many lies, so much deception. There has never been anything like it, and we're going to have a special prosecutor." Clinton responded that "it is awfully good that someone with the temperament of Donald Trump is not in charge of the law in our country." Trump interjected: "Because you'd be in jail."[82] After the election, he reassured people that he did not want to investigate the Clintons. He lied. He meant what he said the first time. The Mueller report confirms Trump's vendetta: "According to Sessions, the President asked him to reverse his recusal so that Sessions could direct the Department of Justice to investigate and prosecute Hillary Clinton. . . . Sessions listened but did not respond, and he did not reverse his recusal or order an investigation of Clinton."[83] Trump complained in public, tweeting: "Attorney General Jeff Sessions has taken a VERY weak position on Hillary Clinton crimes (where are E-mails & DNC server) & Intel leakers!"[84] A few months later, he repeated the complaint: "Everybody is asking why the Justice Department (and FBI) isn't looking into all of the dishonesty going on with Crooked Hillary & the Dems."[85]

Trump often says that his purported foes are guilty of "treason," even though they have done nothing that meets the constitutional definition of the term. At a 2019 press conference, a journalist reminded him that treason is a capital crime and asked: "You've accused your adversaries of treason. Who specifically are you accusing of treason?" A normal president would have recoiled from the implication that he wanted to put his critics to death. Instead, Trump said matter-of-factly: "Well, I think a number of people. And I think what you look is that they have unsuccessfully tried to take down the wrong person." He went on to name names, including former

FBI Director James Comey and former Acting Director Andrew McCabe.[86] NBC's Chuck Todd asked Press Secretary Sarah Sanders for a clarification, saying, "he's accused James Comey of treason. Does he expect Jim Comey to be arrested?" Sanders did not deny it: "Again, we're going to let the attorney general make that determination as he gets to the conclusion of this investigation."[87]

Just as Trump yearns to weaponize the law against his perceived enemies, he also tries to twist it in favor of his friends and business interests. He has a long history here. In 1992, an Indiana jury convicted heavyweight boxer Mike Tyson of raping an 18-year-old woman, and Trump tried to influence the sentencing. He urged authorities not to send Tyson to prison and instead let him keep fighting, with some of the proceeds going to rape victims. Why did the persecutor of the Central Park Five suddenly develop such a soft spot for rapists? He had a business relationship with Tyson, whose Atlantic City prizefights had been profitable for Trump properties. Under the proposed arrangement, Trump could keep making money from Tyson, which was especially important at a time when he was having financial difficulties. He failed. "An offer to buy someone out of prison or out of a sentence is not appropriate," said a spokesperson for the prosecution, adding that Trump's idea "is something that the prosecutor's office does not take seriously."[88] A reporter asked Trump about his double standard: "If your sister was raped by a millionaire, would you encourage her to accept a big bundle of cash to forget everything?" Trump replied: "I think every individual situation is different."[89]

When he became president, he continued to show selective skepticism about criminal prosecutions. In 2018, he commented on the indictments of GOP House members Duncan Hunter of California and Chris Collins of New York, who happened to be the first two House members to endorse his candidacy in 2016. "Two long running, Obama era, investigations of two very popular Republican Congressmen were brought to a well publicized charge, just ahead of the Mid-Terms, by the Jeff Sessions Justice Department. Two easy wins now in doubt because there is not enough time. Good job Jeff."[90] Although he did not get Justice to drop these cases, his comment was dumbfounding. He was openly criticizing the prosecution not because of the law or the evidence, but because of the potential harm to political allies. (He need not have fretted, because both indicted members won reelection.)

The president enjoys broad power to issue pardons for federal offenses. As Chief Justice William Howard Taft wrote, "Our Constitution confers this discretion on the highest officer in the nation in confidence that he will not abuse it."[91] Trump has abused it. In the spring of 2017, he asked Attorney General Jeff Sessions whether the federal government could drop a criminal case against Joe Arpaio, a political ally and former Arizona sheriff who had defied a judge's order to stop detaining people just because he thought they might be undocumented immigrants. Sessions advised Trump that dropping the case would be inappropriate.[92] After a judge convicted Arpaio, Trump skipped the customary review process and pardoned him. "No one is above the law and the individuals entrusted with the privilege of being sworn law officers should always seek to be beyond reproach in their commitment to fairly enforcing the laws they swore to uphold," said Senator John McCain of Arizona. "The President has the authority to make this pardon, but doing so at this time undermines his claim for the respect of rule of law as Mr. Arpaio has shown no remorse for his actions."[93]

Trump also pardoned Dinesh D'Souza, author of books attacking Obama and Hillary Clinton, and British publisher Conrad Black, who had written a glowing work titled *Donald J. Trump: A President Like No Other*. The favoritism toward pro-Trump writers appalled legal scholars. Another pardon, involving former California Assembly GOP leader Pat Nolan, was less controversial because Nolan had devoted his post-prison life to criminal justice reform. But Nolan may have also curried Trump's favor by citing the Mueller investigation as an example of how prosecutors "decide who they're going to prosecute and then hunt for a crime."[94]

TAKE CARE

In their sentencing memorandum in the case of Trump fixer Michael Cohen, federal prosecutors said of hush-money payments to a porn star and a Playboy model: "Cohen acted with the intent to influence the 2016 presidential election. Cohen coordinated his actions with one or more members of the campaign [and] as Cohen himself has now admitted, with respect to both payments, he acted in coordination with and at the direction of Individual-1."[95] Donald Trump was "Individual-1." Someone who orders an underling to commit a crime is also guilty of that crime, so federal prosecutors believed that Trump had committed a felony. They did not act against Trump, probably because Justice Department guidelines prevent the indictment of a sitting president. Some also believed that the House cannot impeach him for actions that he took before becoming president. But his offenses continued after he assumed office. As president, he reimbursed Cohen for the hush money and encouraged Cohen to give misleading testimony about the arrangement. Members of Congress might reasonably conclude that this behavior violated his constitutional duty to take care that the laws be faithfully executed.

In his 2019 testimony, Cohen admitted that he had previously lied about Trump Tower Moscow. Again, he was acting at the president's behest. "Mr. Trump did not directly tell me to lie to Congress. That's not how he operates. In conversations we had during the campaign, at the same time I was actively negotiating in Russia for him, he would look me in the eye and tell me there's no business in Russia and then go out and lie to the American people by saying the same thing. In his way, he was telling me to lie."[96] CNN law enforcement analyst James Gagliano said in a tweet: "I was once assigned to FBI Organized Crime Squad in Queens, NY. Can't begin to number amount of Mob cooperators who described their abilities to interpret Mob Boss's orders in exact same manner."[97]

Trump was bitter about Cohen's decision to become a cooperator. Inadvertently, though, he reinforced the Mafia comparison. In December 2018, Trump tweeted: "Remember, Michael Cohen only became a 'Rat' after the FBI did something which was absolutely unthinkable & unheard of until the Witch Hunt was illegally started. They BROKE INTO AN ATTORNEY'S OFFICE! Why didn't they break into the DNC to get the Server, or Crooked's office?"[98] As anyone who has seen *Goodfellas* would know, Trump was adopting gangland language. Former prosecutor Andrew McCarthy, a conservative who supported Trump, cautioned in a tweet: "Sir, in mobster lingo, a 'rat' is a witness who tells prosecutors real incriminating info. Perhaps a different word? Searches of lawyer's offices common enough that DOJ has a procedure for them. Here it yielded evidence of crimes you said he should be jailed for. You should stop."[99]

In an interview with Fox News, Trump acknowledged his decades-long familiarity with gangsters. "This whole thing about flipping, they call it, I know all about flipping," he said of Cohen's plea negotiations. "For 30, 40 years I've been watching flippers. Everything's wonderful and then they get 10 years in jail and they— they flip on whoever the next highest one is, or as high as you can go." He added: "I've had many friends involved in this stuff. It's called flipping and it almost ought to be illegal."[100] The justice system depends on plea negotiations, which account for 90 percent of outcomes in federal criminal cases.[101] Getting criminals to testify against one another is a vital part of the fight against organized crime. As prosecutor Rudy Giuliani explained during a 1986 case: "The people who know best about what was going on inside a cesspool of corruption like this one are the people who were wallowing in it."[102] A ban on "flipping" would hobble such prosecutions and benefit the mob.

Trump implicitly threatened Cohen's family. In late 2018, he tweeted about Cohen's request for leniency, alleging that he had made up stories and he had already made a deal to get "his wife and father-in-law (who has the money?) off Scott Free [sic]."[103] In a January 2019 interview with Jeanine Pirro of Fox News, he repeated his claim about a deal, adding: "He should give information maybe on his father-in-law, because that's the one that people want to look at." When Pirro asked him for the man's name, he said: "I don't know, but you'll find out, and you'll look into it because nobody knows what's going on over there."[104] (Cohen's father-in-law, Fima Shusterman, was a Ukrainian immigrant with a 1993 conviction related to money laundering.[105]) At the very least, Trump was encouraging a television network to investigate a private citizen. At worst, he was hinting that federal prosecutors should do so. Either way, he was trying to scare Cohen. "I have seen mobsters in Mafia cases do this and gang leaders," a former prosecutor told *ABA Journal.* "But they wouldn't tell the news; we'd pick it up in a wiretap. Nobody would come out and say these things—the gangsters know better."[106] If Trump were indictable, obtaining a conviction for witness intimidation might be uncertain because of the difficulty of proving intent. There is much less question that Trump was again failing in his constitutional duty. A president who took his oath seriously would have refrained from such activity and encouraged Cohen to tell the whole truth.

Trump flouted his duty on other occasions. On January 26, 2017, he learned that his national security adviser Michael Flynn had lied to the FBI about contacts with the Russian ambassador. The next day, he invited FBI Director James Comey to a private dinner at the White House. "I need loyalty. I expect loyalty," he told Comey. Reflecting on his earlier work as a prosecutor of gangsters, Comey later wrote: "To my mind, the demand was like Sammy the Bull's Cosa Nostra induction ceremony—with Trump, in the role of the family boss asking me if I have what it takes to be a 'made man.'"[107] At another meeting a few weeks later, Trump told Comey: "I hope you can see your way clear to letting this go, to letting Flynn go. He is a good guy. I hope you can let this go."[108]

Comey did not let it go, and Trump eventually fired him. The day of the firing, the White House insisted that Trump was following a departmental recommendation to terminate Comey for mishandling the 2016 Clinton email investigation. That claim was false. Trump had already made up his mind to fire Comey no matter what Justice said.[109] He then blew his own cover story. On May 10, 2017, he told Russian officials in the Oval Office: "I just fired the head of the F.B.I. He was crazy, a real nut job. I faced great pressure because of Russia. That's taken off."[110] And he told NBC's Lester Holt: "And in fact, when I decided to just do it, I said to myself—I said, you know, this Russia thing with Trump and Russia is a made-up story."[111]

After the Comey firing, the Justice Department named Robert Mueller to take over the probe of Russian election interference. When the media reported that Mueller was also investigating whether Trump had obstructed justice, Trump responded by . . . obstructing justice. He ordered White House counsel Donald McGahn to tell the Acting Attorney General to sack Mueller. McGahn did not carry out the order. Later, after the news media reported that McGahn had threatened to resign rather than take part in a Mueller firing, Trump pressed McGahn to deny that he had ever made such a demand. McGahn declined, and the account in the Mueller report is worth quoting at length:

> The President also asked McGahn in the meeting why he had told Special Counsel's Office investigators that the President had told him to have the Special Counsel removed. McGahn responded that he had to and that his conversations with the President were not protected by attorney-client privilege. The President then asked, "What-about these notes? Why do you take notes? Lawyers don't take notes. I never had a lawyer who took notes." McGahn responded that he keeps notes because he is a "real lawyer" and explained that notes create a record and are not a bad thing. The President said, "I've had a lot of great lawyers, like Roy Cohn. He did not take notes."[112]

Throughout the investigation and afterward, Trump continued to undercut top law enforcement officials. "I have done a great service for our country when I fired James Comey because he was a bad cop, and he was a dirty cop, and he lied. He really lied."[113] He also criticized Mueller many times. He even took a swipe at Christopher Wray, the man he named to succeed Comey at the FBI. In an interview, he told George Stephanopoulos that it was not necessary for campaign operatives to tell the FBI about offers of information by foreigners. When Stephanopoulos replied that the "FBI director said that is what should happen," Trump said: "the FBI director is wrong, because frankly it doesn't happen like that in life."[114]

Newt Gingrich, Rudy Giuliani, and other surrogates amplified Trump's efforts to discredit law enforcement officials. In 1998, however, Gingrich had a different point of view. He said on the House floor that "the American people have the right to expect that the rule of law will prevail, that no one is above the law."[115] He also told a political meeting: "There is something profoundly demeaning and destructive to have the White House systematically undermine an officer of the Department of Justice. And when I watch these paid hacks on television, to be quite honest, I am sickened by how unpatriotically they undermine the Constitution of the United States on behalf of their client."[116]

TRUMP AND THE LAW

Trump broke the law. He directed the hush money scheme that landed Michael Cohen in prison. In several different ways, he acted to obstruct the investigations of his conduct. Some of his defenders say that he could not have committed obstruction, because there was no "underlying offense." In a series of tweets, Representative Justin Amash (R-MI) knocked down this argument, pointing out that the Mueller investigation revealed many crimes. In any event, he further explained why obstruction of justice need not hinge on the prosecution of an underlying crime. "Prosecutors might not charge a crime precisely *because* obstruction of justice denied them timely access to evidence that could lead to a prosecution. If an underlying crime were required, then prosecutors could charge obstruction of justice only if it were unsuccessful in completely obstructing the investigation. This would make no sense."[117]

Trump supporters have also argued that Trump could not have obstructed justice at all because the president is the federal government's chief law enforcement officer. This assertion is a new version of the old Nixon line, "When the president does it, that means it is not illegal." The Mueller report offered a rebuttal: "Under applicable Supreme Court precedent, the Constitution does not categorically and permanently immunize a President for obstructing justice through the use of his Article II powers." Because of departmental policy, it did not recommend indictment, but added, "if we had confidence after a thorough investigation of the facts that the President clearly did not commit obstruction of justice, we would so state. Based on the facts and the applicable legal standards, we are unable to reach that judgment. Accordingly, while this report does not conclude that the President committed a crime, it also does not exonerate him." It hinted at impeachment as a remedy: "The conclusion that Congress may apply the obstruction laws to the President's corrupt exercise of the powers of office accords with our constitutional system of checks and balances and the principle that no person is above the law."[118]

Trump rejected this view. When George Stephanopoulos asked him if a president could obstruct justice, he said: "A president can run the country. And that's what happened, George. I run the country, and I run it well."[119] *I run the country*—seldom has a president voiced a viewpoint more at odds with the Constitution. Though the presidency has great power for good or ill, its occupant is still just the temporary steward of one of the branches of one of the 89,000-plus governments of the United States. As Madison explained at great length, the Founders designed a system whereby all three branches of the federal government would check one another, and the states would provide an additional check on federal authority. The powers of government would be strictly limited so that free individuals could control their own lives. In other words, the whole point was that no single person could "run the country."

In the early months of the Trump administration, advisers and members of Congress tried to school him in the separation of powers and the limits of presidential authority. Nevertheless, he persisted. Trump seems to regard the government as his private property and its officials as his servants. He refers to the military's highest-ranking officers as "my generals" and House Republican leaders as "my Kevin" and "my Steve."[120] Those who fail to do his bidding are disloyal to the country, he thinks, because they are disloyal to him. In November 2019, Judge Paul Friedman explained why this attitude is especially ominous in the case of the judiciary:

> [W]ith respect to litigation challenging his emergency declaration respecting the border wall, the President predicted adverse rulings in the district courts and in the Ninth Circuit. He called the Ninth Circuit "a complete and total disaster, . . . out of control." But, he said, "hopefully we'll get a fair shake" in the Supreme Court; in fact, on one occasion, he said, "we'll win in the Supreme Court," perhaps to suggest that he expects the five Justices appointed by Republican presidents invariably will vote to uphold decisions made by his Administration. "If it's my judges," he said during the campaign, "you know how they're going to decide." This is not normal. And I mean that both in the colloquial sense and in the sense that this kind of personal attack on courts and individual judges violates all recognized democratic norms. [121]

5

A DECENT RESPECT TO THE OPINIONS OF MANKIND

In 1630, John Winthrop told his fellow Massachusetts settlers: "We shall be as a city upon a hill, the eyes of all people are upon us." Though Winthrop was addressing his own community, Americans have taken the underlying sentiment to apply to the country as a whole. The drafters of the Declaration knew that they had a global audience, so they wrote that "a decent respect to the opinions of mankind requires that they should declare the causes which impel them to the separation." They also started the bill of particulars against King George by pronouncing, "let Facts be submitted to a candid world." As Lincoln later said at Gettysburg, the Declaration dedicated the nation to the proposition that all men are created equal. In human history, it was unprecedented to dedicate a nation to ideas instead of blood and soil. The ideas that set us apart were liberty and democracy, as well as equality. Thomas Paine wrote in *Common Sense*: "Every spot of the old world is overrun with oppression. Freedom hath been hunted round the globe. Asia, and Africa, have long expelled her. Europe regards her like a stranger, and England hath given her warning to depart. O! receive the fugitive, and prepare in time an asylum for mankind."

It almost came apart during the Civil War. In 1861, historian Allen Guelzo points out, the United States was the only example of a large-scale democracy in the world. Monarchs and autocrats had crushed other struggles for rule by the people. "If the American democracy shattered itself because seven states weren't willing to abide by the outcome of the presidential election, then every one of those kings, emperors and dictators would be able to say to their nations, 'See what democracy gets you? Instability. Disorder.'"[1] A victory for Jefferson Davis and Robert E. Lee would have been a triumph for tyrants everywhere. Lincoln understood the stakes: "We shall nobly save or meanly lose the last best hope of earth."[2]

In the 20th century, Americans leaders wanted our ideas to extend around the globe. On the 175th anniversary of the Declaration, Harry Truman said; "[T]he ideas on which our Government is founded—the ideas of equality, of God-given rights, of self-government-are still revolutionary. Since 1776 they have spread around the world." He emphasized the importance of being a model for other countries: "Today, more than ever before, it is important that we continue to make progress in expanding our freedoms and improving the opportunities of our citizens. To do so is to strengthen the hopes and determination of free men everywhere."[3] In his 1961 inaugural, John F. Kennedy also referred back to the Declaration: "And yet the same revolutionary beliefs for which our forebears fought are still at issue around the globe—the belief that the rights of man come not from the generosity of the state, but from the hand of God." JFK saw a special responsibility for the United States: "Let every nation know, whether it wishes us well or ill, that we shall pay any price, bear any burden, meet any hardship, support any friend, oppose any foe, in order to assure the survival and the success of liberty."[4]

American behavior has often clashed with American ideals. At times, selfish and base motives have driven foreign and military policy. Lincoln denounced the Mexican American War as "unnecessary and unconstitutional," and a century later, Harry Truman laid a wreath at a memorial to Mexican heroes of that war. At other times, good intentions have mingled with poor judgment and skewed intelligence to produce catastrophic results. Vietnam comes to mind. And even when leaders have combined noble motives with practical wisdom, they have had to deal with the world as it is, meaning that the United States has always done business with undemocratic regimes.

Yet for all of our faults, mistakes, sins, and compromises, Americans continue to believe that our country has a special place and mission in the world. At its best, this belief inspires efforts to make the United States worthy of its exceptional self-image. In examples ranging from the Marshall Plan to the fight against HIV/AIDS in Africa, the United States has led with an open hand instead of an iron fist. These efforts serve our self-interest, properly understood. The United States is safer and more prosperous when other countries like its people and admire its virtues.

Though they have not always used the term, American political leaders have generally embraced American exceptionalism. After coming under criticism for suggesting ambivalence about the concept, President Obama took care to proclaim it. "What makes us special—a lot of times we talk about American exceptionalism," he said in 2013, "what makes us the envy of the world has not just been our ability to generate incredible wealth for a few people, it's the fact that we've given everybody a chance to pursue their own true measure of happiness. That's who we are."[5] The following year, he told West Point graduates: "I believe in American exceptionalism with every fiber of my being. But what makes us exceptional is not our ability to flout international norms and the rule of law, it is our willingness to affirm them through our actions."[6]

It is rare for major public figures to deny or disparage American exceptionalism. That is why Trump's comments on the subject are worth a very close look.

TRUMP VERSUS AMERICAN EXCEPTIONALISM

In 2013, Vladimir Putin derided President Obama's endorsement of American exceptionalism. In an op-ed for the *New York Times*, he wrote: "It is extremely dangerous to encourage people to see themselves as exceptional, whatever the motivation."[7] American political figures reacted with indignation, and even Obama's fiercest GOP congressional critics said that they found Putin's comments to be insulting.[8] Putin did get applause from one American celebrity: Donald Trump. On Greta Van Susteren's Fox News show the next day, Trump discussed Putin and the op-ed:

> And it really makes him look like a great leader, frankly. And when he criticizes the president for using the term "American exceptionalism," if you're in Russia, you don't want to hear that America is exceptional. . . . And that's basically what Putin was saying is that, you know, you use a term like "American exceptionalism," and frankly, the way our country is being treated right now by Russia and Syria and lots of other places and with all the mistakes we've made over the years, like Iraq and so many others, it's sort of a hard term to use. But other nations and other countries don't want to hear about American exceptionalism. They're insulted by it. And that's what Putin was saying.[9]

On other cable news programs, Trump gleefully claimed that Putin had scored points on President Obama. He told CNBC's Maria Bartiromo that Putin "is really embarrassing the United States, and he's embarrassing the president. . . . He's making him look like he's the professor and the president is a schoolchild. . . . It makes the president look very weak and very ineffective. Frankly, it makes it look like he doesn't know what he's doing."[10] On CNN, he said to Piers Morgan: "We have a president who's been outplayed by Putin to an extent that nobody has ever seen and we look very bad as a country and certainly he's looking very bad."[11]

Trump's comments triggered little commentary at the time.. Still, it was extraordinary that he was praising Putin, belittling President Obama, and saying that American exceptionalism was offensive to countries such as Russia. By this point, it was clear that the Putin regime was an adversary. In 2012, Republican nominee Mitt Romney had said that Russia "is without question our number one geopolitical foe, they fight for every cause for the world's worst actors."[12] Though some Democrats criticized Romney's comment, they eventually acknowledged its accuracy.

It was bad enough that Trump sided with a foreign adversary against the president of his own country. Even worse, stayed with that side. Three years later, at a tea party event in Texas, the moderator asked him what he apparently thought was a softball question about American exceptionalism. Trump let loose with a diatribe against the whole concept. "I don't like the term. I'll be honest with you. People say, 'Oh he's not patriotic.' Look, if I'm a Russian, or I'm a German, or I'm a person we do business with, why, you know, I don't think it's a very nice term."[13]

Trump then revealed what he thought exceptionalism means. "First of all, Germany is eating our lunch. So they say, 'Why are you exceptional? We're doing a lot better than you.'" Trump was defining national status in purely material terms: in his mind, being "exceptional" meant nothing more than being richer than other countries. He was thus breaking with a centuries-old American tradition that emphasized our commitment to the principles of the Declaration. In the example that he mentioned, he was also garbling the facts. The United States had a higher gross domestic product per capita than Germany. It did run a trade deficit with Germany, but it made no sense for him to suggest that German trade policy caused it. As German Chancellor Angela Merkel had to explain to him in 2017, Germany does not have a trade policy separate from the European Union.

Trump went on: "I want to take everything back from the world that we've given them. We've given them so much." He was playing to the common misperception that a huge share of the federal budget goes to foreign aid. (The real figure is around 1 percent.) Living up to the nation's ideals of generosity and service, Americans have given massive amounts of private aid through organizations such as CARE and the Salvation Army. If he really wanted to take back everything that American has given to the world, he would insist that all of these organizations send debt collectors around the globe, demanding the return of charitable contributions. (Perhaps he knows some Mafiosi who could help.) Seriously, shutting down American generosity to the world's needy would ruin our ideals and tarnish our international image.

He continued: "When I see these politicians get up [and say], 'the American exceptionalism'—we're dying. We owe 18 trillion in debt. I'd like to make us exceptional. And I'd like to talk later instead of now. Does that make any sense?" No. It takes effort to make sense out of this jumble of words. One could try to reconstruct this passage into something coherent by focusing on the impact of our mounting federal debt. Trump probably would not want to make this argument today, however. The figure that he cited in 2015 was gross federal debt, and by that yardstick, he is a miserable failure. By 2019, it was more than $22 trillion, and the projected figure for 2029 is $34 trillion.[14]

At other times, Trump has suggested that America is not a very good nation, let alone an exceptional one. During the 2016 campaign, David Sanger of the *New York Times* asked if he would press the Turkish government about its violations of civil liberties. Trump replied:

> I think right now when it comes to civil liberties, our country has a lot of problems, and I think it's very hard for us to get involved in other countries when we don't know what we are doing and we can't see straight in our own country. We have tremendous problems when you have policemen being shot in the streets, when you have riots. . . . When you have all of the things that are happening in this country—we have other problems, and I think we have to focus on those problems. When the world looks at how bad the United States is, and then we go and talk about civil liberties, I don't think we're a very good messenger.[15]

Take a second look at this phrase: "how bad the United States is." Trump was talking about violent crime, which pervaded the hellish New York landscape of the 1970s and 1980s. As the previous chapter noted, however, crime rates had been plunging since the 1990s, and by the time he ran for president New York was safer in many ways than London.[16] Notably, Trump paid no attention to the focus of the reporter's question, which was civil liberties. In its 2016 international survey, Freedom House scored the United States very high in the protection of civil liberties. As we also saw in the last chapter, Trump did not consider this accomplishment to be a good thing, as he had long complained about the rights of criminal defendants.[17]

A much more disquieting problem with Trump's comment was the implied moral equivalence between the United States and autocratic regimes. This country is far from perfect, and for an example of gross injustice, remember the Central Park Five. Trump was not just acknowledging our faults. He was suggesting that a country with a flawed but deeply rooted commitment to human rights is equivalent to one that wantonly puts political dissidents behind bars. The former, he concluded, has no right to judge the latter. Trump is ignorant of history, so he probably did not know that he was parroting an argument that the Soviet Union used to make. Jeane Kirkpatrick, who served as President Reagan's ambassador to the United Nations, wrote that the Soviet technique was to hold Western democracies to abstract, absolute standards and always find them wanting. "The Soviets can always claim 'We are no worse than you. Even if we are a lawless society, you too are a lawless society, we are no worse than you.' This is the 'logic' of the doctrine of moral equivalence."[18]

Fittingly, Trump applied the same moral equivalence to a veteran of the KGB. When he said in an interview that he wanted to get along with Vladimir Putin, Fox News personality Bill O'Reilly cautioned him that Putin is a killer. Trump did not care: "There are a lot of killers. Do you think our country is so innocent? Do you think our country is so innocent?"[19]

TRUMP AND RUSSIA

Trump is weak—morally weak, intellectually weak, and physically weak. He compensates by adoring toughness, or at least its outward appearance. In the 2016 campaign, he retweeted a quotation that expressed this affinity: "It is better to live one day as a lion than 100 years as a sheep."[20] When reporters told him that the line came from Mussolini, he said that he did not care. Trump's toughness tropism helps explain why he is such a Putin fanboy. Over the past two decades, Putin's government has killed and jailed political opponents, strangled freedom of the press, taken foreign territory by force, and given aid to other autocratic regimes. What the American tradition would revile as cruel despotism, Trump sees as "strength." Putin tops it off with flamboyant displays of bare-chested masculinity, which Trump venerates.

Trump has had his eye on Putin for a long time. In 2013, he staged the Miss Universe Pageant in Russia and tweeted this odd message: "Do you think Putin will be going to The Miss Universe Pageant in November in Moscow—if so, will he become my new best friend?"[21] There is no evidence that Putin attended the event, but Trump's admiration was undiminished. The next year, he told Jeffrey Lord: "I had the Miss Universe contest in Moscow recently, six months ago, and Putin, by the way, treated us unbelievably well. And it was at that time that Putin said, 'Who do they think they are saying they're exceptional?' And I understand that."[22] In another 2014 interview, he endorsed sanctions for the Russian invasion of Crimea, but continued to compare Putin favorably to President Obama: "I mean, Putin has eaten Obama's lunch, therefore our lunch, for a long period of time. I just hope that Obama, who's not looking too good, doesn't do something very foolish and very stupid to show his manhood."[23]

In December 2015, Putin made a point of saying that Trump was "bright and talented." Trump answered in kind: "It is always a great honor to be so nicely complimented by a man so highly respected within his own country and beyond."[24] At the time, Trump was on speaking terms with Joe Scarborough and phoned into his MSNBC program. "When people call you 'brilliant' it's always good," Trump said, "especially when the person heads up Russia." Scarborough pointed out that Putin "is a person who kills journalists, political opponents and invades countries, obviously that would be a concern, would it not?" Trump was nonchalant: "He's running his country, and at least he's a leader, unlike what we have in this country." When Scarborough repeated that Putin kills journalists, Trump answered with moral equivalence: "Well, I think that our country does plenty of killing, too, Joe." Trump later gave a ritual condemnation of murdering journalists, but added: "I've always felt fine about Putin. He's a strong leader. He's a powerful leader."[25]

As questions about Russia mounted in 2016, Trump contradicted his previous claims to a relationship with Putin, denying that he knew the man. He also said he had no dealings with Russia although Michael Cohen was pursuing a deal to build Trump Tower Moscow. All the same, he stuck to his praise for Putin. When Matt Lauer asked him about his previous warm words for the Russian leader, he said, "Well, he does have an 82 percent approval rating."[26] The answer was consistent with his belief that might—or in this case, popularity—makes right. He failed to consider, though, that the number might have overstated Putin's popularity, since it is hard to get honest survey answers in a country where political critics end up dead. In response to a question about Russian hacking, Trump mixed dishonesty with a fresh helping of moral equivalence: "Well, nobody knows that for a fact. But do you want me to start naming some of the things that President Obama does?" Trump finished with another paean to Russian "strength" and another slap at the American president: "I mean, the man has very strong control over a country. And that's a very different system and I don't happen to like the system. But certainly in that system he's been a leader, far more than our president has been a leader."[27]

Among Putin's most significant acts was the 2014 annexation of Crimea. President Obama and other world leaders condemned it as an act of raw aggression. In a 2016 interview, Trump took a more tolerant view, claiming that "the people of Crimea, from what I've heard, would rather be with Russia than where they were. And you have to look at that, also. Now, that was under—just so you understand, that was done under Obama's administration. . . . Crimea has been taken. Don't blame Donald Trump for that."[28] A couple of years later, when a reporter asked if he accepted Russia's annexation of Crimea, he said: "We're going to have to see."[29] He reportedly told G7 leaders that Crimea is Russian because its people speak Russian.[30]

The first-ever acknowledged meeting between Trump and Putin took place at a 2017 international summit in Germany. Trump reportedly took his interpreter's notes and ordered her not to tell anyone what they had said.[31] At a dinner on the same day, he and Putin had a private chat with no other Americans present. Their third meeting took place in November of that year at the Asia-Pacific Economic Cooperation Meeting in Da Nang, Vietnam. Aboard Air Force One, after the event, a reporter asked Trump if he had pressed Putin about Russian interference with the 2016 election. "He just—every time he sees me, he says, 'I didn't do that,'" Trump answered. "And I believe—I really believe that when he tells me that, he means it. But he says, 'I didn't do that.' I think he's very insulted by it, if you want to know the truth."[32]

After a fraudulent Russian election in March 2018, Trump called Putin to congratulate him on his "victory," although aides had prepared a briefing book that said in all-capital letters: "DO NOT CONGRATULATE."[33] John McCain observed on Twitter: "An American president does not lead the Free World by congratulating dictators on winning sham elections. And by doing so with Vladimir Putin, President Trump insulted every Russian citizen who was denied the right to vote in a free and fair election."[34]

In July 2018, Trump had his notorious Helsinki press conference with Putin. He struck the moral equivalence chord once again, and linked tensions in bilateral relations to the Mueller probe: "I hold both countries responsible. I think that the United States has been foolish. I think we've all been foolis. . . . I do feel that we have both made some mistakes. I think that the probe is a disaster for our country. I think it's kept us apart. It's kept us separated." On the issue of election interference, he again gave the benefit of the doubt to Putin. "My people came to me, Dan Coats, came to me and some others they said they think it's Russia. I have President Putin. He just said it's not Russia. I will say this: I don't see any reason why it would be." He latter implausibly claimed that he meant to say "wouldn't be," but his other comments in Helsinki showed that his faith lay with the Russian autocrat. "I have great confidence in my intelligence people but I will tell you that President Putin was extremely strong and powerful in his denial today and what he did is an incredible offer. He offered to have the people working on the case come and work with their investigators."[35] That reaction was like welcoming Al Capone's help in investigating the St. Valentine's Day Massacre. In one way, though, Trump was right: *incredible* means "unworthy of belief."

Putin gloated. When a reporter asked if he had wanted Trump to win the 2016 election, he said: "Yes, I did. Yes, I did. Because he talked about bringing the U.S.-Russia relationship back to normal." Trump's craven performance appalled most Americans who saw it. Representative Will Hurd (R-TX), a former CIA agent, said: "I've seen Russian intelligence manipulate many people over my professional career and I never would have thought that the US President would become one of the ones getting played by old KGB hands."[36]

Perhaps Trump's most despicable comment on Russia came as an informal aside. At a 2019 White House press availability, a reporter asked about policy toward Afghanistan. Trump rambled for a while, then referred to the Soviet Union's 1979 invasion. "The reason Russia was in Afghanistan was because terrorists were going into Russia. They were right to be there."[37] Putin might have approved of that historical revisionism, but no respectable American commentators did. "Right to be there? We cannot recall a more absurd misstatement of history by an American President," wrote the *Wall Street Journal* editorial board. "The Soviet Union invaded Afghanistan with three divisions in December 1979 to prop up a fellow communist government."[38] The United States spent billions to help the Afghan resistance, and Reagan cited the Soviet defeat as one of his key accomplishments. There is no other way to put it: Trump was retrospectively taking sides against his own country.

The Russians knew what they were getting. According to the Senate Intelligence Committee, an employee of their social media operation described reactions to Trump's election: "On November 9, 2016, a sleepless night was ahead of us. And when around 8 a.m. the most important result of our work arrived, we uncorked a tiny bottle of champagne . . . took one gulp each and looked into each other's eyes. . . . We uttered almost in unison: 'We made America great.'"[39] On the same night, the Mueller report reveals, the head of Russia's sovereign wealth fund received a mysterious text message: "Putin has won."[40]

A WEAKNESS FOR STRONGMEN

Many writers have suggested that Putin must have compromising information—*kompromat*—about Trump's personal life or, more likely, his finances. Future revelations may well bear out this speculation, but there is another reason for Trump's deference to Putin. Not only in Russia but all over the world, Trump finds much to like in leaders who mock the democratic principles that Americans hold dear. He has a weakness for strongmen.

This aspect of his character is nothing new. In 1989, peaceful protesters, mostly students, occupied Tiananmen Square in Beijing. They built a version of the Statue of Liberty and read a translation of the Declaration of Independence. Chinese troops put down the demonstration by force, and to this day, no one knows how many protesters died. Most Americans saw Tiananmen Square as a case study in the evils of dictatorship. Donald Trump saw it as an illustration of "strength." In a 1990 *Playboy* interview, he said: "When the students poured into Tiananmen Square, the Chinese government almost blew it. Then they were vicious, they were horrible, but they put it down with strength. That shows you the power of strength. Our country is right now perceived as weak . . . as being spit on by the rest of the world."[41] *Almost blew it?* Did he think it would have been bad for the Chinese to permit free speech? And why did he follow that statement with a reference to the United States? Did he regard China as a role model? A little later in the interview, he hinted that the 41st president should be more like the Chinese leaders: "I like George Bush very much and support him and always will. But I disagree with him when he talks of a kinder, gentler America. I think if this country gets any kinder or gentler, it's literally going to cease to exist."

Presidents George H. W. Bush and George W. Bush both waged war against Iraq. The 2003 invasion was extremely controversial, but few Americans have had anything good to say about Saddam Hussein, universally acknowledged as a mass murderer. Trump, who falsely claimed to have opposed the invasion from the start, is an exception. During a 2016 campaign speech, he said of Saddam: "He was a bad guy—really bad guy. But you know what he did well? He killed terrorists. He did that so good. They didn't read them the rights. They didn't talk. They were terrorists."[42] Trump was gratuitously taking a swipe at the due process of law while presenting an upside-down picture of Saddam, who was a state sponsor of terrorism. Another speech was even worse: "Then Saddam Hussein throws a little gas. Everyone goes crazy. Oh, it's because of gas."[43] *A little gas?* In the late 1980s, Saddam launched attacks against dozens of Kurdish villages, using them to test chemical weapons. In the worst attack, in the city of Halabja, mustard gas and nerve agents killed at least 3,000 people.

Like Saddam, North Korea's Kim Jong Un is a sadistic dictator. A United Nations report listed some of his crimes: "extermination, murder, enslavement, torture, imprisonment, rape, forced abortions and other sexual violence, persecution on political, religious, racial and gender grounds, the forcible transfer of populations, the enforced disappearance of persons and the inhumane act of knowingly causing prolonged starvation."[44] And as with Saddam, Trump's view of Kim was initially of the "horrible but admirably strong" variety. "If you look at North Korea, this guy, I mean, he's like a maniac, OK? And you've got to give him credit. How many young guys—he was like 26 or 25 when his father died—take over these tough generals. . . . It's incredible. He wiped out the uncle. He wiped out this one, that one. I mean, this guy doesn't play games."[45] *Give him credit?*

Early in his presidency, Trump went through his "fire and fury" phase, disparaging Kim as "Little Rocket Man" and tweeting a weirdly phallic warning: "North Korean Leader Kim Jong Un just stated that the 'Nuclear Button is on his desk at all times.' Will someone from his depleted and food starved regime please inform him that I too have a Nuclear Button, but it is a much bigger & more powerful one than his, and my Button works!"[46] Belligerence abruptly gave way to a summit, where Kim made a favorable impression. Trump soon reverted to his previous attitude, praising Kim with words that echoed his earlier comments about Putin. When Bret Baier of Fox News asked about Kim's record of murdering people, Trump said: "Hey, when you take over a country, tough country, with tough people, and you take it over from your father, I don't care who you are, what you are, how much of an advantage you have. If you can do that at 27 years old, I mean that's one in 10,000 that could do that. . . . I think we understand each other." Baier interjected that Kim had done bad things. "Yeah, but so have a lot of other people done some really bad things," Trump replied. "I mean, I could go through a lot of nations where a lot of bad things were done."[47] The next day, Trump spoke to Steve Doocy, also of Fox News. "He's the head of a country, and I mean he's the strong head," Trump said. "Don't let anyone think anything different. He speaks and his people sit up at attention. I want my people to do the same."[48] Trump later claimed that he was kidding about the last part, though the video does not suggest a jocular demeanor.

At a rally in Wheeling, West Virginia, Trump said: "And then we fell in love, OK? No, really. He wrote me beautiful letters. And they're great letters. We fell in love." He anticipated criticism of his remarks by falling back on his theme of popularity-makes-right. "Now, they'll make—they'll say, 'Donald Trump said they fell in love. How horrible. How horrible is that? So unpresidential.' [laughter] And I always tell you, it's so easy to be presidential. But instead of having 10,000 people outside trying to get into this packed arena, we'd have about 200 people standing right there. OK? [applause]"[49]

Trump seemed willing to overlook or excuse Kim's abuses of human rights, even when they involved Americans. In 2019, he commented on the death of college student Otto Warmbier, who underwent torture in North Korea and then died in 2017 after the regime sent him back to the United States in a coma. "I don't believe he [Kim] would have allowed that to happen. It just wasn't to his advantage to allow that to happen. Those prisons are rough, they're rough places and bad things happened. But I really don't believe that he was—I don't believe he knew about it. . . . He tells me that he didn't know about it, and I will take him at his word."[50]

A few months after those comments, he talked about a news report that Kim's half-brother had been a CIA informant before his assassination, which Kim had almost certainly ordered. "I see that, and I just received a beautiful letter from Kim Jong Un," Trump said. "I think the relationship is very well, but I appreciated the letter. I saw the information about the CIA with regard to his brother or half-brother, and I would tell him that would not happen under my auspices. I wouldn't let that happen under my auspices. I just received a beautiful letter from Kim Jong Un."[51] With this casual statement, he stood with Kim against the US intelligence community, which would now have a tougher time recruiting intelligence assets in North Korea.

The world is full of other autocrats that Trump is ready to befriend.

After taking power in 2016, President Rodrigo Duterte of the Philippines instigated the extrajudicial killing of thousands of people in his country. Though ostensibly part of a "war on drugs," the slaughter took out political opponents as well as suspected drug dealers.[52] In a call with Duterte, Trump said: "I just wanted to congratulate you because I am hearing of the unbelievable job (you're doing) on the drug problem." Duterte claimed that he had to act harshly for the sake of his nation. Trump answered with a dig at President Obama: "I . . . fully understand that and I think we had a previous president who did not understand that." He concluded by inviting the dictator to the White House and telling him, "You are a good man."[53]

Duterte had long justified the killing of journalists, at least when there was a pretext of corruption: "Just because you're a journalist you are not exempted from assassination, if you're a son of a bitch."[54] The killings continued during his tenure. At a meeting with Trump in Manila, Duterte answered reporters' questions: "We will be talking on matters of interest to both the Philippines and—with you around, guys, you're the spies. Yes, you are."[55] Trump smirked at the comment.

Trump excuses the rule of strongmen by referring to the difficulties that they confront. He used similar language about two autocrats who visited the United States. He said of Egypt's Abdel Fatah al-Sisi: "I just want to let everybody know, in case there was any doubt, that we are very much behind President al-Sisi. He's done a fantastic job in a very difficult situation."[56] Awaiting the Egyptian leader at an international summit, he called out, "Where's my favorite dictator?"[57] In New York, he met with Turkey's Recep Tayyip Erdogan: "And it's a great honor and privilege—because he's become a friend of mine—to introduce President Erdogan of Turkey. He's running a very difficult part of the world. He's involved very, very strongly, and frankly, he's getting very high marks."[58] In 2019, Trump gave a green light for Erdogan's incursion into northern Syria to drive out the Kurds. After Erdogan had carried out the operation and agreed to suspend further action, Trump said: "So you have a 22-mile strip. And for many, many years, Turkey—in all fairness, they've had a legitimate problem with it. They had terrorists. They had a lot of people in there that they couldn't have. They've suffered a lot of loss of lives also. And they had to have it cleaned out."[59] If the positive allusion to ethnic cleansing were not enough, Trump then tweeted: "Just spoke to President @RTErdogan of Turkey. He told me there was minor sniper and mortar fire that was quickly eliminated. He very much wants the ceasefire, or pause, to work. Likewise, the Kurds want it, and the ultimate solution, to happen."[60] It is not clear whether Trump understood the history of the phrase "ultimate solution."

Trump has a soft spot for Saudi Arabia, the first foreign country that he visited as president. Saudi Arabia has always committed abuses of human rights, which got much worse during the first two years of the Trump administration. In October 2018, Saudi agents murdered Jamal Khashoggi in Istanbul. He was a *Washington Post* columnist and outspoken critic of the Saudi regime. Although the killing of a US resident was a blatant effort to silence opposition, Trump shied from meaningful action. Trump called Crown Prince

Mohammed bin Salman "a strong person, he has very good control."[61] Even after the CIA concluded that the prince had ordered the murder, Trump put dollar signs ahead of principles:

> After the United States, Saudi Arabia is the largest oil producing nation in the world. They have worked closely with us and have been very responsive to my requests to keeping oil prices at reasonable levels—so important for the world. As President of the United States I intend to ensure that, in a very dangerous world, America is pursuing its national interests and vigorously contesting countries that wish to do us harm. Very simply it is called America First![62]

In a Reuters interview, he continued to oppose economic sanctions: "I really hope that people aren't going to suggest that we should not take hundreds of billions of dollars that they're going to siphon off to Russia and to China, primarily those two, instead of giving it to us."[63] Senator Bob Corker (R-TN), chair of the Senate Foreign Relations Committee, criticized Trump's decision. "It's un-American," he said. "When we provide aid to other countries, we do so because we want to see good things happen in those countries. We espouse American values around the world. And to say, 'Well, no. They're going to buy some arms for us and so it's OK to kill a journalist,' sends exactly the wrong message about who we are as a country."[64] It fell to a French leader to school the American president in American ideals. "Patriotism is the exact opposite of nationalism: nationalism is a betrayal of patriotism," said French President Emmanuel Macron at a Paris event marking the 100th anniversary of the end of World War I. "By pursuing our own interests first, with no regard to others,' we erase the very thing that a nation holds most precious, that which gives it life and makes it great: its moral values."[65]

EMOLUMENTS

At a 2015 campaign rally in Mobile, Alabama, Trump shamelessly admitted: "Saudi Arabia, I get along great with all of them, they buy apartments from me, they spend $40 million, $50 million. Am I supposed to dislike them?"[66] His ties to the Saudis went back decades. In 1991, when he was deep in debt, he sold his yacht to a Saudi prince for $20 million. A few years later, the prince bought a stake in Trump's Plaza Hotel. In 2001, the Kingdom of Saudi Arabia paid $4.5 million for the 45th floor of his Trump World Tower.[67] The business dealings continued after his election. Lobbyists for the Saudi government reserved blocks of rooms at his expensive Washington hotel, buying 500 nights over a span of three months.[68] Trump hotels in New York and Chicago also saw an inflow of Saudi visitors.[69]

It is not just Saudi Arabia. A review by NBC news found that representatives of at least 22 foreign governments appear to have spent money at Trump Organization hotels, restaurants, golf clubs, and other properties.[70] For instance, public records indicate that at least nine governments bought or rented property in Trump buildings or communities: Kuwait, Iraq, Saudi Arabia, China, Malaysia, Slovakia, Thailand, India, and the European Union.

There are connections to foreign governments even when they are not directly spending the money. The homepage of a Trump-branded property in the Philippines says: "Rising in the Philippines' most prestigious financial and commercial district is a name synonymous with unparalleled service, quality and real estate. Trump Tower at Century City—the country's most amenitized residential high-rise and Manila's definitive landmark."[71] The licensing deal for the hotel made millions for Trump. Right after the 2016 election, Duterte announced that he was appointing Trump's Filipino business partner as special envoy to the United States for trade, investment, and economic affairs. The partner then flew to New York for a private meeting at Trump Tower with Trump's children.[72]

The Trump Organization website includes this description of a property in Turkey: "Trump Towers, Istanbul, Sisli is a landmark in the historic city of Istanbul. With two towers rising in Mecidiye-koy, one of the city's most vibrant areas, the property captures the utmost in luxury."[73] When it opened in 2012, Ivanka Trump tweeted: "Thank you Prime Minister Erdogan for joining us yester-day to celebrate the launch of #TrumpTowers Istanbul!"[74] Erdogan was president five years later, when he arranged a dubious referen-dum that strengthened his autocratic power. After Trump congratu-lated him, *Mother Jones* reminded readers that Trump had once done an interview with Steve Bannon where he admitted: "I have a little conflict of interest 'cause I have a major, major building in Istanbul. It's a tremendously successful job. It's called Trump Tow-ers—two towers, instead of one, not the usual one, it's two."[75]

In some cases, Trump customers are influential foreign figures, former leaders, or aspiring office-holders. A *Washington Post* report found that patrons of the Trump International Hotel included exiled Thai prime ministers, a Nigerian presidential candidate, and the leader of an Iraqi order of Sufi Muslims who spent 26 nights at an extremely expensive suite.[76]

Many of Trump's transactions potentially fall afoul of the Con-stitution. The Foreign Emoluments Clause (Article. I, section 9, clause 8) states: "[N]o Person holding any Office of Profit or Trust under [the United States], shall, without the Consent of the Con-gress, accept of any present, Emolument, Office, or Title, of any kind whatever, from any King, Prince, or foreign State." In lawsuits, plaintiffs argued that Trump's dealings with foreigners violated this clause.[77] The litigation will turn on complicated and technical points of constitutional interpretation. The relevant case law is limited pre-cisely because previous presidents took pains to avoid the appear-ance of conflicts of interest. Jimmy Carter, for instance, put his peanut business into a blind trust. Whatever the outcome in court, however, it is clear that Trump has violated the spirit of the law. The Framers included the Emoluments Clause because they worried that foreign benefits and payments would prejudice the judgment of public officials toward their benefactors. In the case of the presi-dent, wrote Hamilton, the idea was that he would "have no pecuni-ary inducement to renounce or desert the independence intended for him by the Constitution."[78] Trump asked rhetorically about the Saudis: "Am I supposed to dislike them?" No, but neither is he supposed to favor them because they have put money in his pocket.

Such conflicts of interest damage the country's reputation. When foreign leaders think that they can buy favor with the government by enriching the president and his family, they see America not as a city on a hill but as a bazaar in a swamp.

THE UGLY AMERICAN

At the American battlefield memorial in Normandy, a visitor can see inscribed quotations about war. One is from General Mark Clark: "If ever proof were needed that we fought for a cause and not for conquest, it could be found in these cemeteries. Here was our only conquest: all we asked . . . was enough . . . soil in which to bury our gallant dead." By the middle of the 20th century, Americans thought that their country should fight for liberty, not loot. After World War II, the United States agreed to the Fourth Geneva Convention, forbidding the hostile acquisition of resources from occupied territory.[79] Trump has a different view. As early as 2011, he tweeted: "I still can't believe we didn't take the oil from Iraq."[80] Two years later, he said it again: "I still can't believe we left Iraq without the oil."[81] He repeated the claim throughout the 2016 campaign and did not stop when he became president. In his ill-famed remarks at the Central Intelligence Agency on the day after he took office, he said: "The old expression, 'To the victor belong the spoils'—you remember. I always used to say, keep the oil. I wasn't a fan of Iraq. I didn't want to go into Iraq. But I will tell you, when we were in, we got out wrong. And I always said, in addition to that, keep the oil."[82] Ominously, he offered a side remark to CIA Director Mike Pompeo: "Maybe you'll have another chance." He kept at it throughout his administration, reportedly raising the prospect with the Iraqi prime minister.[83]

Treaties are the law of the land, and the chief executive has a constitutional duty to execute the laws faithfully. So Trump was cheerfully discussing a violation of the presidential oath as well as international law. He was also reinforcing a charge that America's global critics had long made: that the United States is a pirate country that cares only for its own enrichment. *Pravda* could not have said it more effectively than Trump.

He has soiled our national image in other ways. Just as he praises murderous dictatorships, he insults democracies and their leaders. In the wake of a 2017 terror attack, London Mayor Sadiq Khan condemned the terrorists and told the people of his city that they should not be alarmed at the surge of police activity that would follow. Trump attacked him on Twitter: "At least 7 dead and 48 wounded in terror attack and Mayor of London says there is 'no reason to be alarmed!'"[84] As he was heading to London in 2019, he tweeted: " Kahn [sic] reminds me very much of our very dumb and incompetent Mayor of NYC, de Blasio, who has also done a terrible job— only half his height."[85] At the 2017 Conservative Political Action Conference, he quoted an invisible friend to attack Muslim immigration to France: "I have a friend—he's a very, very substantial guy. He loves the City of Lights. He loves Paris. For years, every year, during the summer, he would go to Paris—it was automatic— with his wife and his family. I hadn't seen him in a while. And I said, Jim, let me ask you a question: How's Paris doing? 'Paris? I don't go there anymore. Paris is no longer Paris.'"[86]

Sometimes his remarks about other countries end up revealing his lack of knowledge. In a fundraising speech, he bragged that he made up information in a meeting with Canadian Prime Minister Justin Trudeau. He insisted that the United States had a trade deficit with Canada without knowing whether we actually did. "Nice guy, good-looking guy, comes in—'Donald, we have no trade deficit.' He's very proud because everybody else, you know, we're getting killed . . . . So, he's proud. I said, 'Wrong, Justin, you do.' I didn't even know. . . . I had no idea. I just said, 'You're wrong.'"[87] He claimed that he turned out to be right, which he was not: the United States had a trade surplus with Canada, just as Trudeau said. And when he was running for president, he said that immigration had made Brussels a "hellhole" but later tried to make nice: "Belgium is a beautiful city."[88]

Presidents have tried to preserve the image of national unity by refraining from attacks on domestic political opponents while overseas. Not Trump. During a 2018 visit to American troops stationed in Iraq, he said: "You know, when you think about it, you're fighting for borders in other countries, and they don't want to fight—the Democrats—for the border of our country. It doesn't make a lot of sense."[89] During a 2019 trip to Japan, he quoted Kim: "North Korea fired off some small weapons, which disturbed some of my people, and others, but not me. I have confidence that Chairman Kim will keep his promise to me, & also smiled when he called Swampman Joe Biden a low IQ individual, & worse. Perhaps that's sending me a signal?"[90] And he claimed that his invisible Japanese friends agreed with him about his political opponents: "Great fun and meeting with Prime Minister @AbeShinzo. Numerous Japanese officials told me that the Democrats would rather see the United States fail than see me or the Republican Party succeed—Death Wish!"[91] His most disgraceful insult came in Normandy on the 75th anniversary of D-Day—an event where he was duty bound to focus on the sacrifices of Americans in uniform instead of his own petty grudges. With the headstones of a military cemetery in the background, he told Laura Ingraham of Fox News that Robert Mueller—a recipient of the Bronze Star and Purple Heart—"just made such a fool out of himself."[92]

THE FACE HE SHOWS THE WORLD

One group of world leaders does consider Trump to be a role model of sorts: autocrats and would-be strongmen. In at least 15 countries, authoritarian rulers have used Trump's "fake news" line to delegitimize political opponents.[93] One such leader is Hungary's Viktor Orban, who called his country's leading independent news portal "a fake news factory."[94] After Trump welcomed Orban to the White House, he reportedly said, "It's like we're twins."[95]

In other corners of the world, people do not associate Trump with anything good. For years, Gallup has been posing a question to adults all over the world: "Do you approve or disapprove of the job performance of the leadership of the United States?" In 2016, the last year of President Obama's tenure, adults in more than 130 countries and areas gave American leadership a median approval rating of 48 percent. After Trump's first year in office, that number had plunged to 30 percent, and a year later, it was virtually unchanged at 31 percent. [96]

This shift reflects the words and deeds that this chapter has recounted, but it also stems from those that previous chapters covered as well. The technology of the 21st century makes it easy for people all over the world to follow events in the United States, and they do not like what they see. His dishonesty is among his most recognizable traits around the globe. So is his record on human rights. The nation's reputation for defending individual liberty, once quite strong, has dropped considerably in international surveys by the Pew Research Center. [97]

In another survey, this one of experts in foreign affairs, 93 percent say the United States is less respected by other countries today compared with the past. [98] One might dismiss this result as the opinion of left-leaning academics, but a survey of rank-and-file Americans shows a similar concern. According to Dina Smeltz and colleagues at the Chicago Council on Global Affairs: "As interactions with allies have strained over the past year, majorities of Americans say that relations with other countries are worsening (56%) and that the United States is losing allies (57%). In addition, 59 percent of Americans say that the United States is less respected now than it was 10 years ago, with 21 percent saying it is more respected now." [99] They quote one survey respondent: "I think the world is laughing at us."

That comment was not just a figure of speech. In the fall of 2018, Trump addressed the United Nations General Assembly. At one point in his speech, he said: "In less than two years, my administration has accomplished more than almost any administration in the history of our country." Audience members laughed in his face. [100]

UKRAINE

In the summer and fall of 2019, Americans started to learn that Trump had squeezed the government of Ukraine for political dirt. As a partial transcript of a July 25 phone call showed, he asked Ukrainian President Volodymyr Zelensky to "do us a favor" by investigating the Ukrainian business dealings of Joseph Biden's son, as well as a crackpot conspiracy theory that Ukraine had interfered in the 2016 election.[101] Trump and his defenders claimed that the demand merely reflected a deep concern about exposing corruption overseas. That claim was absurd. Throughout his entire career, the only thing that Trump ever wanted to know about corruption was how he could benefit from it. In 2012, he complained to CNBC about the Foreign Corrupt Practices Act; "Now every other country goes into these places, and they do what they have to do. It's a horrible law, and it should be changed. I mean, we're like the policemen for the world. It's ridiculous."[102] At a press availability after the scandal broke, a reporter asked: "Have you asked foreign leaders for any corruption investigations that don't involve your political opponents? That is, are there other cases where you've asked for corruption investigations?" Trump could not think of one: "You know, we would have to look."[103] Trump was not fighting corruption. He was abusing presidential power for political gain.

His actions helped Russia. For years, Ukraine has been fighting Russian-backed separatist militias. Trump put a hold on military aid to Ukraine, but had to relent when his pressure scheme came to light. During that hold, American diplomats William Taylor and Kurt Volker went to the front line of the conflict. "The commander thanked us for security assistance, but I was aware that this assistance was on hold, which made me uncomfortable," Taylor testified. "Ambassador Volker and I could see the armed and hostile Russian-led forces on the other side of the damaged bridge across the line of contact. Over 13,000 Ukrainians had been killed in the war, one or two a week. More Ukrainians would undoubtedly die without the U.S. military assistance."[104] In the weeks to follow, more Ukrainians did perish.[105]

On September 25, Trump met with President Zelensky in New York. At a joint press availability, he made this astonishing comment: "And I really hope that Russia—because I really believe that President Putin would like to do something. I really hope that you and President Putin get together and can solve your problem. That would be a tremendous achievement. And I know you're trying to do that."[106] The stunned, nauseated look on Zelensky's face said it all: Trump had just suggested a moral equivalence between the invader and the invaded. Once again, he had given Putin what he wanted.

If anyone in the world still thought that the Trump administration stood for American exceptionalism, acting chief of staff Mick Mulvaney offered a correction. In a press conference, he candidly admitted that the call to the Ukrainians amounted to a quid pro quo. "And I have news for everybody: Get over it. There's going to be political influence in foreign policy."[107]

6

OUR LIVES, OUR FORTUNES, AND OUR SACRED HONOR

James Madison asked, "what is government itself, but the greatest of all reflections on human nature? If men were angels, no government would be necessary."[1] He and other members of the Founding generation believed that human potential for evil required effective governmental powers. But they also believed in limiting those powers. Accordingly, they adopted the principles of federalism, bicameralism, and the separation of powers, as well as bills of rights at the state and federal levels. Underlying their support for limited government was their confidence that Americans, most of the time, could overcome the dark side of human nature and behave decently. In his Farewell Address, George Washington said: "It is substantially true that virtue or morality is a necessary spring of popular government. The rule, indeed, extends with more or less force to every species of free government. Who that is a sincere friend to it can look with indifference upon attempts to shake the foundation of the fabric?"[2] John Adams famously wrote: "Our Constitution was made only for a moral and religious People. It is wholly inadequate to the government of any other."[3] At the Virginia ratifying convention, Madison asked: "Is there no virtue among us? If there be not, we are in a wretched situation. No theoretical checks—no form of government can render us secure."[4] If the people lacked certain moral qualities, he declared in *Federalist 55*, "nothing less than the chains of despotism can restrain them from destroying and devouring one another."[5]

The moral sense includes such elements as fairness, sympathy, self-control, and duty.[6] Fairness is about the Golden Rule: do unto others as you would have them do unto you. Sympathy is the capacity to take part in other people's feelings, to experience sorrow for their misfortune. Self-control is the ability to restrain impulses, emotions, and desires, to rein in all kinds of greed. And duty is faithfulness to one's obligations, especially those that carry a steep cost. These elements help explain why Americans typically do not kill, rob, or cheat their neighbors even when there is no chance of getting caught. As novelist Robert Heinlein put it: "I believe in my fellow citizens. Our headlines are splashed with crime yet for every criminal there are 10,000 honest, decent, kindly men. If it were not so, no child would live to grow up. Business could not go on from day to day. Decency is not news. It is buried in the obituaries, but is a force stronger than crime."[7]

The president of the United States needs a moral sense more than anyone else, which is why Alexander Hamilton wanted the office "filled by characters pre-eminent for ability and virtue."[8] Despite all the safeguards that the Founders built into the Constitution, a chief executive can do great and lasting harm by abusing the immense powers of the office. Moreover, that person's behavior can bring the government into disrepute and set a poor example for the people. Of course, moral perfection is an impossible standard. All presidents have had their faults and failings, sometimes grievous ones. But they have generally tried to show themselves as worthy of the esteem of their fellow citizens. George Washington was acutely aware of his hot temper and other flaws, so he made a lifelong project of building a character that others could admire. As a teenager, he copied out 110 rules of civility and decent behavior, and until the end of his days, he strove to follow those rules. Presidents who behaved badly in private still tried to act with decorum in public. Lyndon Johnson was nasty and crude in the Oval Office, but restrained his tone and language when he spoke to the American people.

A sense of duty is especially important. Presidents must honor the spirit of our democratic system, observing norms that fill in where the spare language of the Constitution is silent. Washington embodied this principle. In his everyday activities as president, he took pains to avoid the trappings of monarchy while maintaining the dignity of his office and defending its legitimate prerogatives. "There is scarcely an action, the motive of which may not be subject to a double interpretation," he explained in a letter. "There is scarcely any part of my conduct, which may not hereafter be drawn into precedent."[9] His successors followed his precedents and built upon them.

Washington was great because of his moral strength and commitment to duty, concepts that are foreign to Donald Trump. When he toured Mount Vernon in 2019, he showed more interest in Washington's personal wealth than his presidential accomplishments. At one point, he reportedly voiced puzzlement as to why Washington did not name the estate after himself: "If he was smart, he would've put his name on it. You've got to put your name on stuff or no one remembers you."[10]

Trump is deficient in the other elements of the moral sense. It is hard to think of another president who was so indifferent to fairness, so bereft of sympathy, and so shameless in his lack of self-control. The problem is not just that he is a bad man who does bad things, but that he is oblivious to moral concepts. When he writes "Bad!" in a tweet, he is merely referring to something that fails to serve his interests. He has no idea that *sacrifice* means giving up something of value for the sake of others. Khizr Khan, the father of an Army captain who died in combat, gave a fiery 2016 convention speech that addressed Trump: "You have sacrificed nothing and no one."[11] When George Stephanopoulos asked Trump to respond, he said: "I think I've made a lot of sacrifices. I work very, very hard. I've created thousands and thousands of jobs, tens of thousands of jobs—built great structures. I've done—I've had—I've had tremendous success. I think I've done a lot." Stephanopoulos asked him if those things were genuine sacrifices. "Oh, sure. I think they're sacrifices. I think, when I can employ thousands and thousands of people, take care of their education, take care of so many things, . . . I raised, and I have raised, millions of dollars for the vets."[12] Making a great deal of money is not a sacrifice, especially when it involves cheating workers, contractors, vendors, and customers. His "charity" also involved cheating, too.

Trump's defenders might say that his bad character is a private matter, unrelated to his public actions. But Trump himself has thrust it into public view. For decades, he has flaunted his greed and immorality and has made little effort to change since taking the oath of office. Trump's dishonor has left a mark on the government and the people around him.

FAIRNESS AND RIGGED SYSTEMS

The word *rigged* appears in more than a hundred of Trump's tweets. He deploys it whenever he is frustrated with an outcome in business or politics. For example, he repeatedly claimed that the Emmy awards were rigged because his reality show failed to win one. The complaints are phony: Trump does not care about fairness, only winning. For all his adult life, he has tried to rig processes to his advantage, usually abusing the law and sometimes breaking it.

Perhaps his first major adult decision consisted of cheating his way out of the Vietnam-era military draft. As mentioned earlier, his father reportedly arranged for a Queens podiatrist to write him a dubious medical excuse claiming that he had bone spurs. As with other forms of cheating, this act had consequences, because somebody else had to take Trump's place in Vietnam. Trump's replacement was probably a working-class man without any college education—the kind of person he claimed to champion in the 2016 campaign.

After he graduated from Wharton, he joined his father's business. He made the news by discriminating against African Americans in apartment rentals, but he cheated many other people as well. Michael Cohen testified about Trump's approach to vendors and contractors: "It should come as no surprise that one of my more common responsibilities was that Mr. Trump directed me to call business owners, many of whom are small businesses, that were owed money for their services and told them that no payment or a reduced payment would be coming. When I asked Mr. Trump—or when I told Mr. Trump of my success, he actually reveled in it."[13] There is plenty of corroboration. A 2016 *USA Today* review found more than 200 mechanic's liens by contractors and employees who claimed that Trump, his properties, or his companies owed them money for their work. That figure was surely just a tiny sample. The Trump technique was to stiff individuals and companies, tie them up in court, and then wait until they either gave up or went broke.[14] In several high-profile cases, he abused bankruptcy law to renege on his debts. It took one small business three years to recover money for its work on the Trump Taj Mahal in Atlantic City. The firm nearly went under, and in the end, got only 30 cents on the dollar. "Trump crawled his way to the top on the back of little guys, one of them being my father," said the current co-owner and daughter of the company founder. "He had no regard for thousands of men and women who worked on those projects. He says he'll make America great again, but his past shows the complete opposite of that."[15]

In a 2015 debate, Chris Wallace pointed out that his bankruptcies had cost his lenders billions of dollars. Trump saw nothing wrong. "I have used the laws of this country just like the greatest people that you read about every day in business have used the laws of this country, the chapter laws, to do a great job for my company, for myself, for my employees, for my family, et cetera." He exulted in what he had done: "I made a lot of money in Atlantic City, and I'm very proud of it." He disparaged the people whose money he took: "Let me just tell you about the lenders. First of all, these lenders aren't babies. These are total killers. These are not the nice, sweet little people that you think, OK?"[16] As usual, he was lying. In a 2009 case, unsecured creditors, including low-level investors, got less than a penny on the dollar, for claims against Trump Entertainment Resorts. "He defaulted, and he walked away," said an 87-year-old man who had lost $91,000 in retirement savings. The man's wife added that Trump "did do great. He walked away with our money."[17]

With the help of his lawyers and political contacts, he unfairly exploited programs meant to benefit others. On September 11, 2001, he told radio station WWOR: "Forty Wall Street actually was the second-tallest building in downtown Manhattan, and it was actually before the World Trade Center the tallest, and then when they built the World Trade Center it became known as the second-tallest, and now it's the tallest."[18] On this tragic day, Trump was thinking less about the suffering of his fellow Americans than about the relative value of his own property (and his claim about its height was not close to being true).[19] He soon figured out a way to make money from 9/11, collecting $150,000 in federal recovery grants that Congress had earmarked for small businesses.[20] During the 2016 campaign, he claimed that he had received the money for helping others recover from the attacks. That claim was false. Records showed that his company sought the "small business" funds to cover cleanup, rent loss, and repair.[21]

Trump also abused eminent domain, the government's power to take property for public use. In the mid-1990s, Trump planned to build a limousine parking lot in Atlantic City, so he bought some nearby properties. But three owners, including an elderly widow, refused to sell. So he had the Casino Reinvestment Development Authority (CRDA) make her an offer. When she declined, CRDA went to court to claim her property under eminent domain. With the help of the Institute for Justice, the widow and her neighbors fought back and eventually won, but it took them several years.[22] Trump later applauded the Supreme Court's infamous *Kelo* decision, which held the door open for such abuses of eminent domain. As one conservative commentator wrote: "*Kelo* was a dreadful decision. It had anti-private property rights, anti-capitalist and anti-growth stains all over it, and the political system is repudiating it (as it should) just about everywhere. . . . To put it simply: *Kelo* was un-American." The writer was Lawrence Kudlow, who would go on to work in the Trump White House.[23]

Trump University was such a flagrant fraud that it has become a national punchline. But it was no joke to the people who spent thousands of dollars on worthless courses. During the 2016 campaign, he vowed that he would keep fighting lawsuits relating to the scam, but then he settled. In typical Trump fashion, there was an asterisk. Trump had dragged out the class-action litigation for so long that some former students had died while waiting to get their money back. For instance, an 85-year-old man passed away in January 2017 before receiving a refund for his $34,995 Trump University "mentorship program" tuition.[24]

Trump takes pride in avoiding taxes. At a 2016 debate, Hillary Clinton noted that he had failed to disclose his returns and "the only years that anybody's ever seen were a couple of years when he had to turn them over to state authorities when he was trying to get a casino license, and they showed he didn't pay any federal income tax." Trump cut in: "That makes me smart."[25] When Trump got a $10 million tax refund while slashing employee pay, recalled Michael Cohen in congressional testimony, "he said that he could not believe how stupid the government was for giving 'someone like him' that much money back."[26] He was not merely making cynical use of lawful tax loopholes. A 2018 investigation by the *New York Times* found: "President Trump participated in dubious tax schemes during the 1990s, including instances of outright fraud, that greatly increased the fortune he received from his parents."[27]

Cohen himself pleaded guilty to evading taxes, and in his sentencing memorandum, federal prosecutors seemed to be sending a signal to Trump. They said that a prison sentence would send "the important message that even powerful individuals cannot cheat on their taxes and lie to financial institutions with impunity, because they will be subject to serious federal penalties." They added that the United States loses billions because tax cheats— "who otherwise take full advantage of all that taxes bring, such as schools, paved roads, transit systems, and Government buildings—shirk their responsibilities as American taxpayers."[28] In at least one instance, a Trump tax scheme imposed specific costs on specific people. He and his siblings set up a phony business to pad the cost of things that their father bought for his buildings, and they divided the money among themselves, thereby evading gift taxes. The inflated cost also enabled them to charge more for rent-regulated apartments. "The higher the markup would be, the higher the rent that might be charged," Trump's brother Robert admitted in a deposition.[29] The Trumps eventually sold the buildings, but the artificially high rents became part of the basis for future rent increases. Because of the Trumps' unfairness, thousands of renters have long kept paying more than they should.

The grift goes on. Just before he became president, Trump said that he would not divest from interests in the Trump Organization. He then brazenly used his office and political status to make money, creating unprecedented conflicts. Foreign emoluments, which the previous chapter discussed, were just part of the sordid picture. During his first two years in office, at least 13 special interest groups spent money at Trump properties at about the same time they were lobbying the White House.[30] Meanwhile, Republican candidates and campaign committees laid out more than $4 million at Trump properties, with more than a quarter of the money coming from Trump's campaign coffers.[31] People who thought they were contributing to political causes were actually making a rich man richer.

After his election, his Mar-a-Lago resort doubled its initiation fee to $200,000. Buyers expected something for their money. At least eight current or former members received nominations or appointments to important federal offices.[32] "The Mar-a-Lago club has turned into a pay-for-access to the president club, with a president with almost no knowledge of governmental policy," the head of Public Citizen told *The Guardian*. "If you can whisper in his ear and tell him anything, he may well think it's sensible and he may well act upon it."[33] In 2019, the House Veterans Affairs Committee opened an investigation into a trio of Mar-a-Lago members. The committee chair wrote: "Top Department [of Veterans Affairs] officials apparently treated these Mar-a-Lago members as having decision-making authority, and emails demonstrate these powerful men weighed in on candidates to lead the Veterans Health Administration, and organized meetings and summits between VA and commercial entities."[34]

Trump used official travel and communications to promote his interests. He visited his properties hundreds of times, thus bringing them more attention. In planning a 2019 trip to Ireland, the White House sought to arrange a meeting with the prime minister at Trump International Golf Links, Doonbeg. The prime minister objected, so they settled on a gathering at the airport. Trump did visit his property, however, and in a press availability with the prime minister, he worked in a plug for it: "I thought this would be the best place. I love to come to Ireland and stay at Doonbeg."[35] In 2019, he announced plans to host the G-7 international summit at his Doral, Florida, golf resort. He changed his mind after this obviously corrupt move drew criticism from across the political spectrum.

Alexander Hamilton warned us about someone like Trump. "An avaricious man, who might happen to fill the office, looking forward to a time when he must at all events yield up the emoluments he enjoyed, would feel a propensity, not easy to be resisted by such a man, to make the best use of the opportunity he enjoyed while it lasted, and might not scruple to have recourse to the most corrupt expedients to make the harvest as abundant as it was transitory."[36]

SYMPATHY

We have already seen Trump's stunning lack of sympathy for disabled people, including his own great-nephew. He also lacks sympathy for women who do not meet his ideal of physical perfection. The terms that he has publicly hurled at specific women include: "ugly," "fat," "horseface," "pig," "dog," and "extremely unattractive," among many others.[37] Worse yet, he has insulted women who have credibly accused him of sexual assault and harassment. In 2016, he told a cheering rally that one accuser "would not be my first choice, that I can tell you."[38] In 2019, he dismissed E. Jean Carroll's statement that he had raped her in the 1990s. "I'll say it with great respect: Number one, she's not my type. Number two, it never happened. It never happened, OK?"[39] Trump not only hurts his targets, but girls and women in general. For boys and young men, he is setting an obnoxious example that echoes through playgrounds, schoolrooms, and workplaces all over the country. He has never shown a moment's concern that his words and deeds may be metastasizing.

There is no evidence that he has much sympathy for anyone at all. In 2008, he told Howard Stern about an old man who fell during a ball at Mar-a-Lago. "So what happens is, this guy falls off right on his face, hits his head, and I thought he died. And you know what I did? I said, 'Oh my God, that's disgusting,' and I turned away," Trump said. "I couldn't, you know, he was right in front of me and I turned away. I didn't want to touch him . . . he's bleeding all over the place, I felt terrible. You know, beautiful marble floor, didn't look like it. It changed color. Became very red." Marines attending the ball carried the old man out. Trump acknowledged that he ordered a cleanup but forgot to check whether the old man died. "It's just not my thing."[40]

After Khizr Khan criticized him at the 2016 Democratic convention, Trump kept going after him and his wife. A campaign adviser reportedly warned him: "You do know you just attacked a Gold Star family?" Trump asked, "What's that?"[41] He did not care enough to learn that the term refers to relatives of Americans who have died in battle. He carried this lack of sympathy into the Oval Office. In an October 17, 2017, radio interview, he said, "I think I've called every family of somebody that's died and it's the hardest call to make. . . . I've called virtually everybody. . . . I can tell you my policy is I've called every one of them."[42] That claim was far from accurate, and the White House did not even have an updated list of those who had died. Presidential aides scrambled to get such a list and make good on his claim.[43] The goal was not to offer condolences but simply to contain a bad media narrative.

As this example indicates, Americans expect their president to show sympathy for the suffering of others. Trump has a hard time faking it. When he held a White House meeting for survivors of the Parkland school shooting, he needed note cards to feign a human response. A photographer caught him holding White House station-ery with five talking points written in black marker: "'1. What would you most want me to know about your experience?' '2. What can we do to help you feel safe?' and '5. I hear you.'"[44] (His fingers covered the fourth.)

Most normal human beings express sympathy through acts of kindness and giving, and the United States ranks among the most charitable nations in the world.[45] Many Americans of modest means dig deep to donate their time and money, and billionaires such as Bill Gates have given a big portion of their wealth to the needy. Trump is different, seeing charity as strictly transactional. When New York Military Academy, his high school alma mater, was fac-ing financial trouble in 2010, a fellow alumnus asked Trump for a $7 million contribution. Trump replied: "What do I get for my $7 million?" The school was willing to name buildings after him, but he rejected the plea: "It's not a good business proposition," he said.[46]

Trump knows that Americans believe in charity, so his strategy has always been to look charitable without being charitable. In the fall of 1996, the Association to Benefit Children held a New York ribbon-cutting event for a new nursery school serving AIDS-af-fected children. Trump barged his way onto the podium so that he would appear in news photographs sitting alongside major donors. He had never given a dime to the charity.[47]

In 2016, his campaign tried to back up his claim to be an "ardent philanthropist" by listing thousands of purported Trump contribu-tions. The *Washington Post* found that none of the donations on the list came from Trump's personal funds. Many of the gifts that the Trump camp cited were such things as free rounds of golf that his courses gave for charity auctions and raffles.[48] The *Post* did find some contributions that Trump had once made, but none since 2009. And of the pre-2009 giving, about 70 percent went to the Trump Foundation. From then on, the foundation got its money entirely from other sources.[49]

Although he had stopped donating personal funds, Trump might have been able to claim credit for organizing a charitable enterprise—if the foundation had been on the level. It was not. Trump used its assets to pay off legal obligations, to promote Trump properties, and to buy personal items. In 2007, for instance, he used $20,000 of foundation money to buy a six-foot-tall painting of himself at a fundraiser auction.[50] In 2018, as a result of a lawsuit by the New York Attorney General, the foundation agreed to dissolve under judicial supervision. Attorney General Barbara Underwood said: "Our petition detailed a shocking pattern of illegality involving the Trump Foundation—including unlawful coordination with the Trump presidential campaign, repeated and willful self-dealing, and much more. This amounted to the Trump Foundation functioning as little more than a checkbook to serve Mr. Trump's business and political interests."[51] In 2019, the New York Supreme Court ordered him to pay $2 million in damages.

As with Trump's other misdeeds, there are victims. Every fraudulent charity undercuts the credibility of the entire nonprofit sector, making it harder for legitimate organizations to raise money. Even worse, it also tainted the Eric Trump Foundation, which once had a fair reputation for supporting cancer research. A donation from the father's foundation to the son's foundation ended up in the coffers of Trump's businesses.[52]

After Trump entered the presidential race, he started making personal contributions again, or at least he promised to do so. In January 2016, he skipped a GOP primary debate and instead held a televised fundraiser for veterans, where he proudly claimed to have given the group a million dollars. Trump did not write a check until months later, and only after the media raised questions about whether he had gone back on his commitment. When David Farenthold of the *Washington Post* asked him if he made the donation in response to the criticism, he said: "You know, you're a nasty guy. You're really a nasty guy. I gave out millions of dollars that I had no obligation to do."[53] More recently, Trump has donated his government salary to charities. But the amount is small compared with the millions that he has made from corruptly using the presidency for his business interests.

Trump's sympathy deficit has affected his conduct in office. After a hurricane struck Puerto Rico in 2017, Trump made the obligatory trip to the disaster area. "I hate to tell you, Puerto Rico, but you've thrown our budget a little out of whack because we've spent a lot of money on Puerto Rico," he said before adding for cover, "and that's fine."[54] In a bizarre scene, he tossed rolls of paper towels to survivors as if they were wedding bouquets. Even though thousands died in the months after the storm, he insisted that the federal response was a roaring success and that the death toll was minimal. "The missing part was empathy," former homeland security adviser Thomas Bossert later told the *New York Times*. "I wish he'd paused and expressed that instead of just focusing on the response success."[55] Trump's coldness to Puerto Rico entailed more than optics. He tweeted: "Puerto Rico got 91 Billion Dollars for the hurricane, more money than has ever been gotten for a hurricane before, & all their local politicians do is complain & ask for more money. The pols are grossly incompetent, spend the money foolishly or corruptly, & only take from USA."[56] He lied: actual federal aid was barely one-tenth the amount he claimed. He had held up additional disaster funds for months, but he nonetheless followed with another tweet: "The best thing that ever happened to Puerto Rico is President Donald J. Trump."[57]

If the Puerto Rico hurricane response was a case of incompetence and neglect, family separation was a case of deliberate cruelty. In 2018, the administration announced a "zero tolerance" policy for illegal immigration, which forced the separation of migrant children from their families. (It had actually been separating families for months before the announcement.) When Laura Ingraham asked Attorney General Jeff Sessions if the administration meant family separation as a deterrent, he said, "So yes, hopefully people get the message and come through the border at the port of entry and not break across the border."[58] John Kelly, then serving as Trump's chief of staff, was more direct, saying that "a big name of the game is deterrence." When a reporter asked if it was cruel to separate children from their mothers, Kelly said, "I wouldn't put it quite that way. The children will be taken care of—put into foster care or whatever."[59] As it turned out, "whatever" included forcing children to sleep on the bare floor of metal cages. As a series of horror stories turned public opinion against the policy, Trump showed no sympathy, instead raising fears about the adults who brought the children. "They could be murderers and thieves and so much else," he said. "We want a safe country, and it starts with the borders, and that's the way it is."[60] But as the policy generated opposition from Republicans and even his own family members, he backed down.

SELF-CONTROL

"America the Beautiful" includes a verse that gives voice to a long-standing ideal: "America! America!/God mend thine every flaw/ Confirm thy soul in self-control/Thy liberty in law!" Holding George Washington as an exemplar, the members of the Founding generation placed great emphasis on restraint, steadiness, and temperance. Americans have traditionally expected such characteristics in a chief executive. As head of state as well as head of government, the president embodies the nation's respectability and legitimacy. A rash and undignified president makes the country look bad. As we saw in the previous chapter, Trump has caused reputational damage to the United States.

Presidential impulsiveness has more direct costs. Hamilton cautioned against "a disgraceful and ruinous mutability in the administration of the government,"[61] which would make it hard for Americans to understand public policy and act accordingly. Hamilton's description could fit the Trump regime. Trump makes and unmakes policy on the fly, confusing citizens, and hindering negotiations with other officials. He promised lawmakers that he would work for gun control, then retreated under pressure from the National Rifle Association. He angrily told the Senate Democratic leader that he would shut down the government to get funding for his border wall, then blamed the Democrats when the shutdown took place. By 2019, the mutability of Trump's policy views had reached the point where aides routinely ignored his more outlandish orders in hopes that he would soon forget.[62] There is one worrisome exception to this pattern. Uniformed military officers are duty bound to follow orders from the commander in chief, so if he impulsively decided to launch missiles, then the missiles would fly.

Some presidents, such as compulsive adulterers John Kennedy and Lyndon Johnson, have lacked self-control in their personal lives. Some writers observe that private sins do not necessarily spill over into public life.[63] With Trump, though, that distinction is meaningless. Throughout his pre-presidential career, he advertised his louche lifestyle, telling the media about his purported sexual adventures and appearing in soft-core *Playboy* videos (albeit fully clothed).[64] Just before the 2016 election, the *Access Hollywood* tape showed Trump delighting in his sexual impulses. "You know, I'm automatically attracted to beautiful—I just start kissing them. It's like a magnet. Just kiss. I don't even wait. And when you're a star, they let you do it. You can do anything. Grab 'em by the pussy. You can do anything."[65] He offered a forced and insincere "apology" and then responded to additional stories of his sexual harassment not only by insulting the women but by threatening to sue them. Sexual harassment is a pervasive problem in American society. It has reached into the military, where women find it difficult to report harassment by superiors. It does not help them that their commander in chief is America's most notorious harasser, and that he has gotten away with it.

Trump's lack of self-control has had other public consequences. The humiliation of his wives never troubled him, so exposure of his infidelity was hardly much of a threat—that is, until he was running for president. Some of the Christian conservatives who had stuck with him after *Access Hollywood* might have ditched him after hearing that he had cheated on Melania right after she gave birth. So he directed Michael Cohen to make the hush money payments that later came to light and landed Cohen in prison.

Unchecked impulses may draw the scrutiny of foreign intelligence officers who seek compromising information. Salacious stories about Trump sex videos are unverified and seem improbable. Another Trump impulse—greed—is a much more likely vulnerability. In the 1990s, Trump's weak management skills combined with his reckless spending to produce corporate bankruptcies. Ivanka Trump said of that time: "I remember once my father and I were walking down Fifth Avenue and there was a homeless person sitting right outside of Trump Tower and I remember my father pointing to him and saying, 'You know, that guy has $8 billion more than me,' because he was in such extreme debt at that point, you know?"[66] Because he was such a deadbeat, American banks shunned him. He later got financing from foreign sources such as Deutsche Bank. According to *New York Times* reporter David Enrich, Trump-connected transactions set off alerts in a Deutsche Bank computer system that flags suspicious activity. Compliance staff members drafted reports for submission to the Treasury Department's Financial Crimes Enforcement Network. Bank executives never sent the reports.[67] The details of these dealings could prove damaging to Trump, either because they involve violations of the law or because they would show that he is less wealthy than he has claimed. Either way, possession of such information could give foreign entities a great deal of leverage over Trump. Presidents do not undergo background checks for security clearances, but if they did, Trump would surely flunk. According to the National Counterintelligence and Security Center, "foreign influence" is the top reason for clearance problems, followed by "financial considerations."[68]

DUTY

At a minimum, duty involves a willingness to exert oneself and accept tough aspects of a job such as candidly dealing with unwelcome news. During the summer of 2016, Trump posted 16 different tweets with the promise, "I will work hard and never let you down."[69] More specifically, he pledged that he would be so devoted to duty that he would not have time for his golf courses in Scotland and Miami: "I love golf, but if I were in the White House, I don't think I'd ever see Turnberry again I don't think I'd ever see Doral again. I don't ever think I'd see anything—I just want to stay in the

White House and work my ass off, make great deals, right?"[70] During the first two and a half years of his presidency, he visited golf courses at least 198 times.[71] As of November 2019, he had done so on 23 percent of the days that he had been in office.[72]

Leaked copies of his schedule revealed that he spent about 60 percent of his "workday" in unscheduled "Executive Time," much of which goes to watching cable television.[73] Trump often skips in-person intelligence briefings and barely glances at written materials from national security aides.[74] And worse still, he rejects information that is not consistent with his attitudes, and he has openly insulted intelligence officials for providing it. In January 2019, he tweeted: "Perhaps Intelligence should go back to school!"[75] Former CIA brief David Priess told NBC: "This is the first president that the intelligence community has had to deal with whose instinctive departure point is not the truth. He goes from his belief first."[76]

Some duties are unique to the president, especially the constitutional responsibility to "take care that the laws be faithfully executed." We have already seen how Trump has violated this duty by obstructing justice, inviting foreign interference in our elections, and advising Border Patrol officers to lie to judges. After the 2018 Democratic takeover of the House, he also stonewalled legitimate congressional inquiries and requests for information. Undoubtedly the remainder of his tenure will supply other examples.

Over and above the duty to the letter of the Constitution, a president also has broader responsibilities to the democratic system itself.[77] One is respect for the rights of Americans. We have seen how he has tried to use the machinery of government against his political opponents, but his rhetoric is just as disturbing. In 2019, he tweeted: "Do you believe that the Failing *New York Times* just did a story stating that the United States is substantially increasing Cyber Attacks on Russia. This is a virtual act of Treason by a once great paper so desperate for a story, any story, even if bad for our Country."[78] National security officials told the *Times* that they had no security concerns with the report. Trump accused the paper of a capital crime because of another revelation: the officials were reluctant to tell Trump about the details of the operation, lest he either scuttle it or reveal sensitive information to the Russians.[79] Around the same time, the premiere of a new film prompted reporters to ask him about his role in railroading the Central Park Five. He refused to acknowledge the violation of their rights. "You have people on both sides of that," he said. "They admitted their guilt."[80]

Acceptance of responsibility is another duty of the commander in chief and head of the executive branch. "The buck stops here," read the famous sign on Harry Truman's desk. After the Bay of Pigs, Kennedy said: "There's an old saying that victory has 100 fathers and defeat is an orphan. Further statements, detailed discussions, are not to conceal responsibility because I'm the responsible officer of the Government."[81] Trump, by contrast, always tries to blame others for bad outcomes. After Navy SEAL Willian "Ryan" Owens died during a secret mission in Yemen, the commander in chief pointed at the brass: "Well, this was a mission that was started before I got here. This was something that was, you know, just— they wanted to do. And they came to see me and they explained what they wanted to do, the generals, who are very respected. My generals are the most respected that we've had in many decades, I would—I believe. And they lost Ryan."[82] He blamed his predecessor for his family separation policy at the border: "You know, under President Obama you had separation. I was the one that ended it."[83] Wrong: in contrast to his "zero tolerance" policy, family separations rarely occurred under Obama. Perhaps Trump's most telling abdication of responsibility came when reporters asked him about the 2019 government shutdown. Turning Truman's famous saying on its head, he said: "The buck stops with everybody."[84]

As head of state, the president has to serve all the people, not just co-partisans. As head of a political party, the president must often fight with the opposing party. These roles are always in tension, but chief executives have usually tried to reconcile them by refraining from practices such as calling names or making partisan comments at nonpartisan events. Trump crosses these lines all the time. He regularly attacks "Crooked Hillary" Clinton, "Crazy Nancy" Pelosi, and "Crying Chuck" Schumer. He tosses partisan red meat into places where it does not belong, including a gathering of Boy

Scouts. Introducing Secretary of Health and Human Service Tom Price at the 2017 Boy Scout Jamboree, Trump said, "hopefully, he's going to get the votes tomorrow to start our path toward killing this horrible thing known as Obamacare that's really hurting us, folks. By the way, you going to get the votes? He'd better get them. He'd better get them. Oh, he'd better—otherwise, I'll say, Tom, you're fired." And then he free-associated about Michigan in the 2016 election. "My opponent didn't work hard there, because she was told [AUDIENCE BOOS], she was told she was going to win Michigan, and I said, well, wait a minute, the car industry is moving to Mexico."[85] Even worse than goading teens and preteens into booing a former secretary of state, he brought partisanship right into the Pentagon. "The federal government remains shut down because Congressional Democrats refuse to approve border security," he said to uniformed military and civilian staff of the Defense Department in January 2019. "The Party has been hijacked by the open borders fringe within the Party. The radical left becoming the radical Democrats."[86]

Trump's attitude toward John McCain offers a fitting summary of his character and his scorn for presidential duty. McCain's courage and integrity stood in stark contrast to Trump's cowardice and sleaze. During the 2008 fall campaign, McCain treated his opponent with respect, swatting down the fears that Trump would later stoke. At a town hall meeting, McCain sought to reassure an audience member who said that he was "scared" of an Obama presidency: "I have to tell you he is a decent person and a person that you do not have to be scared (of) as president of the United States." To a woman who said that she could not trust Obama because he was an "Arab," he replied: "No, ma'am, no ma'am. He's a decent family man, citizen that I just happen to have disagreements with on fundamental issues, and that's what this campaign's all about." And to questioners who said that he should hit Obama harder, he said: "We want to fight and I will fight. But we will be respectful. I admire Senator Obama and his accomplishments. I will respect him."[87] McCain was a loyal American leader who showed how to express loyal opposition. Trump resented him for it. Four years later, he complained in a tweet: "The @BarackObama campaign keeps high-lighting a web video of John McCain being nice & respectful"—as if respect were a bad thing.[88]

Trump kept lashing out. "He's not a war hero," he said in 2015 of McCain. "He was a war hero because he was captured. I like people who weren't captured."[89] It struck many people as odd that a man who had dodged the Vietnam draft—and lied about it—would belittle an American hero who had endured years of torture in Vietnam and passed up early release out of duty to his comrades. Lindsey Graham tweeted: "If there was ever any doubt that @realDonaldTrump should not be our commander in chief, this stupid statement should end all doubt."[90] He continued: "At the heart of @realDonaldTrump statement is a lack of respect for those who have served—a disqualifying characteristic to be president."[91]

In 2017, McCain enraged Trump by casting the decisive vote against a Republican healthcare bill, and giving a thumbs-down gesture for emphasis. McCain could not have had ulterior political motives for the vote, because he knew that he would never run for office again. He had just learned that he had an aggressive brain cancer that would kill him. Instead of acknowledging that McCain had cast a vote on principle, Trump repeatedly attacked him, often with insults that had nothing to do with the healthcare issue. The attacks continued as McCain lay on his death bed, and even after he died. Three postmortem tweets tell us much about their author:

- "Spreading the fake and totally discredited Dossier 'is unfortunately a very dark stain against John McCain.' Ken Starr, Former Independent Counsel. He had far worse 'stains' than this, including thumbs down on repeal and replace after years of campaigning to repeal and replace!"[92]
- "So it was indeed (just proven in court papers) 'last in his class' (Annapolis) John McCain that sent the Fake Dossier to the FBI and Media hoping to have it printed BEFORE the Election. He & the Dems, working together, failed (as usual). Even the Fake News refused this garbage!"[93]

- "He was horrible with what he did with repeal and replace. What he did to the Republican party and to the nation and to sick people who could have had great healthcare, was not good. So I'm not a fan of John McCain and that's fine."[94]

For comparison, consider Lyndon B. Johnson and Robert F. Kennedy, whose deep mutual hatred left a mark on Democratic Party politics throughout the 1960s. LBJ cursed RFK in private, but was always circumspect in his public comments about his rival. And when RFK lay dying from an assassin's bullet, Johnson spoke to the nation: "At this moment, the outcome is still in the balance. We pray to God that He will spare Robert Kennedy and will restore him to full health and vigor. We pray this for the Nation's sake, for the sake of his wife and his children, his father and his mother, and in memory of his brother, our beloved late President."[95] Unlike Trump, he did not subsequently whine about a dead man who had opposed his policies. Johnson knew how to talk like a president, buttoning up his private feelings for the sake of the country.

In 2019, the Trump White House was planning a presidential trip to Japan. Staffers asked the Navy to keep the U.S.S. *John S. McCain* out of sight during the visit. Contradicting initial denials from the White House, the Navy eventually acknowledged that it had received a request to minimize the warship's visibility, but that it kept all ships in their proper places. It probably irked Trump that the Navy responded this way. John McCain once explained the difference between the Trump mindset and the military mindset: "He is in the business of making money and he has been successful both in television as well as Miss America and others. I was raised in a military family. I was raised in the concept and belief that duty, honor, country is the lodestar for the behavior that we have to exhibit every single day."[96]

THE FISH ROTS FROM THE HEAD DOWN

The president has a responsibility to seek the best people for jobs in the executive branch. In the 18th-century prose of *Federalist 76*, Hamilton wrote that the chief executive should "investigate with care the qualities requisite to the stations to be filled, and to prefer with impartiality the persons who may have the fairest pretensions to them."[97] Anyone entering the White House with a normal human sense of duty would try to meet this standard. Trump did not. His 2016 transition process was scandalously slapdash, and when it came to researching potential appointees, he delegated much of the work to young and inexperienced staffers at the Republican National-al Committee. Even their cursory review of potential nominees revealed red flags. The vetting form for Scott Pruitt, under consideration as EPA administrator, warned about "allegations of coziness with big energy companies." Representative Tom Price (R-GA), a contender for Health and Human Services secretary, reportedly faced "criticisms of management ability." [98] Trump did not care. He appointed both of them anyway, and both eventually had to resign in disgrace. Many other officials also got into trouble as well. Trump had promised to drain the swamp, but all he did was bring in more alligators.

For Trump, a key consideration in personnel choices is loyalty— not loyalty to the Constitution and laws of the United States, but personal loyalty to Donald Trump. He will favor job candidates who flatter him and parrot his views, even if they are unfit. In 2019, he planned to nominate a pair of sycophants to the Federal Reserve, and their qualifications were so poor that they ran into opposition from otherwise-compliant Republican senators. They pulled out. Trump did name a highly competent chair of the Federal Reserve, but then his policies diverged from Trump's preferences. Disregarding the century-old principle of Federal Reserve independence and talking like a mob boss chewing out an unruly henchman, Trump said: "Here's a guy, nobody ever heard of him before, and now I made him, and he wants to show how tough he is? O.K. Let him show how tough he is."[99]

Trump's contempt for the rule of law sends powerful signals throughout the executive branch. From her departmental account, HUD official Lynne Patton retweeted a defense of Secretary Ben Carson that also attacked Representative Alexandria Ocasio-Cortez (D-NY). Her Twitter post likely violated the Hatch Act, which forbids federal employees to use government time or resources for political activities. "Just retweeted this amazing tweet from both of my Twitter accounts—professional and personal," she then wrote on Facebook. "It may be a Hatch Act violation. It may not be. Either way, I honestly don't care anymore. These people are determined to try to ruin and discredit a good man."[100] Under criticism for disregarding the law, she then tweeted: "What part about 'I don't give a shit' don't you understand?"[101]

After Trump aide Kellyanne Conway attacked Joe Biden, reporters pointed out to her that the Office of Special Counsel (OSC) had found that some of her previous comments violated the Hatch Act. Conway was dismissive. "Blah, blah, blah," she said. "If you're trying to silence me through the Hatch Act, it's not going to work. Let me know when the jail sentence starts."[102] In mid-June, OSC recommended her removal:

> Ms. Conway's disregard for the restrictions the Hatch Act places on executive branch employees is unacceptable. If Ms. Conway were any other federal employee, her multiple violations of the law would almost certainly result in removal from her federal position by the Merit Systems Protection Board. As a highly visible member of the Administration, Ms. Conway's violations, if left unpunished, send a message to all federal employees that they need not abide by the Hatch Act's restrictions. Her actions erode the principal foundation of our democratic system—the rule of law.[103]

"In interview after interview, she uses her official capacity to disparage announced candidates, which is not allowed," said Special Counsel Henry Kerner, a Trump appointee. "What kind of example does that send to the federal workforce? If you're high enough up in the White House, you break the law, but if you're a postal carrier or a regular federal worker, you lose your job?"[104] The chief executive saw no problem, however, and Conway stayed on the job.

When future dictionaries define the term "bad influence," they need only show a picture of Donald J. Trump. Some of his underlings and appointees were obviously bad right from the start, as is clear from the felonies of campaign chair Paul Manafort and national security adviser Michael Flynn. More generally, he brings out the worst in the people around him, baring their weaknesses and encouraging their darkest impulses. His administration rewards obsequious praise for the boss and discourages critical thinking about issues. Following the president's lead, political appointees expect that they should be harshly partisan, legal restrictions be damned. For Trump, there is no such thing as right and wrong, only winning and losing. In his eyes, the winners are strong, and the losers are weak. When he conveyed to subordinates under investigation that they should "stay strong," he was not urging them to show moral courage by telling the truth. Instead, he was adopting Mafia language suggesting that they could beat the rap if only they did not rat him out. His example teaches that ethical transgressions are no big deal, unless they hurt Trump. In place of "always do right," the operative motto is "never get caught."

As Michael Gerson writes, "Trumpism is an easygoing belief system that indulges and excuses the stiffing of contractors, the conning of students, the bilking of investors, the exploitation of women and the practices of nepotism and self-dealing. A faith that makes losing a sin will make cheating a sacrament."[105]

7

NEW GUARDS FOR THEIR FUTURE SECURITY

"**T**rumpism" does not have much of a future as a coherent political philosophy. Trump has never articulated a comprehensive set of principles, and most of his issue positions have had the lifespan of a mayfly. During the 2016 campaign, he made the risible claim that he could eliminate the federal debt in eight years, and then blithely put it on a path to even larger increases. He threatened North Korea with fire and fury, then fell in love with the butcher of Pyongyang. First, NATO was obsolete, then it was not. Foreign trade is the sole issue on which he has been more or less consistent, talking up tariffs as early as the 1980s, then imposing them in the first years of his presidency. But protectionism is a weak spine for a long-term program because it has practically no intellectual foundation. If there is one point of agreement among economists across the ideological spectrum, it is that protectionism is a foolish approach that harms the people that it is supposed to help. In 2016, the University of Chicago Booth School of Business asked a panel of top economic experts whether it would be a good idea to encourage domestic production by adding new or higher import duties on products such as air conditioners and cars. In response, 93 percent "disagreed" or "strongly disagreed."[1] The rest did not answer. Not a single respondent called it a good idea.

Some writers and Trump officials have projected their ideas onto the Trump screen but with minimal success. Secretary of State Mike Pompeo has tried to root Trump's foreign policy in the concept of American exceptionalism.[2] There is just one problem: as we saw earlier in this book, Trump has explicitly, emphatically, and repeatedly repudiated that very idea. If anything has guided his actions on the world stage, it is not an intellectual framework but an emotional attachment to foreign strongmen. As with trade protectionism, it is hard to see how this impulse could supply the basis for a political program. Except for the alt-right extremists who chanted "Russia is our friend" at Charlottesville, few Americans put support for autocracy at the top of their political agenda. Trump's crowds cheer him in spite of this attitude, not because of it.

Trump has done little to build a political movement that promotes anything other than Trump. He has raised money for the GOP, but at least part of his motivation has been to line his own pockets. In mid-2019, the *Washington Post* reckoned that of all the fundraisers or donor events that Trump had attended as president, about a third had taken place at his own properties.[3] Trump has shown no interest in long-term party-building or in developing organizations that will outlive him.

It would have been unwise to expect anything else. Trump's ghostwritten book, *The Art of the Deal*, suggested his attitude toward planning: "You can't be imaginative or entrepreneurial if you've got too much structure. I prefer to come to work each day and just see what develops."[4] Trump lives for the present and for himself. He would never understand the old saying that society grows great when old men plant trees whose shade they know they will never see. In 2017, aides tried to tell him that his economic policies would bloat the federal debt. Noting that the problem would become critical only after he left office, he reportedly shrugged, "Yeah, but I won't be here."[5]

Trump's indifference to the future represents a break with American tradition, which has always called on our leaders to think about generations to come. The Preamble to the Constitution promised to "secure the blessings of liberty to ourselves and our posterity." It might shock the self-styled "King of Debt" that George Washington warned against red ink, "ungenerously throwing upon posterity the burden which we ourselves ought to bear."[6] In 1989, President George H. W. Bush looked back at his early predecessors: "And if you look back, one thing is so striking about the way the Founding Fathers looked at America. They didn't talk about themselves. They talked about posterity. They talked about the future. And we, too, must think in terms bigger than ourselves."[7]

Trump does not think in terms bigger than himself, but like the blast of a dirty bomb, his impact will spread wide and last long.

FOLLOWERS

GOP consultant Rick Wilson put it best: everything Trump touches dies. The first casualties of the Trump regime have been people close to him: staffers, appointees, and political allies. Some have ended up in legal trouble. Many more have stained their public images. Trump does not have some mystical aura that curses those who stand behind him; instead, the harm comes from the conditions that he imposes on them. As before in this volume, the Mafia sheds some light on how Trump works. To become a "made man," a gangster must first commit a contract murder. As far as we know, Trump does not require his minions to kill, but he does make them lie, cheat, publicly defend ridiculous statements, or at very least, abase themselves by offering oleaginous compliments to the boss. Take Sean Spicer, for instance. Before serving Trump as press secretary, he had a decent reputation as a Republican communications professional. On his first full day on the job in 2017, Trump ordered him to claim that his inauguration audience was the biggest in history, which was provably false. Spicer quickly became a laughingstock. His successor, Sarah Sanders, was worse. She dissembled remorselessly, and only when Mueller's team put her under oath did her façade crack a little. In a press interview, she had said that rank-and-file FBI agents had lost confidence in James Comey. Under penalty of perjury, Sanders admitted to investigators that she had made the remark "in the heat of the moment" and that it "was not founded on anything."[8] In other words, she had lied. Steve Mnuchin, after a career dealing with actual numbers in the financial services industry, prophesied that the 2017 Trump tax cut would pay for itself by stimulating the economy. The prediction was ridiculous on its face, and the tax cut predictably caused the Treasury to hemorrhage red ink. In the oleaginous compliment category, it would be hard to top 2020 campaign manager Brad Parscale, who tweeted that "Only God could deliver such a savior to our nation."[9] To any serious Christian, such language is not just offensive, but blasphemous.

No doubt these people will make money in the future. Even as their bank accounts swell, their reputations will rot. Their cringeworthy comments are tattooed onto the public record, and the technology of the 21st century will make them easy to find. Whatever else Sanders, Parscale, and company may do in life, any search of their records will instantly reveal what they said and did for Trump. Power and money are fleeting. Shame lasts forever.

Will the damage engulf GOP at the ballot box? Republican optimists might point to the aftermath of the Nixon administration. The party took major losses in the 1974 midterm election that followed Watergate, and some pundits speculated that the GOP might go the way of the Whigs. As soon as 1976, however, there were signs of recovery, as Gerald Ford came surprisingly close to winning a full term under adverse circumstances. The 1978 midterm endowed the congressional party with fresh blood and new issues; and two years later, Reagan's victory reversed the narrative and prompted talk of a Republican realignment. So if the GOP can get back on its feet after Nixon, Republicans might ask, why should they worry now? The answer lies in a fundamental difference between Nixon and Trump. Whereas Watergate crimes took place in secret, Trump's un-American words and actions are out in the open. Most Nixon-era Republicans did not take part in Watergate and did not see the conclusive evidence of the president's guilt until the scandal's final days. Today's Republican politicians know who Trump is, and they know what they are doing when they support him. His stench will stick to them.

Two features of the American electoral system limit the short-term harm to the GOP. First is the distribution of the vote in House races. Democratic support is concentrated in urban areas, where lopsided margins mean many wasted Democratic votes. GOP support has a more efficient distribution. In Senate elections, equal representation of states means that the lightly populated GOP states of Wyoming and Alaska have the same number of seats as the mega-states of California and New York.

In the long run, though, Trump has greased the way for Republican decline. A 2018 AP poll found that most Americans between the ages of 15 and 35 think that he is racist, dishonest, and "mentally unfit" for office.[10] In 2018, the Pew Research Center found that 59 percent of Millennial voters (born between 1981 and 1996) identified or leaned Democratic, compared with only 32 percent who sided with the GOP.[11] Americans born since 1996 have similar views.[12] Party identification tends to last, so we can expect that GOP vote share will shrink as the rising generations vote in larger numbers and older ones die off. Trump is not entirely responsible for this trend, of course. Democrats have a built-in advantage because younger generations are more ethnically and racially diverse than their elders. But that is also a reason why Trump's pandering to racists is especially repugnant to young people. By joining hands with him, Republican politicians are making themselves more repulsive to the electorate of the future.

Their choice is partly a matter of belief, partly a response to GOP primary voters. Trump encouraged dark impulses both among elected officials and the electorate. At *The Atlantic*, Eliot Cohen acknowledged the presence of such impulses among his fellow conservatives. Many of them, he said, had hoped the civil rights movement, changing social norms, and rising levels of education "had eliminated the germs that produced secession, lynching, and Indian massacres. Instead, those microbes simply went into dormancy, and now, in the presence of Trump, erupt again like plague buboes—bitter, potent, and vile."[13]

Trump is helping turn his followers against the foundations of their own country. In 2016, Maine Governor Paul LePage said: "Sometimes, I wonder that our Constitution is not only broken, but we need a Donald Trump to show some authoritarian power in our country and bring back the rule of law because we've had eight years of a president, he's an autocrat, he just does it on his own, he ignores Congress and every single day, we're slipping into anarchy."[14] In a 2018 Ipsos survey, 59 percent of Republicans either agreed or strongly agreed with the statement "America needs a strong leader willing to break the rules."[15] (Only 22 percent of Democrats answered the same way.) Perhaps the most vivid evidence emerged on July 4, 2017, when National Public Radio tweeted the Declaration of Independence line by line. The network got angry responses from Trump supporters, who did not recognize the source and thought that NPR was attacking the president.[16]

TOCQUEVILLE'S WARNING

Another problem stems from Trump's alliance with evangelical Christians. It was an odd coupling from the start. Trump had always acted as if the Ten Commandments were a bucket list. He swindled his customers, cheated on all three of his wives, and lied about nearly everything. Despite his nominal status as a Presbyterian, he showed little familiarity with the Christian faith. "Donald Trump has no knowledge of the Bible at all. It might as well be a paper brick to him," said embittered former aide Omarosa Manigault Newman, an ordained Baptist minister. "'We love the Bible. It's the best,' he said during the campaign. 'We love *The Art of the Deal*, but the Bible is far, far superior.' How would he know? He says he never reads the Bible. . . . Nothing has more meaning to Donald than himself."[17] After Trump said that public schools should give their students the "option" of studying the Bible, Reverend David Lewicki tweeted: "I was @realDonaldTrump's pastor for 5 years @MarbleChurch. I assure you, he had the 'option' to come to Bible study. He never 'opted' in. Nor did he ever actually enter the church doors. Not one time."[18]

Indeed, Trump denies a core teaching of Christianity just as directly as he spurns human equality and American exceptionalism. Jesus said: "But I tell you, love your enemies and pray for those who persecute you" (Matthew 5:44). Perhaps His most famous saying is: "If someone slaps you on one cheek, turn to them the other also" (Luke 6:29). Recall from the discussion of the Central Park Five that Trump proclaimed that we needed more hatred, not less. In 2012, he tweeted: "When someone attacks me, I always attack back . . . except 100x more. This has nothing to do with a tirade but rather, a way of life!"[19] Lest anyone miss the point about Trump's rejection of Jesus' words, see a tweet from 2013: "What happened to 'turn the other cheek?' Sorry, not a believer!"[20]

Evangelical leaders knew that Trump was as un-Christian as he was un-American, but he offered them power and judicial appointments. They took the Faustian bargain, then rationalized it. Some claimed without evidence that he was growing in faith. Others likened him to the biblical King David, a flawed instrument of God's will. Jerry Falwell Jr., president of Liberty University, said: "God called King David a man after God's own heart even though he was an adulterer and a murderer."[21] Franklin Graham, son of Billy Graham, also embraced Trump. Many years before, however, he explained why evangelicals should be wary of comparisons between David and a sinful president:

> But forgiveness is not the end of David's story. Huge consequences followed immediately. The prophet Nathan confronted David with the news that while his life would be spared, the life of his child would be extinguished after just seven days on earth. Bathsheba's husband and others were killed in an attempt to cover up the illicit affair. David, who confessed his sin when confronted by Nathan (perhaps God's special prosecutor), also witnessed a bloody coup attempt by his own son, Absalom. He was never the same king.[22]

For people who cared about the lessons of the Gospel, Trump's presidential actions were more troubling than his private degeneracy. Russell Moore, president of the Ethics and Religious Liberty Commission of the Southern Baptist Convention, tweeted: "The reports of the conditions for migrant children at the border should shock all of our consciences. Those created in the image of God should be treated with dignity and compassion, especially those seeking refuge from violence back home. We can do better than this."[23] Falwell responded: "Who are you @drmoore? Have you ever made a payroll? Have you ever built an organization of any type from scratch? What gives you authority to speak on any issue? I'm being serious. You're nothing but an employee—a bureaucrat."[24] One wonders what Falwell would think of an itinerant carpenter.

Trump, as any other Republican president would, named judges that evangelical leaders liked. But he made false claims about other things that he had accomplished. A federal law effectively forbids tax-exempt churches and charitable organizations from endorsing political candidates. He told a closed-door meeting that he had gotten rid of the law, which was not true. He also used apocalyptic language to stir fear and hatred of the Democrats. "This Nov. 6 election is very much a referendum on not only me, it's a referendum on your religion, it's a referendum on free speech and the First Amendment." If Republicans lose Congress, he said, "they will overturn everything that we've done and they'll do it quickly and violently, and violently. There's violence. When you look at Antifa [a left-wing fringe movement] and you look at some of these groups—these are violent people."[25]

Trump corrupts his evangelical audiences by getting them to accept—even approve—hateful words. At the 2019 Faith and Freedom conference, he spoke about changes in the makeup of the Senate: "We needed 60 votes, and we had 51 votes. And sometimes, you know, we had a little hard time with a couple of them, right? (Laughter.) Fortunately, they're gone now. They've gone on to greener pastures. (Laughter.) Or perhaps, far less green pastures, but they're gone. . . . Very happy they're gone."[26] Among Republicans who departed the Senate in 2018, Trump's most visible opponents were Jeff Flake and John McCain, both of Arizona. Flake's replacement was a Democrat, so it is unlikely that Trump could be "happy" about that seat change. Though he did not say so expressly, it is hard to escape the conclusion that he was talking about John McCain. So in front of people who professed to be Christians, Trump was gloating over the death of a war hero and strongly suggesting ("far less green pastures") that he had gone to Hell. Attendees laughed.

The Constitution forbids religious tests for public office, so presidents of the United States need not belong to a particular religion, or any religion at all. But it is bad for the country when a president actively discredits religion, as Trump has done. Christians began to cheer for Donald Trump without qualification and a chorus of other believers decried that support as immoral, wrote Mark Galli at *Christianity Today*. "The Christian leaders who have excused, ignored, or justified his unscrupulous behavior and his indecent rhetoric have only given credence to their critics who accuse them of hypocrisy."[27] A leading evangelical told the *Washington Post*: "When you Google evangelicals, you get Trump. When people say what does it mean to be an evangelical, people don't say evangelism or the gospel. There's a grotesque caricature of what it means to be an evangelical."[28]

Gallup has long asked whether religion can solve "all or most of today's problems," or if it is "old-fashioned and out of date." Back in 1957, Americans preferred the first answer by a 75-point margin, 82–7 percent.[29] That margin gradually narrowed over the decades, but between 2017 and 2018, it dropped sharply—from 21 points (55–34) to seven (46–39). Author Mark Silk asks rhetorically: "What is it about the Trump era that has led a smaller percentage of Americans than ever to think that religion can answer today's problems and a larger percentage than ever to think that it is old-fashioned and out of date?"[30] As with the GOP, Trump is hardly the only reason for religion's problems, but he makes them worse. It is hard to convince people that religion stands for love and charity when key religious leaders extol a man who is so mean and selfish. The Falwells and Grahams of the world are confirming what Alexis de Tocqueville wrote more than a century and a half ago: when religion allies itself with political power, it "sacrifices the future for the present." A faith "cannot share the material strength of the rulers without being burdened with some of the animosity roused against them. . . . It does not need their support in order to live, and in serving them it may die."[31]

OVER THERE

In 2018, a group of former military officers and defense officials issued a report saying: "America has progressed and regressed. But we have, over our history and in the course of our individual lifetimes, seen moral growth in this country. This is not only a source of great pride, but it is also something we treasure as security experts. It is the nucleus of America's strength."[32] To halt or reverse that moral growth is to weaken America for the future.

Trump's bad moral example has spread beyond our borders, providing perverse guidance to authoritarians around the world. In particular, his dismissal of inconvenient reality as "fake news" has caught on among strongmen. In response to reports of prison deaths, Syrian president Bashar al-Assad said that "we are living in a fake-news era." President Nicolás Maduro of Venezuela attacked the global media for "lots of false versions, lots of lies," saying "this is what we call 'fake news' today." In Myanmar, which is killing Rohingya Muslims, a security official said "there is no such thing as Rohingya," adding: "It is fake news." In Russia, a foreign ministry spokeswoman told a CNN journalist to "stop spreading lies and fake news."[33]

When democracy declines, Trump shrugs. During a photo opportunity with President Andrzej Duda of Poland, a reporter asked about democratic backsliding in the country. Trump said: "I'm not concerned. I know the President very well. I know the people and the leadership of Poland very well. I'm not concerned at all. By the way, Poland is doing so well and they know if they do backslide, they won't be doing well like they're doing right now. They've probably never done better economically." Duda told the reporter: "Someone cheated you. There is no problems with democracy in Poland. Really. Everything is excellent." Trump said: "That's what I hear. Okay?"[34]

Trump's lack of concern for America's moral standing was on panoramic display during his 2019 trip to the G-20 summit in Osaka, Japan. He met Crown Prince Mohammed bin Salman, calling the Saudi dictator "a friend of mine" and saying that he had done "really, a spectacular job."[35] He praised the prince's work for women. Although Saudi Arabia had recently allowed women to drive, it continues to oppress them in most other ways and remains a notorious abuser of human rights in general. At a press conference, a reporter asked him about the prince's role in the murder of journalist Jamal Khashoggi. Trump lied, claiming that "nobody so far, has pointed directly a finger at the future King of Saudi Arabia."[36] Actually, the CIA had done so months earlier. When another reporter pointed out that the agency had concluded that the prince had ordered or authorized the killing, Trump lied again: "I cannot comment on intelligence community." Nonsense: he had commented on the intelligence community many times, often to insult its leaders. Trump kept trying to change the subject to American business deals with Saudi Arabia, claiming that they created a million American jobs—a figure that he made up.

As he sat for photographs with Vladimir Putin at the start of their meeting, Trump referred to journalists: "Get rid of them. Fake news is a great term, isn't it?" he said. "You don't have this problem in Russia but we do." Putin answered in English: "We also have. It's the same."[37] Since Putin first became president in 2000, 42 journalists had been killed in Russia. Of those 42 people, the data indicate 26 of them were victims of murder.[38] Putin probably blessed these killings. Trump's timing made his wisecrack even more ghastly, as it came exactly one year after a gunman opened fire in a Maryland newsroom, killing five staffers.

When the pair took questions, a reporter asked Trump if he would tell Putin not to meddle in the 2020 election. "Yes, of course, I will. Don't meddle in the election, please," he said, playfully wagging a finger. "Don't meddle in the election."[39] The smirks on their faces indicated that they both saw the question of election interference as a joke. Speaking to reporters later, he repeated an assertion from his infamous Helsinki press conference: "You know we've talked about it before. You know he denies it totally, by the way. Just to—I mean, how many times can you get somebody to deny something? But he has, in the past, denied it. He's denied it also publicly."[40]

Trump garnished the trip with a surprise visit to yet another murderous autocrat, Kim Jong Un, stepping into the demilitarized zone and becoming the first sitting president to set foot in North Korea. He told Kim that "it's just an honor to be with you."[41] Kim had reportedly executed some of his diplomatic officials after his previous summit, but Trump did not ask about their fate. Before heading home, Trump stopped at Osan Air Force Base, where he again violated norms against bringing partisan politics across the water's edge and onto military facilities. He bragged about increasing the military budget: "And that wasn't easy because, I will tell you—this is not a political speech, but the Democrats were not going to give it to you. That I can tell you. They weren't going to give it to you, folks. They weren't going to. They want open borders and the hell with the military. That's not good."[42]

Trump did all of those things over just a few days in June.

Meanwhile, he was continuing to harm America's standing in the world. A poll of 20,000 people around the globe ranked the United States as the 27th most trustworthy country, down from 17th just three years before.[43] When the Pew Research Center surveyed 22 nations, it found that a median of 45 percent of respondents saw American power and influence as a major threat, up from 38 percent the year before and 25 percent in 2013, under President Obama. This trend occurred together with declines in favorable views of the United States and confidence in its president to do the right thing regarding world affairs.[44]

OUR FUTURE SECURITY

Classical Western liberalism is the philosophy of liberty and natural rights, the ideas that animated the Declaration of Independence. In a 2019 interview, Vladimir Putin said: "The liberal idea has become obsolete. It has come into conflict with the interests of the over-whelming majority of the population."[45] Putin reiterated the point after the Osaka summit. "The liberal idea has started eating itself," he said at a news conference. "Millions of people live their lives, and those who propagate those ideas are separate from them."[46] A normal American president would have responded to such a direct attack on our Founding ideas. Trump did not. When reporters asked him about it, he did not understand the question. "His comments to the *Financial Times*, right before arriving here, was that Western-style liberalism is obsolete," said a reporter "I know you probably haven't read the interview. Do you think that's true?" Trump acted as if the question was about leftist California politicians, and he used the occasion to take potshots at fellow Americans: "I mean, he sees what's going on. And I guess, if you look at what's happening in Los Angeles, where it's so sad to look; and what's happening in San Francisco and a couple of other cities which are run by an extraordinary group of liberal people. . . . But he does see things that are happening in the United States that would—would probably preclude him from saying how wonderful it is."[47]

Trump brings to mind an old joke. *Question: is ignorance worse than apathy? Answer: I don't know and I don't care.* Whether his comments on Western liberalism grew out of ignorance, apathy, or both, they were appalling—yet the American public did not display the revulsion that one might expect. In part, the muted response reflected the limited media coverage: Trump's failure to defend liberal democracy was just one story out of many in an eventful week. It also represented the need for better civic education in the United States. One reason why Trump has gotten away with so much is that so many Americans lack a strong understanding of the historical precedents that he is shattering, the democratic norms that he is violating, the republican principles that he is trashing. Popular culture fills this well-documented vacuum in civic knowledge. If you think that *House of Cards* was an accurate depiction of Washington politics, then Trump's behavior may seem tame by comparison: after all, he is not personally shoving investigative reporters into the path of oncoming trains.

Improving civic education would not mean drills on the details, such as the number of members of the House of Representatives. It would focus on big questions. What did the drafters of the Declaration mean when they wrote that all men are created equal? How does our nation's commitment to liberty and equality make us exceptional? How did George Washington's presidency set standards for how presidents should act? The more that people think about such questions, the more readily they will see how much Trump deviates from the American tradition.

It would be naïve to think that teaching and preaching would be sufficient to safeguard the future of our system. As Madison wrote, "A dependence upon the people is, no doubt, the primary control on the government; but experience has taught mankind the necessity of auxiliary precautions."[48] One set of auxiliary precautions would consist of legislative remedies for Trump-era problems. Early in 2019, the House passed legislation requiring presidents to disclose their tax returns. Another bill would require presidents and vice presidents to disclose and divest any potential financial conflicts of interest. Congress might also consider legislation clarifying that federal anti-nepotism law applies to the White House staff, thus keeping unqualified trust-fund babies such as Jared Kushner and Ivanka Trump off the West Wing roster. On the foreign-interference front, Congress must harden voting and registration systems against electronic tampering. And the example of Paul Manafort should inspire legislation to keep campaigns from sharing private material with foreign governments, and them to report offers of foreign help.[49]

Many reform proposals involve campaign finance laws. Measures to improve the transparency of political contributions might have many beneficial effects, but they would not necessarily prevent the election of un-American demagogues such as Donald Trump. He did not win the 2016 Republican nomination because he spent more than his rivals: Jeb Bush and other candidates spent more.[50] Hillary Clinton outspent him in the general election campaign, both directly and through outside groups.[51]

Whatever specific measures they enact, members of Congress need to remember that they swear an oath to the Constitution, not a president or a party. Regardless of whether they serve in the majority or minority, in-party or out-party, they have a sacred duty to preserve the separation of powers.

Newt Gingrich put it well in 2014:

> The Founding Fathers . . . designed the Constitution to enable the American people to maintain their freedom. They sought a balance of power between the legislative, executive and judicial branches (defined in that order with the legislature first). They would be appalled at the arrogance and hubris of a president who thought he could impose his will against the Congress. They would also stand up to the presidential power-grab at all costs, considering it a profound threat to our system of government. The precedent of such unrestrained executive cannot be allowed to stand.[52]

In 2016, House Republican Leader Kevin McCarthy expressed concern that the institution was not living up to its responsibility: "Unfortunately, we live in a dangerous time, and many of our nation's elected representatives accepted the president's argument, implicitly consenting to his subversion of congressional authority by refusing to block the president's actions. It seems they are happy to hand Congress's constitutional powers to the president as long as the policy that gets enacted suits them."[53]

THE NEAR FUTURE

Trump's opponents would say that the ultimate check on Trump would be his removal from office. There is no doubt that such a move would be appropriate. In his notes on the Constitutional Convention, James Madison recorded his own authoritative thoughts on the subject: "Mr. MADISON thought it indispensable that some provision should be made for defending the Community agst. the incapacity, negligence or perfidy of the chief Magistrate. The limitation of the period of his service, was not a sufficient security. He might lose his capacity after his appointment. He might pervert his administration into a scheme of peculation or oppression."[54] When the House of Representatives voted to impeach him in 2019, Trump and his defenders said that it would overturn the will of the American people. But they neglected to mention that 54 percent of the electorate had voted against Trump in 2016, and a plurality supported Hillary Clinton. By and large, though, Clinton voters accepted the outcome because the electoral college is a constitutional process. So is impeachment.

Because a Republican Senate would be extremely unlikely to convict him in an impeachment trial, however, the most realistic remedy would consist of defeating him in the 2020 election. Trump's lies about "rigged elections" raise the issue of whether he and his followers would be willing to concede. It is not an idle question. On the night of the 2012 election, he initially thought that Romney was winning the popular vote while Obama was winning the electoral vote. He tweeted: "He lost the popular vote by a lot and won the election. We should have a revolution in this country!" He later deleted that tweet, along with its sequel: "The phoney [sic] electoral college made a laughing stock out of our nation. The loser one [sic]!"[55] He did leave up other tweets:

- "We can't let this happen. We should march on Washington and stop this travesty. Our nation is totally divided!"[56]
- "This election is a total sham and a travesty. We are not a democracy!"[57]
- "Lets [sic] fight like hell and stop this great and disgusting injustice! The world is laughing at us."[58]

During the 2016 campaign, he made groundless warnings. "November 8th, we'd better be careful, because that election is going to be rigged," he told Sean Hannity. "And I hope the Republicans are watching closely, or it's going to be taken away from us."[59] At a debate, Chris Wallace asked him if he would accept the results. "I will look at it at the time," Trump said. "I'm not looking at anything now. I'll look at it at the time . . . this is coming from Pew Report and other places millions of people that are registered to vote that shouldn't be registered to vote." (He was referring to a Pew study of voter registration problems, which pointedly did *not* find evidence of fraud.[60]) Wallace followed up, asking if he would commit to coming together after the election for the good of the country. He said: "What I'm saying is that I will tell you at the time. I'll keep you in suspense. OK?"[61] The Russians appeared to approve of his attitude. On the day of the 2016 election, when it still seemed likely that Trump would lose, WikiLeaks sent a private message to Donald Trump Jr.: "We think it is much more interesting if he DOES NOT conceed [sic] and spends time CHALLENGING the media and other types of rigging that occurred—as he has implied that he might do."[62]

As for 2020, he has already hinted that he would not acknowledge the legitimacy of any result other than a Trump victory. In February 2019, he tweeted: "The Dems are trying to win an election in 2020 that they know they cannot legitimately win!"[63] His lawyer Michael Cohen testified that "given my experience working for Mr. Trump, I fear that if he loses the election in 2020 that there will never be a peaceful transition of power."[64] The real danger is not that Trump would barricade himself in the White House but that he would encourage his followers not to accept the outcome. Alexander Hamilton had such a leader in mind when he wrote:

> When a man unprincipled in private life desperate in his fortune, bold in his temper, possessed of considerable talents . . . known to have scoffed in private at the principles of liberty—when such a man is seen to mount the hobby horse of popularity—to join in the cry of danger to liberty—to take every opportunity of embarrassing the General Government & bringing it under suspicion—to flatter and fall in with all the non sense of the zealots of the day—It may justly be suspected that his object is to throw things

into confusion that he may "ride the storm and direct the whirl-wind."[65]

For those of us who study American politics, the Trump admin-istration has been a learning experience, much as horrible injuries are instructive to students of medical science. We have learned that traditions and norms are like internal organs: we only appreciate them when they stop working.

NOTES

I. TRUMP AND THE
AMERICAN TRADITION

1. Philip Bump, "Donald Trump's Falsehood-Laden Press Conference, Annotated," *Washington Post*, July 27, 2016, https://www.washingtonpost.com/news/the-fix/wp/2016/07/27/donald-trumps-falsehood-laden-press-conference-annotated.

2. Adam Goldman, Michael S. Schmidt, and Nicholas Fandos, "F.B.I. Opened Inquiry into Whether Trump Was Secretly Working on Behalf of Russia," *New York Times*, January 11, 2019, https://www.nytimes.com/2019/01/11/us/politics/fbi-trump-russia-inquiry.html.

3. US Department of Justice, Special Counsel's Office, *U.S. v. Viktor Borisovich Netyksho, et al.* (1:18-cr-215, District of Columbia), July 13, 2018, https://www.justice.gov/file/1080281/download; Michael S. Schmidt, "Trump Invited the Russians to Hack Clinton. Were They Listening?" *New York Times*, July 13, 2018, https://www.nytimes.com/2018/07/13/us/politics/trump-russia-clinton-emails.html.

4. US Department of Justice, Special Counsel's Office, *Report on the Investigation into Russian Interference in the 2016 Presidential Election*, March 2019, vol. 1, p. 4, https://www.justice.gov/storage/report.pdf.

5. Justin Wise, "MSNBCs Katy Tur Denies Trump Was Joking When Telling Russia to Get Clinton's Emails," *The Hill*, March 5, 2019, https://

thehill.com/homenews/media/432624-katy-tur-calls-out-trump-for-saying-he-was-joking-when-telling-russia-to-get.

6. Ken Dilanian, Julia Ainsley, and Carol E. Lee, "FBI Warned Trump in 2016 Russians Would Try to Infiltrate His Campaign," NBC News, December 18, 2017, https://www.nbcnews.com/news/us-news/fbi-warned-trump-2016-russians-would-try-infiltrate-his-campaign-n830596.

7. US Department of Homeland Security, "Joint Statement from the Department of Homeland Security and Office of the Director of National Intelligence on Election Security," October 7, 2016, https://www.dhs.gov/news/2016/10/07/joint-statement-department-homeland-security-and-office-director-national.

8. US Department of Justice, Special Counsel's Office, *Report on the Investigation*, vol. 1, p. 5.

9. Presidential Debate at Washington University in St. Louis, Missouri, October 9, 2016, https://www.debates.org/voter-education/debate-transcripts/october-9-2016-debate-transcript.

10. Letter from Donald Trump to Andrew Rozov, October 28, 2015, http://cdn.cnn.com/cnn/2018/images/12/18/attachment.1.pdf.

11. *U.S. v. Michael Cohen* (1:18-cr-850, Southern District of New York), criminal information at https://www.justice.gov/file/1115596/download.

12. "Intelligence Agencies Should Never Have Allowed This Fake News to 'Leak' into the Public. One Last Shot at Me. Are We Living in Nazi Germany?" Donald J. Trump, Twitter post, January 11, 2017, https://twitter.com/realdonaldtrump/status/819164172781060096.

13. Andrew Kent, Ethan J. Leib, and Jed Shugerman, "Faithful Execution and Article II," *Harvard Law Review* 132 (June 2019), https://papers.ssrn.com/sol3/papers.cfm?abstract_id=3260593.

14. US Department of Justice, Special Counsel's Office, *Report on the Investigation*, vol. 2, p.78.

15. "Transcript: Dan Coats Warns the Lights Are 'Blinking Red' on Russian Cyberattacks," National Public Radio, July 18, 2018, https://www.npr.org/2018/07/18/630164914/transcript-dan-coats-warns-of-continuing-russian-cyberattacks.

16. "A Conversation with Christopher Wray," Council on Foreign Relations, April 26, 2019, https://www.cfr.org/event/conversation-christopher-wray-0.

17.   Remarks by President Trump and Prime Minister Pellegrini of the Slovak Republic before Bilateral Meeting, May 3, 2019, https://www.whitehouse.gov/briefings-statements/remarks-president-trump-prime-minister-pellegrini-slovak-republic-bilateral-meeting.

18.   Transcript: ABC News' George Stephanopoulos's Exclusive Interview with President Trump, June 16, 2019, https://www.goodmorningamerica.com/news/story/transcript-abc-news-george-stephanopoulos-exclusive-interview-president-63749144.

19.   Meredith McGraw, "Trump Now Says 'Of Course' He Would Report 'Incorrect' Dirt from Foreign Adversary to FBI," ABC News, June 14, 2019, https://abcnews.go.com/Politics/trump-now-report-incorrect-dirt-foreign-adversary-fbi/story?id=63713574.

20.   Remarks by President Trump before Marine One Departure, October 3, 2019, https://www.whitehouse.gov/briefings-statements/remarks-president-trump-marine-one-departure-67/.

21.   Danielle Allen, *Our Declaration: A Reading of the Declaration of Independence in Defense of Equality* (New York: Liveright, 2014), 116–17.

22.   Glenn Kessler, Salvador Rizzo, and Meg Kelly, "President Trump Made 8,158 False or Misleading Claims in His First Two Years," *Washington Post*, January 21, 2019, https://www.washingtonpost.com/politics/2019/01/21/president-trump-made-false-or-misleading-claims-his-first-two-years.

23.   NBC News, *Meet the Press* transcript, January 22, 2017, https://www.nbcnews.com/meet-the-press/meet-press-01-22-17-n710491.

24.   NBC News, *Meet the Press* transcript, August 19, 2018, https://www.nbcnews.com/meet-the-press/meet-press-august-19-2018-n901986.

25.   Harry V. Jaffa, *Crisis of the House Divided: An Interpretation of the Issues in the Lincoln-Douglas Debates* (Garden City, NY: Doubleday, 1959), 351–52.

26.   Bill Carter, "Trump Redevelops His Own Series," *New York Times*, August 31, 2005, https://www.nytimes.com/2005/08/31/arts/television/trump-redevelops-his-own-series.html.

27.   Alexander Hamilton, letter, *Dunlap and Claypoole's American Daily Advertiser*, August 28, 1794, https://founders.archives.gov/documents/Hamilton/01-17-02-0130.

28. Excerpts from Joint Deposition, George P. Kent, Deputy Assistant Secretary of State Bureau of European and Eurasian Affairs, House Perma-

nent Select Committee on Intelligence, House Committee on Oversight
and Reform, and House Committee on Foreign Affairs, October 15, 2019,
https://intelligence.house.gov/uploadedfiles/20191107_-
_kent_transcript_excerpts_final_-_9188369.pdf.

29. John F. Kennedy, Address to a Joint Convention of the General
Court of the Commonwealth of Massachusetts, January 9, 1961, https://
www.americanrhetoric.com/speeches/jfkcommonwealthmass.htm.

30. Remarks by President Trump before Marine One Departure, January 10, 2019, https://www.whitehouse.gov/briefings-statements/remarks-
president-trump-marine-one-departure-30.

31. Kevin Liptak, "Trump on China's Xi Consolidating Power: 'Maybe
We'll Give That a Shot Some Day,'" CNN, March 8, 2018, https://
www.cnn.com/2018/03/03/politics/trump-maralago-remarks/index.html.

32. For his multiple changes of party registration, see: "Donald Trump
Twice Dumped Republican Party," *The Smoking Gun*, August 6, 2015,
http://www.thesmokinggun.com/documents/celebrity/trump-a-republican-
for-now-908431. For his issue reversals, see Jeremy Diamond, "Abortion
and 10 Other Donald Trump Flip-Flops," CNN, April 1, 2016, https://
www.cnn.com/2016/03/31/politics/donald-trump-positions-flip-flops/in-
dex.html.

33. Donald Trump, "Trump: Europe Is Terrific Place for Investment,"
CNN, January 22, 2013, http://edition.cnn.com/2013/01/22/business/opin-
ion-donald-trump-europe.

34. Bret Stephens, "Don't Dismiss President Trump's Attacks on the
Media as Mere Stupidity," *Time*, February 18, 2017, updated February 26.
http://time.com/4675860/donald-trump-fake-news-attacks.

35. John Bowden, "'Art of the Deal' Co-Writer: Trump Will Resign So
He Doesn't 'Lose,'" *The Hill*, March 19, 2017, https://thehill.com/blogs/
ballot-box/334188-art-of-the-deal-ghostwriter-trump-will-resign-so-he-
doesnt-lose.

36. Margaret Talev and Jennifer Jacobs, "Trump Defends Invite to
Philippines' Duterte Amid Drug War," Bloomberg News, May 1, 2017,
https://www.bloomberg.com/news/articles/2017-05-01/trump-defends-in-
vite-to-philippines-duterte-amid-drug-war-toll.

37. Michael Scherer, "Read President Trump's Interview with TIME
on Truth and Falsehoods," *Time*, March 23, 2017, http://time.com/
4710456/donald-trump-time-interview-truth-falsehood.

38. Alexander Hamilton, *Federalist 68*, http://avalon.law.yale.edu/18th_century/fed68.asp.

39. Thomas Jefferson, Inaugural Address, March 4, 1801, online by Gerhard Peters and John T. Woolley, The American Presidency Project, https://www.presidency.ucsb.edu/node/201948.

40. Abraham Lincoln, Cooper Union Address, February 27, 1860, http://www.abrahamlincolnonline.org/lincoln/speeches/cooper.htm.

41. David Corn, "Donald Trump Says He Doesn't Believe in 'American Exceptionalism,'" *Mother Jones*, June 7, 2017, https://www.motherjones.com/politics/2016/06/donald-trump-american-exceptionalism.

42. Eli Stokols, "Unapologetic, Trump Promises to Make America Rich," *Politico*, May 26, 2016, https://www.politico.com/story/2016/05/unapologetic-trump-promises-to-make-america-rich-223632.

43. Benjamin Franklin, letter to Thomas Cushing, June 4, 1773, https://oll.libertyfund.org/titles/franklin-the-works-of-benjamin-franklin-vol-vi-letters-and-misc-writings-1772-1775/simple.

44. Ronald W. Reagan, address at Republican National Convention, Houston, August 17, 1992, http://www.cnn.com/SPECIALS/2004/reagan/stories/speech.archive/rnc.speech.html.

45. Donald J. Trump, Address Accepting the Presidential Nomination at the Republican National Convention in Cleveland, Ohio, July 21, 2016, online by Gerhard Peters and John T. Woolley, The American Presidency Project, https://www.presidency.ucsb.edu/node/318521.

46. Donald Trump, "Donald Trump Writes Exclusively for the National Enquirer," *National Enquirer*, August 19, 2015, https://www.nationalenquirer.com/real-life/donald-trump-writes-exclusively-national-enquirer.

47. Eli Stokols, "Unapologetic, Trump Promises to Make America Rich," *Politico*, May 26, 2016, https://www.politico.com/story/2016/05/unapologetic-trump-promises-to-make-america-rich-223632.

48. Alexander Hamilton, *Federalist 1*, http://avalon.law.yale.edu/18th_century/fed01.asp.

49. See, for instance, Donald J. Trump, Remarks in an Exchange with Reporters, October 25, 2017, online by Gerhard Peters and John T. Woolley, The American Presidency Project, https://www.presidency.ucsb.edu/node/331564.

50. James Comey, *A Higher Loyalty: Truth, Lies, and Leadership* (New York: Flatiron Books, 2018), 243.

51. Abraham Lincoln, Inaugural Address, March 4, 1861, online by Gerhard Peters and John T. Woolley, The American Presidency Project, https://www.presidency.ucsb.edu/node/202167.

52. Dan Farber, "Obama Explains His Remark about Punishing 'Enemies,'" CBS News, November 1, 2010, https://www.cbsnews.com/news/obama-explains-his-remark-about-punishing-enemies.

53. "Lee Edwards Shares His Life in Pursuit of Liberty with TFAS," The Fund for American Studies, May 17, 2018, https://tfas.org/news/lee-edwards-shares-life-pursuit-liberty-tfas.

54. Jane Mayer, "Donald Trump's Ghostwriter Tells All," *The New Yorker*, July 25, 2016, https://www.newyorker.com/magazine/2016/07/25/donald-trumps-ghostwriter-tells-all.

55. Marc Fisher, "Donald Trump Doesn't Read Much. Being President Probably Wouldn't Change That," *Washington Post*, June 17, 2016, https://www.washingtonpost.com/politics/donald-trump-doesnt-read-much-being-president-probably-wouldnt-change-that/2016/07/17/d2ddf2bc-4932-11e6-90a8-fb84201e0645_story.html.

56. Crossfire transcript, December 23, 1987, Nexis Uni.

57. C. S. Lewis, *Mere Christianity* (New York: HarperOne, 2015 [1952]), 6.

58. Philip Bump, "Under Trump's New Immigration Rule, His Own Grandfather Likely Wouldn't Have Gotten In," *Washington Post*, August 3, 2017, https://www.washingtonpost.com/news/politics/wp/2017/08/03/under-trumps-new-immigration-rule-his-own-grandfather-likely-wouldnt-have-gotten-in.

59. Gwenda Blair, *The Trumps: Three Generations of Builders and a President* (New York: Simon and Schuster, 2015 [2000]), 50, 86.

60. Kate Connolly, "Historian Finds German Decree Banishing Trump's Grandfather," *The Guardian*, November 21, 2016, https://www.theguardian.com/us-news/2016/nov/21/trump-grandfather-friedrich-banished-germany-historian-royal-decree.

61. "Warren Criticizes 'Class' Parades," *New York Times*, June 1, 1927, 16.

62. Mike Pearl, "All the Evidence We Could Find about Fred Trump's Alleged Involvement with the KKK," Vice, March 10, 2016, https://

www.vice.com/en_us/article/mvke38/all-the-evidence-we-could-find-about-fred-trumps-alleged-involvement-with-the-kkk.

63. Will Kaufman, "Woody Guthrie, 'Old Man Trump' and a Real Estate Empire's Racist Foundations,'" *The Conversation*, January 21, 2016, https://theconversation.com/woody-guthrie-old-man-trump-and-a-real-estate-empires-racist-foundations-53026.

64. Jonathan Mahler and Steve Eder, "'No Vacancies' for Blacks: How Donald Trump Got His Start, and Was First Accused of Bias," *New York Times*, August 27, 2016, https://www.nytimes.com/2016/08/28/us/politics/donald-trump-housing-race.html.

65. Blair, *The Trumps*, 171; Wayne Barrett, *Trump: The Greatest Show on Earth* (New York: Regan Arts, 2016 [1992]), 49.

66. Hearings Before the Committee on Banking and Currency, United States Senate: Eighty-Third Congress. July 20, 1954, 409–10, https://www.washingtonpost.com/wp-stat/graphics/politics/trump-archive/docs/fha-investigation-1954-part-1.pdf.

67. Michael D'Antonio, *Never Enough: Donald Trump and the Pursuit of Success* (New York: Thomas Dunne, 2015), 39.

68. David Barstow, Susanne Craig, and Russ Buettner, "Trump Engaged in Suspect Tax Schemes as He Reaped Riches from His Father," *New York Times*, October 2, 2018, https://www.nytimes.com/interactive/2018/10/02/us/politics/donald-trump-tax-schemes-fred-trump.html.

69. Michael Kranish and Marc Fisher, *Trump Revealed* (New York: Scribner, 2016), 37–38.

70. House Committee on Oversight and Government Reform, *Hearing with Michael Cohen, Former Attorney to President Donald Trump*, 116th Cong, 1st sess., February 27, 2019, 14–15, https://docs.house.gov/meetings/GO/GO00/20190227/108969/HHRG-116-GO00-20190227-SD003.pdf.

71. Steve Eder, "Did a Queens Podiatrist Help Donald Trump Avoid Vietnam?" *New York Times*, December 26, 2018, https://www.nytimes.com/2018/12/26/us/politics/trump-vietnam-draft-exemption.html.

72. Michael F. Armstrong, *They Wished They Were Honest: The Knapp Commission and New York City Police Corruption* (New York: Columbia University Press, 2012), vii.

73.   Fred Ferretti, "Italian-American League's Power Spreads," *New York Times*, April 4, 1971, https://www.nytimes.com/1971/04/04/archives/italianamerican-leagues-power-spreads.html.

74.   William Bastone, "Trump Limos Were Built with a Hood Ornament," The Smoking Gun, September 22, 2015, http://www.thesmokinggun.com/documents/celebrity/trump-and-staluppi-092157.

75.   Nicholas Herzeca, "The Hard Hat Riot: The Decline of New York City's White Working-Class and the Origins of the Reagan Democrat," undergraduate thesis, Claremont McKenna College, 2014.

76.   Morris Kaplan, "Major Landlord Accused of Antiblack Bias in the City," *New York Times*, October 16, 1973, 1, https://www.documentcloud.org/documents/2186612-major-landlord-accuse-of-antiblack-bias-in-city.html.

77.   Kranish, *Trump Revealed*, 55.

78.   Michael Kirk, PBS *Frontline* interview with Elyse Goldweber, May 23, 2018, https://www.pbs.org/wgbh/frontline/interview/elyse-goldweber/.

79.   Joseph P. Fried, "Trump Promises to End Race Bias," *New York Times*, June 11, 1975, https://www.nytimes.com/1975/06/11/archives/trump-promises-to-end-race-bias-realty-management-concern-reaches.html.

80.   Harry Hurt III, *Lost Tycoon: The Many Lives of Donald J. Trump* (Brattleboro, VT: Echo Point, 2016 [1993]), 81.

81.   Barrett, *Trump: The Greatest Show on Earth*, 244.

82.   Barrett, *Trump: The Greatest Show on Earth*, 191–92.

83.   David Cay Johnston, *The Making of Donald Trump* (Brooklyn, NY: Melville House, 2017), 45.

84.   Timothy L. O'Brien, *TrumpNation: The Art of Being the Donald* (New York: Grand Central, 2016 [2005]), 67–68.

85.   Marie Brenner, "How Donald Trump and Roy Cohn's Ruthless Symbiosis Changed America," *Vanity Fair*, August 2017, https://www.vanityfair.com/news/2017/06/donald-trump-roy-cohn-relationship.

86.   Kranish and Fisher, *Trump Revealed*, 80–81.

87.   Andrew Kaczynski, "Trump Isn't into Anal, Melania Never Poops, and Other Things He Told Howard Stern," Buzzfeed, February 16, 2016, https://www.buzzfeednews.com/article/andrewkaczynski/trump-isnt-into-anal-melania-never-poops-and-other-things-he#.ldZMnyq0a.

88. Barrett, *Trump: The Greatest Show on Earth*, 278.

89. Michael Kruse, "Trump's Long War with Justice," *Politico*, August 26, 2018, https://www.politico.eu/article/donald-trump-long-war-with-justice-department.

90. Remarks by President Trump on Infrastructure, August 15, 2017, https://www.whitehouse.gov/briefings-statements/remarks-president-trump-infrastructure.

91. Fifth Lincoln-Douglas Debate, Galesburg, Illinois, October 7, 1858, https://www.nps.gov/liho/learn/historyculture/debate5.htm.

92. Jacob T. Levy, "Why Words Matter," The Bulwark, March 16, 2019, https://thebulwark.com/why-words-matter/.

93. Ronald Reagan, Address to the Veterans of Foreign Wars Convention in Chicago, August 18, 1980, online by Gerhard Peters and John T. Woolley, The American Presidency Project, https://www.presidency.ucsb.edu/node/285595

94. Martin Luther King Jr., "I Have a Dream," Address Delivered at the March on Washington for Jobs and Freedom, August 28, 1963, https://kinginstitute.stanford.edu/king-papers/documents/i-have-dream-address-delivered-march-washington-jobs-and-freedom.

95. Daniel Krauthammer, "What Makes America Great?" *The Weekly Standard*, April 28, 2017, https://www.weeklystandard.com/daniel-krauthammer/what-makes-america-great.

96. Jose A. DelReal and Sean Sullivan, "Democrats Fear That Violent Anti-Trump Protesters Are Only Helping Him," *Washington Post*, June 3, 2016, https://www.washingtonpost.com/politics/democrats-fear-that-violent-anti-trump-protesters-are-only-helping-trump/2016/06/03/37b8c17e-299b-11e6-ae4a-3cdd5fe74204_story.html.

97. "Trump: If a Protester Throws a Tomato at Me, 'Knock the Crap Out of Them' [Video]," *Daily Caller*, February 1, 2016, https://dailycaller.com/2016/02/01/trump-if-a-protestor-throws-a-tomato-at-me-knock-the-crap-out-of-them-video.

98. ABC News Oval Office interview with President Trump, June 13, 2019.

99. Testimony of Rudolph Giuliani, United States Senate, Committee on Judiciary, Organized Crime in America, Part 2, S. Hrg. 98-184, pt. 2, July 11, 1983, p. 135, https://congressional-proquest-com.ccl.idm.oclc.org/congressional/docview/t29.d30.hrg-1983-sjs-0080?accountid=10141.

100. Levy, "Why Words Matter."

101. *Ragbir v. Sessions*, 18-cv-236 (KBF) (S.D.N.Y. Jan. 29, 2018), https://www.law.columbia.edu/sites/default/files/microsites/open-university-project/ragbir-v-sessions-iii-et-al-18-cv-236.pdf

102. "Trump: 'I Could Stand in the Middle of Fifth Avenue and Shoot Somebody and I Wouldn't Lose Any Voters,'" RealClearPolitics, January 23, 2016, https://www.realclearpolitics.com/video/2016/01/23/trump_i_could_stand_in_the_middle_of_fifth_avenue_and_shoot_somebody_and_i_wouldnt_lose_any_voters.html.

103. George Washington, Undelivered First Inaugural Address: Fragments, April 30, 1789, https://founders.archives.gov/documents/Washington/05-02-02-0130-0002.

104. First Lincoln-Douglas Debate, Ottawa, Illinois, August 21, 1858, https://www.nps.gov/liho/learn/historyculture/debate1.htm. See also Ramon Lopez, "Answering the Alt-Right," *National Affairs*, Fall 2017, https://www.nationalaffairs.com/publications/detail/answering-the-alt-right

2. WE HOLD THESE TRUTHS

1. James Madison, *Federalist 55*, http://avalon.law.yale.edu/18th_century/fed55.asp.

2. George Washington, Farewell Address, September 19, 1796, online by Gerhard Peters and John T. Woolley, The American Presidency Project, https://www.presidency.ucsb.edu/node/200675.

3. Thomas Jefferson to John Adams, February 28, 1796, https://www.loc.gov/resource/mtj1.020_0708_0709/?st=text.

4. Thomas Jefferson, "Summary View of the Rights of British America," 1774, http://avalon.law.yale.edu/18th_century/jeffsumm.asp.

5. Michiko Kakutani, *The Death of Truth: Notes on Falsehood in the Age of Trump* (New York: Tim Duggan Books, 2018), 52–56.

6. Allen, *Our Declaration*, 161.

7. Alexander Hamilton, *Federalist 31*, http://avalon.law.yale.edu/18th_century/fed31.asp.

8. Abraham Lincoln, letter to Henry L. Pierce and others, April 6, 1859, http://www.abrahamlincolnonline.org/lincoln/speeches/pierce.htm.

9. *Congressional Record* (daily), January 16, 1999, S291.

10. Maggie Haberman, "A President Who Believes He Is Entitled to His Own Facts," *New York Times*, October 18, 2018, https://

www.nytimes.com/2018/10/18/us/politics/donald-trump-foreign-leaders.html.

11. Donald Trump with Tony Schwartz, *The Art of the Deal* (New York: Random House, 2009 [1987]), 58.

12. Jane Mayer, "Donald Trump's Ghostwriter Tells All," *The New Yorker*, July 18, 2016, https://www.newyorker.com/magazine/2016/07/25/donald-trumps-ghostwriter-tells-all.

13. Linda Qiu, "Is Donald Trump's 'Art of the Deal' The Best-Selling Business Book of All Time?" PolitiFact, July 1, 2015, https://www.politifact.com/truth-o-meter/statements/2015/jul/06/donald-trump/donald-trumps-art-deal-best-selling-business-book-/.

14. "Full Text: Donald Trump Announces a Presidential Bid," *Washington Post*, June 16, 2015, https://www.washingtonpost.com/news/post-politics/wp/2015/06/16/full-text-donald-trump-announces-a-presidential-bid.

15. Kendall Taggart and Chris Geidner, "Trump's Lawyer: We Met with Him in Pairs to Avoid Lies," Buzzfeed, October 6, 2016, https://www.buzzfeednews.com/article/kendalltaggart/trumps-lawyer-we-met-with-him-in-pairs-to-avoid-lies.

16. David A. Fahrenthold and Robert O'Harrow Jr., "Trump: A True Story," *Washington Post*, August 10, 2016, https://www.washingtonpost.com/graphics/politics/2016-election/trump-lies/.

17. Deposition of Donald J. Trump, Donald J. Trump v. Timothy L O'Brien, Superior Court of New Jersey, Camden County, December 19, 2007, https://assets.documentcloud.org/documents/2430267/trumps-lawsuit-on-net-worth.pdf.

18. Vivian Yee, "Donald Trump's Math Takes His Towers to Greater Heights," *New York Times*, November 1, 2016, https://www.nytimes.com/2016/11/02/nyregion/donald-trump-tower-heights.html.

19. David A. Fahrenthold and Jonathan O'Connell, "How Donald Trump Inflated His Net Worth to Lenders and Investors," *Washington Post*, March 28, 2019, https://www.washingtonpost.com/graphics/2019/politics/trump-statements-of-financial-condition.

20. Allan Smith, "NY's Attorney General Is One of the Most Powerful in the Nation. That Should Worry Trump," NBC News, April 1, 2019, https://www.nbcnews.com/politics/donald-trump/ny-s-attorney-general-one-most-powerful-nation-should-worry-n985086.

21. Donald J. Trump, Remarks at the Veterans of Foreign Wars of the United States National Convention, Kansas City, Missouri, July 24, 2018, https://www.whitehouse.gov/briefings-statements/remarks-president-trump-veterans-foreign-wars-united-states-national-convention-kansas-city-mo.

22. Speech: Donald Trump, Des Moines, Iowa, December 8, 2016, https://factba.se/transcript/donald-trump-speech-des-moines-ia-december-8-2016.

23. Donald Trump Campaign Rally in Albuquerque, May 24, 2016, https://archive.org/details/FOXNEWSW_20160525_020100_Hannity/start/263/end/323?q=phony+number.

24. Donald Trump Campaign Rally in Las Vegas, CSPAN, October 11, 2015, https://archive.org/details/CSPAN_20151011_171100_Donald_Trump_Campaign_Rally_in_Las_V egas/start/1800/end/1860.

25. Donald J. Trump, Twitter post, June 11, 2017, https://twitter.com/realDonaldTrump/status/873878232264822784.

26. Marc Fisher and Will Hobson, "Donald Trump Masqueraded as Publicist to Brag about Himself," *Washington Post*, May 16, 2016, https://www.washingtonpost.com/politics/donald-trump-alter-ego-barron/2016/05/12/02ac99ec-16fe-11e6-aa55-670cabef46e0_story.html.

27. Eun Kyung Kim, "Donald Trump Denies Posing as Spokesman in Recordings Washington Post Uncovered," *Today*, May 13, 2016, https://www.today.com/news/donald-trump-denies-posing-spokesman-record-ings-washington-post-uncovered-t92421.

28. Paul Moses, "Trump Takes Stand in $1M Pension Trial," *Newsday*, July 13, 1990, 30.

29. Donald J. Trump, Twitter post, February 18, 2018, https://twit-ter.com/realDonaldTrump/status/965202556204003328.

30. "Donald Trump on Russia, Advice from Barack Obama and How He Will Lead," *Time*, December 7, 2016, http://time.com/4591183/time-person-of-the-year-2016-donald-trump-interview.

31. "WATCH: Trump Connects Cruz's Father to Lee Harvey Oswald," Fox News, May 3, 2016, https://insider.foxnews.com/2016/05/03/watch-trump-calls-out-cruzs-father-old-photo-lee-harvey-oswald.

32. Michael Scherer, "Read President Trump's Interview with TIME on Truth and Falsehoods," *Time*, March 23, 2017, http://time.com/4710456/donald-trump-time-interview-truth-falsehood.

33. Donald J. Trump, Twitter post, January 6, 2018. https://twitter.com/realDonaldTrump/status/949619270631256064; Katy Tur and Ali Vitali, "Amid Latest Controversy, Trump Claims 'World's Greatest Memory,'" NBC News, November 24, 2015, https://www.nbcnews.com/politics/2016-election/amid-latest-controversy-trump-claims-worlds-greatest-memory-n468621.

34. Taggart and Geidner, "Trump's Lawyer."

35. Deposition of Donald J. Trump, November 5, 2013, https://www.washingtonpost.com/wp-stat/graphics/politics/trump-archive/docs/nov-13-djt-depo.pdf.

36. CNN Newsroom, February 28, 2016, https://www.cnn.com/videos/politics/2016/02/28/donald-trump-white-supremacists-david-duke-sotu.cnn.

37. Eric Bradner, "Donald Trump Stumbles on David Duke, KKK," CNN, February 29, 2016, https://www.cnn.com/2016/02/28/politics/donald-trump-white-supremacists/index.html.

38. Deposition of Donald J. Trump, December 10, 2015, https://www.washingtonpost.com/wp-stat/graphics/politics/trump-archive/docs/makaeff-v-trump-univ-trump-full-depo.pdf?tid=a_inl_manual.

39. Remarks by President Trump and President Moon Jae-in of the Republic of Korea before Bilateral Meeting, April 11, 2019, https://www.whitehouse.gov/briefings-statements/remarks-president-trump-president-moon-jae-republic-korea-bilateral-meeting.

40. "Trump Says WikiLeaks 141 Times in Month before Election," NBC News, November 16, 2017, https://www.nbcnews.com/dateline/video/trump-says-wikileaks-141-times-in-month-before-election-1096403523611.

41. US Department of Justice, Special Counsel's Office, *Report on the Investigation*, Appendix C, p. C1.

42. Birth Announcements, *The Sunday Advertiser*, August 13, 1961, https://www.newspapers.com/clip/18503640/barack_obama_birth_announcement.

43. Elspeth Reeve, "Trumpdate 2012: The Donald Says He's a Teeny Bit Birther," *The Atlantic*, March 17, 2011, https://www.theatlantic.com/politics/archive/2011/03/trumpdate-2012-donald-says-hes-teeny-bit-birther/348889.

44. "The Laura Ingraham Show—Donald Trump 'Proud' to Be a Birther," March 30, 2011, https://www.youtube.com/watch?v=WqaS9OCoTZs.

45. Seamus McGraw, "Trump: I Have 'Real Doubts' Obama Was Born in U.S.," *Today*, April 7, 2011, https://web.archive.org/web/20151019020819/http://www.today.com/id/42469703/ns/today-today_news/t/trump-i-have-real-doubts-obama-was-born-us.

46. Donald J. Trump, Twitter post, August 6, 2012, https://twitter.com/realDonaldTrump/status/232572505238433794.

47. Jonathan Karl, "The Last Time Donald Trump Talked about 'Birtherism,'" ABC News, September 7, 2016, https://abcnews.go.com/Politics/time-donald-trump-talked-birtherism/story?id=41927366.

48. Donald J. Trump, Twitter post, December 12, 2013, https://twitter.com/realDonaldTrump/status/411247268763676673.

49. "Health Director Loretta Fuddy Died of Cardiac Arrhythmia," *Honolulu Star-Advertiser*, January 13, 2014, https://www.staradvertiser.com/2014/01/13/breaking-news/health-director-loretta-fuddy-died-of-cardiac-arrhythmia.

50. Katie Reilly, "Read Donald Trump's Speech Finally Admitting President Obama Was Born in the U.S.," *Time*, September 16, 2016, http://time.com/4497626/donald-trump-birther-address-transcript.

51. Ryan Nakashima and Barbara Ortutay, "AP Exclusive: Russia Twitter Trolls Deflected Trump Bad News," Associated Press, November 9, 2017, https://apnews.com/fc9ab2b0bbc34f11bc10714100318ae1.

52. Lam Thuy Vo, "Prosecutors Say These Two Russian Troll Accounts Messed with the 2016 Election. Here Are 50 of Their Most Popular Tweets," Buzzfeed, February 16, 2018, https://www.buzzfeednews.com/article/lamvo/russian-troll-tweets.

53. Kathy Frankovic, "Republicans See Little Need for the Russia Investigation," YouGov, December 8, 2017, https://today.yougov.com/topics/politics/articles-reports/2017/12/08/republicans-see-little-need-russia-investigation.

54. Donald J. Trump, The President's News Conference, February 16, 2017, online by Gerhard Peters and John T. Woolley, The American Presidency Project, https://www.presidency.ucsb.edu/node/323569.

55. Donald J. Trump, Twitter post, November 27, 2016, https://twitter.com/realDonaldTrump/status/802972944532209664.

56. Michael D. Shear and Emmarie Huetteman, "Trump Repeats Lie about Popular Vote in Meeting with Lawmakers," *New York Times*, January 23, 2017, https://www.nytimes.com/2017/01/23/us/politics/donald-trump-congress-democrats.html.

57. Remarks by President Trump at a Roundtable Discussion on Tax Reform, White Sulphur Springs, West Virginia, April 5, 2018, https://www.whitehouse.gov/briefings-statements/remarks-president-trump-roundtable-discussion-tax-reform.

58. Saagar Enjeti, Benny Johnson, and Amber Athey, "Full Transcript of Trump's Oval Office Interview with *The Daily Caller*," *The Daily Caller*, November 14, 2018, https://dailycaller.com/2018/11/14/transcript-trump-daily-caller-interview.

59. Speech: Donald Trump Addresses a National Republican Campaign Committee Fundraiser, April 2, 2019, https://factba.se/transcript/donald-trump-speech-rncc-fundraiser-dinner-april-2-2019.

60. US Department of Justice, Fact Sheet: Department of Justice Ballot Access and Voting Integrity Initiative, July 26, 2006, https://www.justice.gov/archive/opa/pr/2006/July/06_crt_468.html.

61. Lisa Rab, "Why Republicans Can't Find the Big Voter Fraud Conspiracy," *Politico*, April 2, 2017, https://www.politico.com/magazine/story/2017/04/why-republicans-cant-find-the-big-voter-fraud-conspiracy-214972.

62. Ariel Malka and Yphtach Lelkes, "In a New Poll, Half of Republicans Say They Would Support Postponing the 2020 Election If Trump Proposed It," *Washington Post*, August 10, 2017, https://www.washingtonpost.com/news/monkey-cage/wp/2017/08/10/in-a-new-poll-half-of-republicans-say-they-would-support-postponing-the-2020-election-if-trump-proposed-it.

63. Hunter Walker, "Donald Trump Just Released an Epic Statement Raging against Mexican Immigrants and 'Disease,'" *Business Insider*, July 6, 2015, https://www.businessinsider.com/donald-trumps-epic-statement-on-mexico-2015-7#ixzz3fF897ElH

64. Alex Nowrasteh, "Immigration and Crime—What the Research Says," Cato at Liberty, July 14, 2015, https://www.cato.org/blog/immigration-crime-what-research-says.

65. Michael T. Light and Ty Miller, "Does Undocumented Immigration Increase Violent Crime?" *Criminology* 56 (2018): 370–401, https://onlinelibrary.wiley.com/doi/epdf/10.1111/1745-9125.12175.

66. Donald J. Trump, Remarks at a "Make America Great Again" Rally in Elko, Nevada, October 20, 2018, online by Gerhard Peters and John T. Woolley, The American Presidency Project, https://www.presidency.ucsb.edu/node/332411.

67. Remarks by President Trump before Marine One Departure, October 22, 2018, https://www.whitehouse.gov/briefings-statements/remarks-president-trump-marine-one-departure-18/.

68. Kenna Richards, "Do Californians Want Out of Sanctuary Cities? Mostly Not," PolitiFact, November 18, 2018, https://www.politifact.com/west-virginia/statements/2018/nov/15/donald-trump/do-californians-want-out-sanctuary-cities-mostly-n/.

69. Remarks by President Trump in Meeting with SBA Administrator Linda McMahonIssued on: March 29, 2019, https://www.whitehouse.gov/briefings-statements/remarks-president-trump-meeting-sba-administrator-linda-mcmahon.

70. Calvin Woodward, "AP Fact Check: Trump Twists Facts of a Migrant Girl's Death," Associated Press, March 29, 2019, https://www.apnews.com/6c3b6169c6514c72a5adccb7af41aa7f.

71. Donald J. Trump, Twitter post, January 27, 2019, https://twitter.com/realDonaldTrump/status/1089519559126802432.

72. Bryan Baker, "Estimates of the Illegal Alien Population Residing in the United States: January 2015," US Department of Homeland Security, December 2018, https://www.dhs.gov/sites/default/files/publications/18_1214_PLCY_pops-est-report.pdf.

73. Philip N. Howard et al., "The IRA, Social Media and Political Polarization in the United States, 2012–2018," Computational Propaganda Research Project, December 2018, pp. 35, 33, https://comprop.oii.ox.ac.uk/wp-content/uploads/sites/93/2018/12/The-IRA-Social-Media-and-Political-Polarization.pdf.

74. I. Bernard Cohen, Science and the Founding Fathers (New York: W.W. Norton, 1995), 14.

75. Cohen, Science and the Founding Fathers, 19–21.

76. Cohen, Science and the Founding Fathers, 269–72.

77. "2018 Fourth Warmest Year in Continued Warming Trend, According to NASA, NOAA," NASA, February 6, 2019, https://climate.nasa.gov/news/2841/2018-fourth-warmest-year-in-continued-warming-trend-according-to-nasa-noaa.

78. Commission on Presidential Debates, September 26, 2016, Debate Transcript, https://www.debates.org/voter-education/debate-transcripts/september-26-2016-debate-transcript.

79. Donald J. Trump, Twitter post, November 6, 2012, https://twitter.com/realDonaldTrump/status/265895292191248385.

80. Donald J. Trump, Twitter post, January 28, 2014, https://twitter.com/realDonaldTrump/status/428414113463955457.

81. "Ozone Layer Protection," Environmental Protection Agency, https://www.epa.gov/ozone-layer-protection.

82. Vanessa Schipani, "Trump on Hairspray and Ozone," Fact-Check.org, May 17, 2016, https://www.factcheck.org/2016/05/trump-on-hairspray-and-ozone.

83. Michael Burke, "Trump Claims Wind Turbine 'Noise Causes Cancer,'" *The Hill*, April 3, 2019, https://thehill.com/homenews/administration/437096-trump-claims-noise-from-windmills-causes-cancer.

84. US Department of Energy, Office of Energy Efficiency and Renewable Energy, "Frequently Asked Questions about Wind Energy," https://www.energy.gov/eere/wind/frequently-asked-questions-about-wind-energy.

85. "American Energy Dominance Means Mass. Wind," April 16, 2018, https://www.whitehouse.gov/articles/american-energy-dominance-means-mass-wind.

86. Howard Markel, "Life, Liberty and the Pursuit of Vaccines," *New York Times*, February 28, 2011, https://www.nytimes.com/2011/03/01/health/01smallpox.html.

87. Thomas Jefferson to G. C. Edward Jenner, May 14, 1806, https://www.loc.gov/item/mtjbib016128.

88. Josh Hafenbrack, "Trump: Autism Linked to Child Vaccinations," *South Florida Sun-Sentinel*, December 28, 2007, https://www.sun-sentinel.com/sfl-mtblog-2007-12-trump_autism_linked_to_child_v-story.html.

89. Paul A. Offit, *Autism's False Prophets: Bad Science, Risky Medicine, and the Search for a Cure* (New York: Columbia University Press, 2008), 45.

90. Donald J. Trump, Twitter post, August 23, 2012, https://twitter.com/realdonaldtrump/status/238717783007977473.

91. Donald J. Trump, Twitter post, March 28, 2014, https://twitter.com/realdonaldtrump/status/449525268529815552.

92. Donald J. Trump, Twitter post, March 27, 2014, https://twitter.com/realDonaldTrump/status/449331076528615424.

93. Donald J. Trump, Twitter post, September 3, 2014, https://twitter.com/realDonaldTrump/status/507158574670573568.

94. CNN Reagan Library Debate Transcript, September 16, 2015, http://cnnpressroom.blogs.cnn.com/2015/09/16/cnn-reagan-library-debate-later-debate-full-transcript.

95. David Edwards, "Trump Warns Fox News Viewers: Autism Caused by Vaccines," Raw Story, April 2, 2012, https://www.rawstory.com/2012/04/trump-warns-fox-news-viewers-autism-caused-by-vaccines.

96. Zack Kopplin, "Trump Met with Prominent Anti-Vaccine Activists during Campaign," *Science*, November 18, 2016, https://www.sciencemag.org/news/2016/11/trump-met-prominent-anti-vaccine-activists-during-campaign.

97. Andrea Peyser, "Anti-Vaxxers Can Go Stick It," *New York Post*, February 19, 2015, https://nypost.com/2015/02/19/anti-vaxxers-can-go-stick-it.

98. Remarks by President Trump before Marine One Departure, April 26, 2019, https://www.whitehouse.gov/briefings-statements/remarks-president-trump-marine-one-departure-40.

99. Betsy Woodruff, "Donald Trump Is Turning Republicans into Anti-Vaxxers," *The Daily Beast*, July 5, 2016, https://www.thedailybeast.com/donald-trump-is-turning-republicans-into-anti-vaxxers?

100. Kathy Frankovic, "Belief in Conspiracies Largely Depends on Political Identity," YouGov, December 27, 2016, https://today.yougov.com/topics/politics/articles-reports/2016/12/27/belief-conspiracies-largely-depends-political-iden.

101. Briony Swire et al., "Processing Political Misinformation: Comprehending the Trump Phenomenon," Royal Society Open Science, March 1, 2017, https://royalsocietypublishing.org/doi/full/10.1098/rsos.160802.

102. David A. Broniatowski et al., "Weaponized Health Communication: Twitter Bots and Russian Trolls Amplify the Vaccine Debate," *American Journal of Public Health*, September 12, 2018, https://ajph.aphapublications.org/doi/10.2105/AJPH.2018.304567.

103. Broniatowski, "Weaponized Health Communication."

104. US Department of Justice, Special Counsel's Office, *Report on the Investigation into Russian Interference in the 2016 Presidential Election*, March 2019, vol. 2, p. 15, https://www.justice.gov/storage/report.pdf.

105. Donald J. Trump, Twitter post, December 12, 2016, https://twitter.com/realDonaldTrump/status/808300706914594816.

106. Todd J. Gillman, "McCaul Disputes Trump on Russian Hacks and 'Rigged' Election Claim," *Dallas Morning News*, October 19, 2019, https://www.dallasnews.com/news/politics/2016/10/19/mccaul-disputes-trump-russian-hacks-rigged-election-claim.

107. Donald J. Trump, Remarks at a Campaign Rally for Senator Luther J. Strange III in Huntsville, Alabama, September 22, 2017, online by Gerhard Peters and John T. Woolley, The American Presidency Project, https://www.presidency.ucsb.edu/node/331317.

108. Peter Baker, Maggie Haberman, and A. G. Sulzberger, "Excerpts from Trump's Interview with the *New York Times*," *New York Times*, February 1, 2019, https://www.nytimes.com/2019/02/01/us/politics/trump-interview-transcripts.html.

109. Office of the Director of National Intelligence, "Assessing Russian Activities and Intentions in Recent US Elections," January 6, 2017, https://www.dni.gov/files/documents/ICA_2017_01.pdf.

110. Remarks by President Trump at the 2019 Conservative Political Action Conference, March 3, 2019, https://www.whitehouse.gov/briefings-statements/remarks-president-trump-2019-conservative-political-action-conference.

111. William J. Bennett, ed., *The Book of Virtues* (New York: Simon and Schuster, 1993), 599.

112. David Wright, "Tillerson Points to U.S. 'Crisis of Ethics and Integrity,'" WBUR, May 17, 2018, https://www.wbur.org/onpoint/2018/05/17/tillerson-vmi-commencement-speech.

3. CREATED EQUAL

1. Allen, *Our Declaration*, 188.

2. Thomas Jefferson, letter to Roger Weightman, June 24, 1826, https://www.loc.gov/exhibits/jefferson/214.html.

3. Abraham Lincoln, "Fragments on Slavery," 1854, http://founding.com/founders-library/american-political-figures/abraham-lincoln/fragments-on-slavery.

4. Sixth Lincoln-Douglas Debate, Quincy, Illinois, October 13, 1858, https://www.nps.gov/liho/learn/historyculture/debate6.htm.

5. S Department of Justice, Special Counsel's Office, Report on the Investigation, vol. I, p. 27, fn70.

6. Alexander H. Stephens, "The Cornerstone Speech," March 21, 1861, https://teachingamericanhistory.org/library/document/cornerstone-speech.

7. George William Hunter, *A Civic Biology* (New York: American Book Company, 1914), 263.

8. Hunter, *A Civic Biology*, 196.

9. Jared Taylor, "Race and Intelligence: The Evidence," American Renaissance, Posted on July 9, 2017, November 1992, https://www.amren.com/news/2017/07/race-and-differences-in-intelligence-evidence.

10. Dinesh D'Souza, "Richard Spencer, Wilsonian Progressive," American Greatness, August 10, 2018, https://outline.com/sTSdtH.

11. Quoted in Thomas J. Main, *The Rise of the Alt-Right* (Washington, DC: Brookings Institution Press, 2018), 128.

12. Main, *The Rise of the Alt-Right*, 127.

13. Lisa Mascaro, "David Duke and Other White Supremacists See Trump's Rise as Way to Increase Role in Mainstream Politics," *Los Angeles Times*, September 29, 2016, https://www.latimes.com/politics/la-na-pol-trump-david-duke-20160928-snap-story.html.

14. Maureen Dowd, "Trump Shrugged," *New York Times*, November 28, 1999, https://www.nytimes.com/1999/11/28/opinion/liberties-trump-shrugged.html.

15. "CNN Late Edition with Wolf Blitzer," March 21, 2004, http://www.cnn.com/TRANSCRIPTS/0403/21/le.00.html.

16. Donald Trump and Robert Kiyosaki, "Why We Want You to Be Rich," 2006, https://youtu.be/hPOCSJ23bh0.

17. Deborah Solomon, "If He Builds It," *New York Times*, March 25, 2009, https://www.nytimes.com/2009/03/29/magazine/29wwln-q4-t.html.

18. Deborah Solomon, Twitter post, January 16, 2017, https://twitter.com/deborahsolo/status/821048406550441984.

19. Phil Han, "Donald Trump: I Have the Genes for Success," CNN, February 11, 2010, http://www.cnn.com/2010/SHOWBIZ/02/11/donald.trump.marriage.apprentice/index.html.

20. Speech: Donald Trump in Mobile, Alabama, August 21, 2015, https://factba.se/transcript/donald-trump-speech-mobile-al-august-21-2015.

21. Donald J. Trump, Twitter post, December 3, 2015, https://twitter.com/realDonaldTrump/status/672389616998227968.

22. D'Antonio, *Never Enough*, 326–27.

23. Catherine Lucey, Zeke Miller, and Jonathan Lemire, "Read the Transcript of AP's Interview with President Trump," Associated Press, October 16, 2018, https://www.apnews.com/a28cc17d27524050b37f4d91e087955e.

24. Katie Rogers, "In the Pale of Winter, Trump's Tan Remains a State Secret," *New York Times*, February 2, 2019, https://www.nytimes.com/2019/02/02/us/politics/trump-tan.html.

25. Nick Paumgarten, "The Death and Life of Atlantic City," *The New Yorker*, August 31, 2015, https://www.newyorker.com/magazine/2015/09/07/the-death-and-life-of-atlantic-city.

26. Michael Isikoff, "Trump Challenged over Ties to Mob-Linked Gambler with Ugly Past," Yahoo, March 7, 2016, https://www.yahoo.com/news/trump-challenged-over-ties-to-mob-linked-gambler-100050602.html.

27. "Trump Plaza Loses Appeal of Discrimination Penalty," United Press International, October 19, 1992, https://www.upi.com/Archives/1992/10/19/Trump-Plaza-loses-appeal-of-discrimination-penalty/1911719467200.

28. Jack O'Donnell, "Donald Trump Says He's 'Never Used Racist Remarks.' I Know Different," *Politico*, November 7, 2018, https://www.politico.com/magazine/story/2018/11/07/donald-trump-says-hes-never-used-a-racist-remark-i-know-different-222314.

29. John R. O'Connell with James Rutherford, *Trumped! The Inside Story of the Real Donald Trump—His Cunning Rise and Spectacular Fall* (New York: Crossroad Press, 2016 [1991]), 115.

30. Marcus Baram, "Donald Trump Was Once Sued by Justice Department for Not Renting to Blacks," *Huffington Post*, April 29, 2011, https://www.huffpost.com/entry/donald-trump-blacks-lawsuit_n_855553.

31. *New York Daily News*, May 1, 1989, at http://apps.frontline.org/clinton-trump-keys-to-their-characters/pdf/trump-newspaper.pdf.

32. Andrew Kaczynski and Jon Sarlin, "Trump in 1989 Central Park Five Interview: 'Maybe Hate Is What We Need,'" CNN, October 10, 2016, https://www.cnn.com/2016/10/07/politics/trump-larry-king-central-park-five/index.html.

33. Oliver Laughland, "Donald Trump and the Central Park Five: The Racially Charged Rise of a Demagogue," *The Guardian*, February 17, 2016, https://www.theguardian.com/us-news/2016/feb/17/central-park-five-donald-trump-jogger-rape-case-new-york.

34. Laughland, "Donald Trump and the Central Park Five."

35. Donald Trump, "Donald Trump: Central Park Five Settlement Is a 'Disgrace,'" *New York Daily News*, June 21, 2014, https://www.nydailynews.com/new-york/nyc-crime/donald-trump-central-park-settlement-disgrace-article-1.1838467.

36. Yusef Salaam, "I'm One of the Central Park Five. Donald Trump Won't Leave Me Alone," *Washington Post*, October 12, 2016, https://www.washingtonpost.com/posteverything/wp/2016/10/12/im-one-of-the-central-park-five-donald-trump-wont-leave-me-alone.

37. US Congress, House, Committee on Natural Resources, Subcommittee on Native American Affairs, Implementation of the Indian Gaming Regulatory Act, 103d Congress, 1st sess., October 5, 1993, 242.

38. "Trump Personally Approved Ads Slamming Indian Tribe: 'This Could Be Good!'" *Los Angeles Times*, June 29, 2016, http://documents.latimes.com/trump-personally-approved-ads-slamming-indian-tribe-could-be-good.

39. Jason Kirk, "The 27 Times Donald Trump Tweeted about Barack Obama Playing Golf Too Much," SBNation, February 3, 2018, https://www.sbnation.com/golf/2017/3/27/15073086/donald-trump-tweets-barack-obama-golf.

40. Donald J. Trump, Twitter post, August 15, 2011, https://twitter.com/realDonaldTrump/status/103158206498476032.

41. Josh Dawsey, "'Want to See the Lincoln Bedroom?': Trump Relishes Role as White House Tour Guide," *Washington Post*, January 28, 2019, https://www.washingtonpost.com/politics/want-to-see-the-lincoln-bedroom-trump-relishes-role-as-white-house-tour-guide/2019/01/28/fe1254b0-20f7-11e9-bda9-d6efefc397e8_story.html.

42. Bethy Fouhy, "Trump: Obama a 'Terrible Student' Not Good Enough for Harvard," Associated Press, April 25, 2011, https://www.nbcnewyork.com/news/local/Trump-Obama-Wasnt-Good-Enough-to-Get-into-Ivy-Schools-120657869.html.

43. House Oversight, *Hearing with Michael Cohen*, 14.

44. House Oversight, *Hearing with Michael Cohen*, 13.

45. Remarks: Donald Trump Delivers a Speech at a Fundraiser in Utica, NY, August 13, 2018, https://factba.se/transcript/donald-trump-remarks-fundraiser-utica-ny-august-13-2018.

46. Donald J. Trump, Twitter post, August 3, 2018, https://twitter.com/realDonaldTrump/status/1025586524782559232.

47. Donald J. Trump, Twitter post, April 30, 2015, https://twitter.com/realDonaldTrump/status/593752475263442944.

48. Donald J. Trump, Twitter post, November 22, 2015, https://twitter.com/realDonaldTrump/status/668520614697820160.

49. Charles Johnson, "We Found Where Donald Trump's 'Black Crimes' Graphic Came From," Little Green Footballs, November 22, 2015, http://littlegreenfootballs.com/article/45291_We_Found_Where_Donald_Trumps_Black_Crimes_Graphic_Came_From.

50. "Torch-Wielding Protesters Gather at Lee Park," *The Daily Progress*, May 13, 2017, https://www.dailyprogress.com/news/local/torch-wielding-protesters-gather-at-lee-park/article_201dc390-384d-11e7-bf16-fb43de0f5d38.html.

51. Sarah Toy, "KKK Rally in Charlottesville Met with Throng of Protesters," *USA Today*, July 8, 2017, https://www.usatoday.com/story/news/nation-now/2017/07/08/kkk-holds-rally-virginia-and-met-protesters/462146001.

52. A. C. Thompson, "A Few Things Got Left out of The Daily Caller's Report on Confederate Monument Rally," Pro Publica, May 31, 2017, https://www.propublica.org/article/things-got-left-out-of-the-daily-callers-report-confederate-monument-rally.

53. Libby Nelson, "'Why We Voted for Donald Trump': David Duke Explains the White Supremacist Charlottesville Protests," Vox, August 12, 2017, https://www.vox.com/2017/8/12/16138358/charlottesville-protests-david-duke-kkk.

54. Donald J. Trump, Remarks on Signing the VA Choice and Quality Employment Act of 2017 in Bedminster, New Jersey, August 12, 2017, online by Gerhard Peters and John T. Woolley, The American Presidency Project, https://www.presidency.ucsb.edu/documents/remarks-signing-the-va-choice-and-quality-employment-act-2017-bedminster-new-jersey.

55. Donald J. Trump, Remarks on Infrastructure and an Exchange with Reporters in New York City, August 15, 2017, online by Gerhard Peters and John T. Woolley, The American Presidency Project, https://www.

presidency.ucsb.edu/documents/remarks-infrastructure-and-exchange-with-reporters-new-york-city.

56. Rosie Gray, "'Really Proud of Him': Alt-Right Leaders Praise Trump's Comments," *The Atlantic*, August 15, 2017, https://www.theatlantic.com/politics/archive/2017/08/really-proud-of-him-richard-spencer-and-alt-right-leaders-praise-trumps-comments/537039.

57. David Duke, Twitter post, August 15, 2017, https://twitter.com/DrDavidDuke/status/897559892164304896.

58. Lindsey Graham, "Graham Statement on Charlottesville," August 16, 2017, https://www.lgraham.senate.gov/public/index.cfm/2017/8/graham-statement-on-charlottesville.

59. David A. Graham, Adrienne Green, Cullen Murphy, and Parker Richards, "An Oral History of Trump's Bigotry," *The Atlantic*, June 2019, https://www.theatlantic.com/magazine/archive/2019/06/trump-racism-comments/588067.

60. Remarks by President Trump before Marine One Departure, April 26, 2019, https://www.whitehouse.gov/briefings-statements/remarks-president-trump-marine-one-departure-40.

61. Donald J. Trump, announcement of candidacy, June 16, 2015, http://www.p2016.org/trump/trump061615sp.html.

62. Anna Flagg, "Is There a Connection between Undocumented Immigrants and Crime?" Marshall Institute, May 13, 2019, https://www.themarshallproject.org/2019/05/13/is-there-a-connection-between-undocumented-immigrants-and-crime.

63. Remarks by President Trump at a California Sanctuary State Roundtable, May 16, 2018, https://www.whitehouse.gov/briefings-statements/remarks-president-trump-california-sanctuary-state-roundtable.

64. President Trump Statement on Government Shutdown, C-SPAN, January 4, 2019, https://www.c-span.org/video/?456701-1/president-trump-confirms-shutdown-months-years.

65. Remarks by President Trump before Marine One Departure, January 6, 2019, https://www.whitehouse.gov/briefings-statements/remarks-president-trump-marine-one-departure-29.

66. Remarks by President Trump during Roundtable Discussion with State, Local, and Community Leaders on Border Security and Safe Communities, January 12, 2019, https://www.whitehouse.gov/briefings-statements/remarks-president-trump-roundtable-discussion-state-local-community-leaders-border-security-safe-communities.

67. Robert A. Stribley, "Our History of Blaming Immigrants for Disease," *Medium*, April 12, 2019, https://medium.com/s/story/our-history-of-blaming-immigrants-for-disease-2cf77c474961.

68. Donald J. Trump, Twitter post, August 5, 2014, https://twitter.com/realdonaldtrump/status/496640747379388416.

69. Donald J. Trump, Twitter post, July 5, 2015, https://twitter.com/realdonaldtrump/status/618229195181826049.

70. Donald J. Trump, Twitter post, December 11, 2018, https://twitter.com/realDonaldTrump/status/1072464107784323072.

71. Donald J. Trump, Twitter post, August 2, 2014, https://twitter.com/realDonaldTrump/status/495531002505494528.

72. Donald J. Trump, Twitter post, September 19, 2014, https://twitter.com/realdonaldtrump/status/513141602064543744.

73. Donald J. Trump, Twitter post, June 19, 2018, https://twitter.com/realdonaldtrump/status/1009071403918864385.

74. Donald J. Trump, Twitter post, April 18, 2018, https://twitter.com/realdonaldtrump/status/986544648477868032.

75. Donald J. Trump, Twitter post, July 27, 2019, https://twitter.com/realdonaldtrump/status/1155073965880172544

76. Donald J. Trump, Twitter post, July 14, 2019, https://twitter.com/realDonaldTrump/status/1150381394234941448?s=20.

77. Donald J. Trump, Twitter post, July 14, 2019, https://twitter.com/realDonaldTrump/status/1150381395078000643?s=20.

78. U.S. Equal Employment Opportunity Commission, "Immigrants' Employment Rights Under Federal Anti-Discrimination Laws," https://www.eeoc.gov/eeoc/publications/immigrants-facts.cfm.

79. Donald J. Trump for President, "Protect the Electoral College," 2019, https://forms.donaldjtrump.com/landing/protect-the-electoral-college.

80. Michael D. Shear and Julie Hirschfeld Davis, "Stoking Fears, Trump Defied Bureaucracy to Advance Immigration Agenda," *New York Times*, December 23, 2017, https://www.nytimes.com/2017/12/23/us/politics/trump-immigration.html.

81. Josh Dawsey, "Trump Derides Protections for Immigrants from 'Shithole' Countries," *Washington Post*, January 12, 2018, https://www.washingtonpost.com/politics/trump-attacks-protections-for-immigrants-from-shithole-countries-in-oval-office-meeting/2018/01/11/bfc0725c-f711-11e7-91af-31ac729add94_story.html.

82. Sarah Churchwell, *Behold America: The Entangled History of "America First" and "The American Dream"* (New York: Basic Books, 2018), 54–55.

83. "White Supremacists Praise Trump's Inflammatory Immigration Remarks," Anti-Defamation League, January 12, 2018, https://www.adl.org/blog/white-supremacists-praise-trumps-inflammatory-immigration-remarks.

84. Maureen Groppe, "What Trump Has Said about Judge Curiel," *Indianapolis Star*, June 11, 2016, https://www.indystar.com/story/news/2016/06/11/what-trump-has-said-judge-curiel/85641242.

85. Alan Rappeport, "That Judge Attacked by Donald Trump? He's Faced a Lot Worse," *New York Times*, June 3, 2016, https://www.nytimes.com/2016/06/04/us/politics/donald-trump-university-judge-gonzalo-curiel.html.

86. Heather Caygle, "Ryan: Trump's Comments 'Textbook Definition' of Racism," *Politico*, June 7, 2016, https://www.politico.com/story/2016/06/paul-ryan-trump-judge-223991.

87. Manu Raju, Eugene Scott, and Deirdre Walsh, "Graham: Trump's Judge Comments 'Un-American.'" CNN, June 7, 2016, https://www.cnn.com/2016/06/07/politics/lindsey-graham-donald-trump/index.html.

88. Patrick Healy, Maggie Haberman, and Jonathan Martin, "Democrats Jump on Allies of Donald Trump in Judge Dispute," *New York Times*, June 6, 2016, https://www.nytimes.com/2016/06/07/us/politics/democrats-trump-presidential-race.html.

89. Julius Krein, "I Voted for Trump. And I Sorely Regret It," *New York Times*, August 17, 2017, https://www.nytimes.com/2017/08/17/opinion/sunday/i-voted-for-trump-and-i-sorely-regret-it.html.

90. "Trump Fires V.A. Secretary Shulkin, Nominates White House Physician," CNN Newsroom, March 29, 2018, http://www.cnn.com/TRANSCRIPTS/1803/29/cnr.06.html.

91. Philip Rucker, Josh Dawsey, and Damian Paletta, "Trump Slams Fed Chair, Questions Climate Change and Threatens to Cancel Putin Meeting in Wide-Ranging Interview with the Post," *Washington Post*, November 27, 2018, https://www.washingtonpost.com/politics/trump-slams-fed-chair-questions-climate-change-and-threatens-to-cancel-putin-meeting-in-wide-ranging-interview-with-the-post/2018/11/27/4362fae8-f26c-11e8-aeea-b85fd44449f5_story.html.

92. Donald J. Trump, Twitter post, October 10, 2017, https://twitter.com/realDonaldTrump/status/917734186848579584.

93. Paul Solotaroff, "Trump Seriously: On the Trail with the GOP's Tough Guy," *Rolling Stone*, September 9, 2015, https://www.rollingstone.com/politics/politics-news/trump-seriously-on-the-trail-with-the-gops-tough-guy-41447.

94. Meghan Keneally, "Donald Trump Offends Some with Comment That Clinton Lacks 'Presidential Look,'" ABC News, September 6, 2016, https://abcnews.go.com/Politics/donald-trump-offends-comment-clinton-lacks-presidential/story?id=41891411.

95. Heidi Evans, "Inside Trumps' Bitter Battle: Nephew's Ailing Baby Caught in the Middle." *New York Daily News*, December 19, 2000, https://www.nydailynews.com/archives/news/trumps-bitter-battle-nephew-ailing-baby-caught-middle-article-1.888562.

96. Barbara Res, "Trump and His Flunkies: Why Aren't Staffers Standing Up to Him?" *New York Daily News*, September 12, 2018, https://www.nydailynews.com/opinion/ny-oped-trump-and-his-flunkies-20180911-story.html.

97. Jose A. DelReal, "Trump Draws Scornful Rebuke for Mocking Reporter with Disability," *Washington Post*, November 26, 2015, https://www.washingtonpost.com/news/post-politics/wp/2015/11/25/trump-blasted-by-new-york-times-after-mocking-reporter-with-disability.

98. Maggie Haberman, "Donald Trump Says His Mocking of *New York Times* Reporter Was Misread," *New York Times*, November 26, 2015, https://www.nytimes.com/2015/11/27/us/politics/donald-trump-says-his-mocking-of-new-york-times-reporter-was-misread.html.

99. Ken Meyer, "Coulter Says Trump Was 'Doing a Standard Retard,' Not Mocking Disabled Reporter," Mediaite, September 1, 2016, https://www.mediaite.com/online/coulter-says-trump-was-doing-a-standard-retard-not-mocking-disabled-reporter.

100. Donald J. Trump, Twitter post, September 4, 2018, https://twitter.com/realDonaldTrump/status/1037173907625832448

101. Interview: Donald Trump on *The Howard Stern Show*, April 16, 2004, https://factba.se/transcript/donald-trump-interview-howard-stern-show-april-16-2004.

102. Interview: Donald Trump on *The Howard Stern Show*, September 23, 2004, https://factba.se/transcript/donald-trump-interview-howard-stern-show-september-23-2004.

103. Gideon Resnick and Asawin Suebsaeng, "Donald Trump Called Deaf Apprentice Marlee Matlin 'Retarded,' Three Staffers Say," *The Daily Beast*, October 13, 2016, https://www.thedailybeast.com/donald-trump-called-deaf-apprentice-marlee-matlin-retarded-three-staffers-say.

104. Maureen Dowd, "Is You Wicked," *New York Times*, May 3, 2003, https://www.nytimes.com/2003/05/07/opinion/is-you-wicked.html.

105. Robert Slater, *No Such Thing as Over-Exposure: Inside the Life and Celebrity of Donald Trump* (Upper Saddle River, NJ: Pearson Prentice Hall, 2005), 197.

106. Statement from President Donald J. Trump on Down Syndrome Awareness Month, October 1, 2017, https://www.whitehouse.gov/briefings-statements/statement-president-donald-j-trump-syndrome-awareness-month.

107. Jamie Weinstein, "Trump on Flag Burning, The 'Superstar' Who Made Him Pro-Life, and Whether He'd Live in the White House," *Daily Caller*, September 3, 2015, https://dailycaller.com/2015/09/03/trump-on-flag-burning-the-superstar-who-made-him-pro-life-and-whether-hed-live-in-the-white-house/.

108. Remarks by President Trump Welcoming the U.S. Olympic Team, April 27, 2018, https://www.whitehouse.gov/briefings-statements/remarks-president-trump-welcoming-u-s-olympic-team/.

109. David Cross, "Take It from a Lawyer with a Disability: Trump's Paralympics Comments Were Offensive," *USA Today*, May 11, 2018, https://www.usatoday.com/story/opinion/2018/05/11/donald-trump-paralympics-disabled-tough-watch-column/599142002.

110. Celeste Katz, "Donald Trump Tried to Limit Street Vendors on Fifth Ave., Including Those Who Were Veterans," *New York Daily News*, August 3, 2015, https://www.nydailynews.com/news/politics/exclusive-donald-trump-push-street-vendors-article-1.2312519.

111. William J. Gorta, "Trump to Mayor: Boot Fifth Ave. Peddlers," *New York Post*, June 18, 2004, https://nypost.com/2004/06/18/trump-to-mayor-boot-fifth-ave-peddlers.

112. *United States of America v. Internet Research Agency LLC* [and 15 others], defendants: case 1:18-cr-00032-DLF, February 18, 2018, https://permanent.access.gpo.gov/gpo89499/file1035477download.pdf.

113. Richard Engel, Kate Benyon-Tinker, and Kennett Werner, "Russian Documents Reveal Desire to Sow Racial Discord—and Violence—in the U.S.," NBC News, May 20, 2019, https://www.nbcnews.com/news/world/

russian-documents-reveal-desire-sow-racial-discord-violence-u-s-n1008051.

114. US Department of Justice, Special Counsel's Office, *Report on the Investigation*, vol. I, p. 29, fn85.

115. Nick Penzenstadler, Brad Heath, and Jessica Guynn, "We Read Every One of the 3,517 Facebook Ads Bought by Russians. Here's What We Found," *USA Today*, May 11, 2018, https://www.usatoday.com/story/news/2018/05/11/what-we-found-facebook-ads-russians-accused-election-meddling/602319002.

116. Peter Aldhous, "Russian Trolls Swarmed the Charlottesville March—Then Twitter Cracked Down," Buzzfeed, August 11, 2018, https://www.buzzfeednews.com/article/peteraldhous/russia-twitter-trolls-charlottesville.

117. Juliana Menasce Horowitz, Anna Brown, and Kiana Cox, "Race in America 2019," Pew Research Center, April 9, 2019, https://www.pewsocialtrends.org/2019/04/09/race-in-america-2019/.

118. Abraham Lincoln, letter to Joshua Speed, August 24, 1855, http://www.abrahamlincolnonline.org/lincoln/speeches/speed.htm

4. THE ADMINISTRATION OF JUSTICE

1. John Adams, Novanglus, February 6, 1775, http://www.let.rug.nl/usa/presidents/john-adams/novanglus-text-february-6-1775.php.

2. Alexander Hamilton, *Federalist 27*, http://avalon.law.yale.edu/18th_century/fed27.asp.

3. 28 US Code § 453, Oaths of Justices and Judges, https://www.law.cornell.edu/uscode/text/28/453.

4. Abraham Lincoln, "The Perpetuation of Our Political Institutions: Address before the Young Men's Lyceum of Springfield, Illinois," January 27, 1838, http://www.abrahamlincolnonline.org/lincoln/speeches/lyceum.htm.

5. Rudolph Giuliani, Opening Remarks to the United Nations General Assembly Special Session on Terrorism," October 3, 2001, https://www.americanrhetoric.com/speeches/rudygiuliani911unitednations.htm.

6. James Madison, *Federalist 62*, http://avalon.law.yale.edu/18th_century/fed62.asp.

7. Jonathan Swan, "Trump's Government of One," Axios, November 5, 2017, https://www.axios.com/trumps-government-of-one-1513306691-b7aed116-84c7-46fa-8375-570948a76374.html.

8. "Trump: 'The Republican Party Is a Total Mess, Just Like Our Country,'" *Fox News Insider*, January 26, 2016, https://insider.foxnews.com/2016/01/26/donald-trump-and-bret-baier-face-special-report-2-days-fox-news-google-gop-debate.

9. Michael Wolff, *Fire and Fury: Inside the Trump White House* (New York: Henry Holt, 2018), 16.

10. Jeremy Diamond, "Trump: Death Penalty for Cop Killers," CNN, December 11, 2015, https://www.cnn.com/2015/12/10/politics/donald-trump-police-officers-death-penalty/index.html.

11. Perhaps he was suggesting that Alito joined a controversial opinion on late-term abortion that his sister had written when they served together on a federal court—but that was also wrong. See Ramesh Ponnuru, "Maryanne Trump Barry vs. Samuel Alito on Abortion," *National Review*, February 26, 2016, https://www.nationalreview.com/corner/maryanne-trump-barry-vs-samuel-alito-abortion.

12. Josh Rogin, "Trump to House Republicans: 'Say Great Things . . . We Love Trump.'" *Washington Post*, July 7, 2016, https://www.washingtonpost.com/opinions/global-opinions/trump-to-house-republicans-say-great-things--we-love-trump/2016/07/07/c487cf2a-447e-11e6-8856-f26de2537a9d_story.html.

13. Sergio Chapa, "Rex Tillerson Makes Rare Public Appearance in Houston," *Houston Chronicle*, December 8, 2018, https://www.chron.com/business/article/Rex-Tillerson-13448868.php.

14. Remarks by President Trump Before Marine One Departure, July 12, 2019, https://www.whitehouse.gov/briefings-statements/remarks-president-trump-marine-one-departure-52/.

15. Remarks by President Trump at Turning Point USA's Teen Student Action Summit 2019. Issued on: July 23, 2019, https://www.whitehouse.gov/briefings-statements/remarks-president-trump-turning-point-usas-teen-student-action-summit-2019/.

16. Kevin McCarthy, "Congress Stands Athwart Obama's Imperial Presidency," *National Review*, March 17, 2016, https://www.nationalreview.com/2016/03/obama-congress-constitution-supreme-court-immigration-lawsuit/.

17. Donald J. Trump, Twitter post, March 21, 2013, https://twitter.com/realDonaldTrump/status/314771578850275329.

18. Alexander Hamilton, *Federalist 69*, http://avalon.law.yale.edu/18th_century/fed69.asp.

19. Alexander Hamilton, *Federalist 70*, http://avalon.law.yale.edu/18th_century/fed70.asp.

20. Alexander Hamilton, *Federalist 65*, http://avalon.law.yale.edu/18th_century/fed65.asp.

21. Remarks by President Trump before Marine One Departure, May 30, 2019, https://www.whitehouse.gov/briefings-statements/remarks-president-trump-marine-one-departure-45.

22. Donald J. Trump, Twitter posts, May 16, 2017, https://twitter.com/realDonaldTrump/status/864436162567471104 andhttps://twitter.com/realDonaldTrump/status/864438529472049152.

23. Remarks by President Trump before Marine One Departure, June 8, 2018, https://www.whitehouse.gov/briefings-statements/remarks-president-trump-marine-one-departure-8.

24. Mary C. Lawton, "Presidential or Legislative Pardon of the President," US Department of Justice, August 5, 1974, https://www.justice.gov/sites/default/files/olc/opinions/1974/08/31/op-olc-supp-v001-p0370_0.pdf.

25. Remarks by President Trump before Marine One Departure, January 10, 2019, https://www.whitehouse.gov/briefings-statements/remarks-president-trump-marine-one-departure-30.

26. Donald J. Trump, Twitter post, March 6, 2019, https://twitter.com/realDonaldTrump/status/1103353074469535750.

27. Jenna Johnson, "Trump Calls for 'Total and Complete Shutdown of Muslims Entering the United States,'" *Washington Post*, December 7, 2015, https://www.washingtonpost.com/news/post-politics/wp/2015/12/07/donald-trump-calls-for-total-and-complete-shutdown-of-muslims-entering-the-united-states/?utm_term=.c248bac1b08f

28. Duane Patterson, "Vice President Dick Cheney on San Bernardino, Obama's Foreign Policy, and Setting History Straight," *Hugh Hewitt Show*, December 5, 2015, https://www.hughhewitt.com/vice-president-dick-cheney-san-bernardino-obamas-foreign-policy-setting-history-straight/#more-29615.

29. Elizabeth Landers, "Governor Nikki Haley Blasts Donald Trump after His South Carolina Visit," CNN, December 9, 2015, https://

www.cnn.com/2015/12/09/politics/nikki-haley-donald-trump-south-carolina/index.html.

30. Andrew Kaczynski, "Stephen Moore Once Slammed Trump's 'Dangerous' Immigration Position, Larry Kudlow Compared It to Worst Parts of World War II," CNN, April 16, 2019, https://www.cnn.com/2019/04/15/politics/kfile-stephen-moore-larry-kudlow-trump.

31. Michael Scherer, "Exclusive: Donald Trump Says He Might Have Supported Japanese Internment," *Time*, December 8, 2015, http://time.com/4140050/donald-trump-muslims-japanese-internment.

32. *Trump v. Hawaii*, 585 US _ (2018), at 38, https://www.supremecourt.gov/opinions/17pdf/17-965_h315.pdf.

33. *Shaughnessy v. Mezei*, 345 US 206 (1953), at 212, https://supreme.justia.com/cases/federal/us/345/206.

34. *Reno v. Flores*, 507 US 292 (1993), at 306, https://supreme.justia.com/cases/federal/us/507/292.

35. Donald J. Trump, Twitter post, June 24, 2018, https://twitter.com/realDonaldTrump/status/1010900865602019329.

36. "Trump, Airing Grievances with Immigration System, Says U.S. Needs to 'Get Rid of Judges,'" CBS News, April 2, 2019, https://www.cbsnews.com/news/president-trump-nato-meeting-secretary-general-jens-stoltenberg-today-live-stream-updates-2019-04-02.

37. Remarks by President Trump at the White House Opportunity and Revitalization Council Meeting, April 4, 2019, https://www.whitehouse.gov/briefings-statements/remarks-president-trump-white-house-opportunity-revitalization-council-meeting.

38. Jake Tapper, "Trump Pushed to Close El Paso Border, Told Admin Officials to Resume Family Separations and Agents Not to Admit Migrants," CNN, April 8, 2019, https://www.cnn.com/2019/04/08/politics/trump-family-separation-el-paso-kirstjen-nielsen/index.html.

39. Nick Miroff and Josh Dawsey, "'Take the Land': President Trump Wants a Border Wall. He Wants It Black. And He Wants It by Election Day," *Washington Post*, August 27, 2019, https://www.washingtonpost.com/immigration/take-the-land-president-trump-wants-a-border-wall-he-wants-it-black-and-he-wants-it-by-election-day/2019/08/27/37b80018-c821-11e9-a4f3-c081a126de70_story.html.

40. Charles V. Bagli, "Trump Paid over $1 Million in Labor Settlement, Documents Reveal," *New York Times*, November 27, 2017, https://

www.nytimes.com/2017/11/27/nyregion/trump-tower-illegal-immigrant-workers-union-settlement.html.

41. James West, "Former Models for Donald Trump's Agency Say They Violated Immigration Rules and Worked Illegally," *Mother Jones*, August 30, 2016, https://www.motherjones.com/politics/2016/08/donald-trump-model-management-illegal-immigration.

42. *New York Daily News*, May 1, 1989, at http://apps.frontline.org/clinton-trump-keys-to-their-characters/pdf/trump-newspaper.pdf.

43. Kaczynski and Sarlin, "Trump in 1989 Central Park Five Interview."

44. NBC News, *Meet the Press* transcript, August 2, 2015, https://www.nbcnews.com/meet-the-press/meet-press-transcript-august-2-2015-n402571.

45. Donald J. Trump, Remarks to Federal, State, and Local Law Enforcement Officers in Brentwood, New York, July 28, 2017, online by Gerhard Peters and John T. Woolley, The American Presidency Project, https://www.presidency.ucsb.edu/documents/remarks-federal-state-and-local-law-enforcement-officers-brentwood-new-york.

46. Email from Chuck Rosenberg, July 29, 2017, https://www.politico.com/f/?id=0000015d-9ecc-d43a-a3dd-bfef0fa60001.

47. Antonia Noori Farzan, "'Shoot Them!': Trump Laughs Off a Supporter's Demand for Violence against Migrants," *Washington Post*, May 9, 2019, https://www.washingtonpost.com/nation/2019/05/09/shoot-them-trump-laughs-off-supporters-demand-violence-against-migrants.

48. Julie Hirschfeld Davis and Michael D. Shear, *Border Wars: Inside Trump's Assault on Immigration* (New York: Simon and Schuster, 2019), 337.

49. Tom LoBianco, "Donald Trump on Terrorists: 'Take out Their Families,'" CNN, December 3, 2015, https://www.cnn.com/2015/12/02/politics/donald-trump-terrorists-families/index.html.

50. "The Fox News GOP Debate Transcript, Annotated," *Washington Post*, March 3, 2016, https://www.washingtonpost.com/news/the-fix/wp/2016/03/03/the-fox-news-gop-debate-transcript-annotated.

51. Damian Paletta and Nick Timiraos, "Trump Reverses His Stance on Torture," *Wall Street Journal*, March 4, 2016, https://www.wsj.com/articles/trump-reverses-his-stance-on-torture-1457116559.

52. Interview with Donald Trump, Anderson Cooper 360, CNN, March 9, 2016, http://www.cnn.com/TRANSCRIPTS/1603/09/acd.01.html.

53. Greg Jaffe, "For Trump and His Generals, 'Victory' Has Different Meanings," *Washington Post*, April 5, 2018, https://www.washingtonpost.com/world/national-security/for-trump-and-his-generals-victory-has-different-meanings/2018/04/05/8d74eab0-381d-11e8-9c0a-85d477d9a226_story.html.

54. Waitman Wade Beorn, "I Led a Platoon in Iraq. Trump Is Wrong to Pardon War Criminals," *Washington Post*, May 9, 2019, https://www.washingtonpost.com/outlook/i-led-a-platoon-in-iraq-trump-is-wrong-to-pardon-war-criminals/2019/05/09/15b10430-71d5-11e9-9eb4-0828f5389013_story.html.

55. Sarah Sanders, Press Briefing by Principal Deputy Press Secretary Sarah Sanders and Treasury Secretary Mnuchin, June 29, 2017, online by Gerhard Peters and John T. Woolley, The American Presidency Project, https://www.presidency.ucsb.edu/documents/press-briefing-principal-deputy-press-secretary-sarah-sanders-and-treasury-secretary.

56. Ben Schreckinger, "Trump on Protester: 'I'd Like to Punch Him in the Face,'" *Politico*, February 23, 2016, https://www.politico.com/story/2016/02/donald-trump-punch-protester-219655.

57. Anna Giaritelli, "Trump: Protesters Should Face Consequences," *Washington Examiner*, March 11, 2016, https://www.washingtonexaminer.com/trump-protesters-should-face-consequences.

58. Zak Cheney-Rice, "Video of Donald Trump Supporter Sucker-Punching a Guy Got Five Sheriff's Deputies Suspended," Mic, March 18, 2016, https://www.yahoo.com/news/video-donald-trump-supporter-sucker-175600036.html.

59. Louis Jacobson, "In Context: Donald Trump's 'Second Amendment People' Comment," PolitiFact, August 9, 2016, https://www.politifact.com/truth-o-meter/article/2016/aug/09/context-donald-trumps-second-amendment-people-comm.

60. Nick Corasaniti and Maggie Haberman, "Donald Trump Suggests 'Second Amendment People' Could Act against Hillary Clinton," *New York Times*, August 9, 2016, https://www.nytimes.com/2016/08/10/us/politics/donald-trump-hillary-clinton.html.

61. Philip Bump, "Donald Trump Says 'Second Amendment People' May Be the Only Check on Clinton Judicial Appointments," *Washington Post*, August 9, 2016, https://www.washingtonpost.com/news/the-fix/wp/

2016/08/09/donald-trump-says-second-amendment-people-may-be-the-only-check-on-clinton-judicial-appointments.

62. Donald J. Trump, Remarks at a "Make America Great Again" Rally, Springfield, Missouri, September 21, 2018, online by Gerhard Peters and John T. Woolley, The American Presidency Project, https://www.presidency.ucsb.edu/documents/remarks-make-america-great-again-rally-springfield-missouri.

63. Alexander Marlow, Matthew Boyle, Amanda House, and Charlie Spiering, "Exclusive— President Donald Trump: Paul Ryan Blocked Subpoenas of Democrats," Breitbart, March 13, 2019, https://www.breitbart.com/politics/2019/03/13/exclusive-president-donald-trump-paul-ryan-blocked-subpoenas-of-democrats.

64. Donald J. Trump, Twitter post, September 29, 2019, https://twitter.com/realDonaldTrump/status/1178477539653771264?s=20.

65. Donald J. Trump, Remarks at a "Make America Great Again" Rally in Missoula, Montana, online by Gerhard Peters and John T. Woolley, The American Presidency Project, https://www.presidency.ucsb.edu/documents/remarks-make-america-great-again-rally-missoula-montana.

66. Donald J. Trump, Twitter post, July 2, 2017, https://twitter.com/realDonaldTrump/status/881503147168071680; David Nakamura, "Trump Appears to Promote Violence against CNN with Tweet," *Washington Post*, July 2, 2017, https://www.washingtonpost.com/news/post-politics/wp/2017/07/02/trump-appears-to-promote-violence-against-cnn-with-tweet.

67. Alayna Treene, "Trump Shares Meme of Train Running over CNN," Axios, August 15, 2017, https://www.axios.com/trump-shares-meme-of-train-running-over-cnn-1513304846-d47ed092-3c93-4cc4-a283-33f53ad1dbb6.html.

68. Faith Karimi, "Pipe Bomb Suspect Cesar Sayoc Describes Trump Rallies as 'New Found Drug,'" CNN, April 24, 2019, https://www.cnn.com/2019/04/24/us/cesar-sayoc-letter-trump-rallies/index.html.

69. Evelyn Rupert, "Trump: Muslim Soldier Was a Hero, but His Father 'Has No Right' to Criticize Me," *The Hill*, July 30, 2016, https://thehill.com/blogs/ballot-box/presidential-races/289894-trump-praises-muslim-soldier-but-says-father-has-no-right.

70. Donald J. Trump, Twitter post, August 14, 2016, https://twitter.com/realDonaldTrump/status/764870785634799617.

71. Donald J. Trump, Remarks Prior to a Meeting with Prime Minister Justin P. J. Trudeau of Canada and an Exchange with Reporter, October

11, 2017, online by Gerhard Peters and John T. Woolley, The American Presidency Project, https://www.presidency.ucsb.edu/documents/remarks-prior-meeting-with-prime-minister-justin-pj-trudeau-canada-and-exchange-with https://www.presidency.

72. A Transcript of Donald Trump's Meeting with the *Washington Post* Editorial Board, *Washington Post*, March 21, 2016, https://www.washingtonpost.com/blogs/post-partisan/wp/2016/03/21/a-transcript-of-donald-trumps-meeting-with-the-washington-post-editorial-board.

73. Donald J. Trump, Twitter post, September 5, 2018, https://twitter.com/realDonaldTrump/status/1037302649199177728.

74. Patrick Anderson, "Trump Blasts Sutton and Media, Raves about Noem during South Dakota Visit," *The Argus Leader*, September 7, 2018, https://www.argusleader.com/story/news/2018/09/07/donald-trump-news-gop-candidate-kristi-noem-fundraiser-2018-event-sioux-falls-visit/1195256002.

75. Donald J. Trump, Twitter post, October 11, 2017, https://twitter.com/realDonaldTrump/status/918267396493922304.

76. Donald J. Trump, Twitter post, October 11, 2017, https://twitter.com/realDonaldTrump/status/918112884630093825.

77. Donald J. Trump, Twitter post, September 4, 2018, https://twitter.com/realDonaldTrump/status/1036991866124861440.

78. Ipsos, "Americans' Views on the Media," August 7, 2018, https://www.ipsos.com/en-us/news-polls/americans-views-media-2018-08-07.

79. Jane Mayer, "The Making of the Fox News White House," *The New Yorker*, March 11, 2019, https://www.newyorker.com/magazine/2019/03/11/the-making-of-the-fox-news-white-house.

80. Walter Pincus and George Lardner Jr., "Nixon Hoped Antitrust Threat Would Sway Network Coverage," *Washington Post*, December 1, 1997, https://www.washingtonpost.com/wp-srv/national/longterm/nixon/120197tapes.htm.

81. Donald J. Trump, Twitter post, June 3, 2019, https://twitter.com/realDonaldTrump/status/1135499002626154496.

82. Commission on Presidential Debates, October 9, 2016, Debate Transcript, https://www.debates.org/voter-education/debate-transcripts/october-9-2016-debate-transcript.

83. US Department of Justice, Special Counsel's Office, *Report on the Investigation*, vol. 2, p. 107.

84. Donald J. Trump, Twitter post, July 25, 2017, https://twitter.com/realDonaldTrump/status/889790429398528000.

85. Donald J. Trump, Twitter post, November 3, 2017, https://twitter.com/realDonaldTrump/status/926403023861141504.

86. Remarks by President Trump on Supporting America's Farmers and Ranchers, May 29, 2019, https://www.whitehouse.gov/briefings-statements/remarks-president-trump-supporting-americas-farmers-ranchers.

87. NBC News, *Meet the Press* transcript, May 26, 2019, https://www.nbcnews.com/politics/meet-the-press/meet-press-may-26-2019-n1010416.

88. Kiley Armstrong, "Trump Cash Offer for Tyson Release Fails," Associated Press, February 14, 1992, https://news.google.com/newspapers?nid=266&dat=19920214&id=bt0rAAAAIBAJ&sjid=VGQFAAAAIBAJ&pg=6071,3882825&hl=en.

89. Armstrong, "Trump Cash Offer."

90. Donald J. Trump, Twitter post, September 3, 2018, https://twitter.com/realDonaldTrump/status/1036681588573130752.

91. *Ex Parte Grossman*, 267 US 87 (1925), at 121, https://supreme.justia.com/cases/federal/us/267/87.

92. Philip Rucker and Ellen Nakashima, "Trump Asked Sessions about Closing Case against Arpaio, an Ally Since 'Birtherism,'" *Washington Post*, August 26, 2017, https://www.washingtonpost.com/politics/trump-asked-sessions-about-closing-case-against-arpaio-an-ally-since-birtherism/2017/08/26/15e5d7b2-8a7f-11e7-a94f-3139abce39f5_story.html.

93. Daniel Chaitin, "John McCain: Trump's Pardon of Joe Arpaio 'Undermines His Claim for the Respect of Rule of Law,'" *Washington Examiner*, August 25, 2017, https://www.washingtonexaminer.com/john-mccain-trumps-pardon-of-joe-arpaio-undermines-his-claim-for-the-respect-of-rule-of-law.

94. Debra J. Saunders, "Trump Flirts with Pardons and Prison Reform," RealClearPolitics, June 3, 2018, https://www.realclearpolitics.com/articles/2018/06/03/trump_flirts_with_pardons_and_prison_reform_137180.html.

95. US Attorney's Office for the Southern District of New York, sentencing memorandum in *United States of America v. Michael Cohen*, December 7, 2018, https://www.lawfareblog.com/document-us-attorneys-office-southern-district-new-york-and-special-counsels-office-file-michael.

96. House Oversight, *Hearing with Michael Cohen*, 10.

97. James A. Gagliano, Twitter post, February 27, 2019, https://twitter.com/JamesAGagliano/status/1100825119411372032.

98. Donald J. Trump, Twitter post, December 16, 2017, https://twitter.com/realDonaldTrump/status/1074313153679450113.

99. Andy McCarthy, Twitter post, December 16, 2018, https://twitter.com/AndrewCMcCarthy/status/1074360328039878657.

100. Brooke Singman, "Trump Rips Cohen for 'Flipping,' Praises Manafort in Exclusive FNC Interview," Fox News, August 23, 2018, https://www.foxnews.com/politics/trump-rips-cohen-for-flipping-praises-manafort-in-exclusive-fnc-interview.

101. John Gramlich, "Only 2% of Federal Criminal Defendants Go to Trial, and Most Who Do Are Found Guilty," Pew Research Center, June 11, 2019, https://www.pewresearch.org/fact-tank/2019/06/11/only-2-of-federal-criminal-defendants-go-to-trial-and-most-who-do-are-found-guilty.

102. Richard J. Meislin, "Jury Deliberates in Friedman Case," *New York Times*, November 23, 1986, https://www.nytimes.com/1986/11/23/nyregion/jury-deliberates-in-friedman-case.html.

103. Donald J. Trump, Twitter post, December 3, 2018, https://twitter.com/realDonaldTrump/status/1069614615510859776.

104. Fox News transcript, January 12, 2018, https://www.foxnews.com/transcript/house-minority-leader-rep-kevin-mccarthy-reacts-to-president-trumps-latest-comments-on-fixing-the-border-crisis.

105. Seth Hettena, "The Dangers of Doing Favors for Donald Trump," *New York Times*, December 10, 2018, https://www.nytimes.com/2018/12/10/opinion/donald-trump-michael-cohen-favors.html.

106. Stephanie Francis Ward, "Legal Experts Weigh in on Trump's Cohen Comments and Whether They Amount to Witness Intimidation," *ABA Journal*, January 15, 2019, http://www.abajournal.com/news/article/following-fox-news-interview-some-wonder-if-president-engaged-in-obstruction.

107. James Comey, *A Higher Loyalty: Truth, Lies, and Leadership* (New York: Flatiron Books, 2018), 237–38.

108. US Department of Justice, Special Counsel's Office, *Report on the Investigation*, vol. 2, p. 3.

109. US Department of Justice, Special Counsel's Office, *Report on the Investigation*, vol. 2, p. 4.

110. Matt Apuzzo, Maggie Haberman, and Matthew Rosenberg, "Trump Told Russians That Firing 'Nut Job' Comey Eased Pressure from Investigation," *New York Times*, May 19, 2017, https://www.nytimes.com/2017/05/19/us/politics/trump-russia-comey.html.

111. "President Trump's Full Interview with Lester Holt: Firing of James Comey," RealClearPolitics, May 11, 2017, https://www.realclearpolitics.com/video/2017/05/11/president_trumps_full_interview_with_lester_holt.html.

112. US Department of Justice, Special Counsel's Office, *Report on the Investigation*, vol. 2, p. 117.

113. Remarks by President Trump before Marine One Departure, January 15, 2019, https://www.whitehouse.gov/briefings-statements/remarks-president-trump-marine-one-departure-31.

114. Transcript: ABC News' George Stephanopoulos' Exclusive Interview with President Trump, June 16, 2019, https://abcnews.go.com/Politics/transcript-abc-news-george-stephanopoulos-exclusive-interview-president/story?id=63749144.

115. *Congressional Record* (daily), April 28, 1998, H 2336, https://www.govinfo.gov/content/pkg/CREC-1998-04-28/html/CREC-1998-04-28-pt1-PgH2335-3.htm.

116. Z. Byron Wolf, "Newt Gingrich, on Book Tour, Declares Special Counsel the 'Tip of the Deep State Spear,'" CNN, June 15, 2017, https://www.cnn.com/2017/06/15/politics/newt-gingrich-bob-mueller-special-counsel-book/index.html.

117. Brett Samuels, "Amash Doubles Down on Trump and Impeachment," *The Hill*, May 20, 2019, https://thehill.com/homenews/house/444613-amash-defends-saying-trump-committed-impeachable-offenses.

118. US Department of Justice, Special Counsel's Office, *Report on The Investigation*, vol. 2, p. 8.

119. Transcript: ABC News' George Stephanopoulos' Exclusive Interview with President Trump.

120. Ashley Parker, "From 'My Generals' To 'My Kevin,' Trump's Preferred Possessive Can Be a Sign of Affection or Control," *Washington Post*, September 16, 2019, https://www.washingtonpost.com/politics/from-my-generals-to-my-kevin-trumps-preferred-possessive-can-be-a-sign-of-affection-or-control/2019/09/16/52480d22-d895-11e9-a688-303693fb4b0b_story.html.

121. Judge Paul L. Friedman, "Threats to Judicial Independence and the Rule of Law," the eleventh annual Judge Thomas A. Flannery Lecture, November 6, 2019, https://www.cnn.com/2019/11/07/politics/judge-paul-friedman-criticize-trump-speech-read/index.html.

5. A DECENT RESPECT TO THE OPINIONS OF MANKIND

1. Allen C. Guelzo, "Abe's Ticking Clock," *New York Post*, April 12, 2011, https://nypost.com/2011/04/12/abes-ticking-clock.

2. Abraham Lincoln, Second Annual Message, December 1, 1862, online by Gerhard Peters and John T. Woolley, The American Presidency Project, https://www.presidency.ucsb.edu/documents/second-annual-message-9.

3. Harry S. Truman, Address at the Ceremonies Commemorating the 175th Anniversary of the Declaration of Independence, July 4, 1951, online by Gerhard Peters and John T. Woolley, The American Presidency Project, https://www.presidency.ucsb.edu/documents/address-the-ceremonies-commemorating-the-175th-anniversary-the-declaration-independence.

4. John F. Kennedy, Inaugural Address, January 20, 1961, online by Gerhard Peters and John T. Woolley, The American Presidency Project, https://www.presidency.ucsb.edu/node/234470.

5. Barack Obama, Remarks at the University of Central Missouri in Warrensburg, Missouri, July 24, 2013, online by Gerhard Peters and John T. Woolley, The American Presidency Project, https://www.presidency.ucsb.edu/documents/remarks-the-university-central-missouri-warrensburg-missouri.

6. Barack Obama, Commencement Address at the United States Military Academy in West Point, New York, May 28, 2014, online by Gerhard Peters and John T. Woolley, The American Presidency Project, https://www.presidency.ucsb.edu/documents/commencement-address-the-united-states-military-academy-west-point-new-york-3.

7. Vladimir V. Putin, "A Plea for Caution from Russia," *New York Times*, September 11, 2013, https://www.nytimes.com/2013/09/12/opinion/putin-plea-for-caution-from-russia-on-syria.html.

8. Gingrich Gibson, "Boehner 'Insulted' by Putin Op-ed," *Politico*, September 12, 2013, https://www.politico.com/story/2013/09/john-boehner-insulted-by-putin-op-ed-096715.

9. Greta Van Susteren, "Vladimir Putin's Op-Ed on Syria; GOP House Freshmen Called to the White House on Syria; CIA Funneling Some Arms to Syrian Rebels," Fox News Network, September 12, 2013, https://advance-lexis-com.ccl.idm.oclc.org/api/document?collection=news&id=urn:contentItem:59BK-7M31-DXH2-64SG-00000-00&context=1516831.

10. Matt Twomey, "Putin Editorial Embarrasses US: Trump," CNBC, September 12, 2013, https://www.cnbc.com/id/101030907.

11. Matt Wilstein, "Donald Trump to Piers Morgan: Obama 'Can't Compete' with Putin's 'Amazing' Op-Ed," Mediaite, September 13, 2013, https://www.mediaite.com/tv/donald-trump-to-piers-morgan-obama-cant-compete-with-putins-amazing-op-ed.

12. Luke Johnson, "Mitt Romney: Russia Is 'Our Number One Geopolitical Foe," *Huffington Post*, March 26, 2012, https://www.huffpost.com/entry/mitt-romney-russia-geopolitical-foe_n_1380801.

13. David Corn, "Donald Trump Says He Doesn't Believe in 'American Exceptionalism,'" *Mother Jones*, June 7, 2016, https://www.motherjones.com/politics/2016/06/donald-trump-american-exceptionalism. Subsequent passages from the speech come from this source.

14. U.S. Congressional Budget Office, *Updated Budget Projections: 2019 to 2019*, p. 7, https://www.cbo.gov/system/files/2019-05/55151-budget_update_0.pdf.

15. "Transcript: Donald Trump on NATO, Turkey's Coup Attempt and the World," *New York Times*, July 21, 2016, https://www.nytimes.com/2016/07/22/us/politics/donald-trump-foreign-policy-interview.html.

16. Justin Fox, "Why London Has More Crime Than New York," Bloomberg, June 19, 2018, https://www.bloomberg.com/opinion/articles/2018-06-19/why-london-has-more-crime-than-new-york.

17. Freedom House, *Freedom in the World 2016*, country report on the United States, https://freedomhouse.org/report/freedom-world/2016/united-states.

18. Jeane Kirkpatrick, "The Myth of Moral Equivalence," *Imprimis*, January 1986, https://imprimis.hillsdale.edu/the-myth-of-moral-equivalence.

19. "Bill O'Reilly's Exclusive Interview with President Trump," February 7, 2017, https://www.foxnews.com/transcript/bill-oreillys-exclusive-interview-with-president-trump.

20. Donald J. Trump, Twitter post, February 28, 2016, https://twitter.com/realDonaldTrump/status/703900742961270784.

21. Donald J. Trump, Twitter post, June 18, 2013, https://twitter.com/realDonaldTrump/status/347191326112112640.

22. Jeffrey Lord, "A Trump Card," *The American Spectator*, June 20, 2014, https://spectator.org/a-trump-card.

23. Eun Kyung Kim, "Donald Trump: 'Putin Has Eaten Obama's Lunch' on Ukraine," *Today*, March 13, 2014, https://www.today.com/news/donald-trump-putin-has-eaten-obamas-lunch-ukraine-2D79372098.

24. Bradford Richardson, "Trump Calls 'Highly Respected' Putin's Comments a 'Great Honor,'" *The Hill*, December 17, 2015, https://thehill.com/blogs/blog-briefing-room/news/263660-trump-calls-highly-respected-putins-comments-a-great-honor.

25. Philip Bump, "Donald Trump Isn't Fazed by Vladimir Putin's Journalist-Murdering." *Washington Post*, December 18, 2015, https://www.washingtonpost.com/news/the-fix/wp/2015/12/18/donald-trump-glad-to-be-endorsed-by-russias-top-journalist-murderer/.

26. Transcript: NBC News Commander-In-Chief Forum, NBC News, September 7, 2016, http://press.nbcnews.com/2016/09/07/transcript-nbc-news-commander-in-chief-forum.

27. Transcript: NBC News Commander-In-Chief Forum.

28. 'This Week' Transcript: Donald Trump, Vice President Joe Biden, and Ret. Gen. John Allen," ABC News, July 31, 2016, https://abcnews.go.com/Politics/week-transcript-donald-trump-vice-president-joe-biden/story?id=41020870.

29. Margaret Talev and Toluse Olorunnipa, "Trump Leaves Door Open to U.S. Recognizing Russia's Crimea Grab," Bloomberg News, June 29, 2018, https://www.bloomberg.com/news/articles/2018-06-29/trump-leaves-door-open-to-u-s-recognizing-russia-s-crimea-grab.

30. Antonio Nardelli and Julia Ioffe, "Trump Told G7 Leaders That Crimea Is Russian because Everyone Speaks Russian in Crimea," Buzzfeed, June 14, 2018, https://www.buzzfeednews.com/article/albertonardelli/trump-russia-crimea.

31. Greg Miller, "Trump Has Concealed Details of His Face-to-Face Encounters with Putin from Senior Officials in Administration," *Washing-*

ton Post, January 13, 2019, https://www.washingtonpost.com/world/national-security/trump-has-concealed-details-of-his-face-to-face-encounters-with-putin-from-senior-officials-in-administration/2019/01/12/65f6686c-1434-11e9-b6ad-9cfd62dbb0a8_story.html.

32. Remarks by President Trump in Press Gaggle Aboard Air Force One en route Hanoi, Vietnam, November 11, 2017, https://www.whitehouse.gov/briefings-statements/remarks-president-trump-press-gaggle-aboard-air-force-one-en-route-hanoi-vietnam.

33. Carol D. Leonnig, David Nakamura, and Josh Dawsey, "Trump's National Security Advisers Warned Him Not to Congratulate Putin. He Did It Anyway," *Washington Post*, March 20, 2018, https://www.washingtonpost.com/politics/trumps-national-security-advisers-warned-him-not-to-congratulate-putin-he-did-it-anyway/2018/03/20/22738ebc-2c68-11e8-8ad6-fbc50284fce8_story.html.

34. John McCain, Twitter post, March 20, 2018, https://twitter.com/SenJohnMcCain/status/976147002244378625.

35. Remarks by President Trump and President Putin of the Russian Federation in Joint Press Conference, Helsinki, July 16, 2018, https://www.whitehouse.gov/briefings-statements/remarks-president-trump-president-putin-russian-federation-joint-press-conference.

36. Rep. Will Hurd, Twitter post, July 16, 2018, https://twitter.com/HurdOnTheHill/status/1018931248457306115.

37. Remarks by President Trump in Cabinet Meeting, January 2, 2019, https://www.whitehouse.gov/briefings-statements/remarks-president-trump-cabinet-meeting-12/.

38. "Trump's Cracked Afghan History," *Wall Street Journal*, January 3, 2019, https://www.wsj.com/articles/trumps-cracked-afghan-history-11546560234.

39. Select Committee on Intelligence, United States Senate, "Report on Russian Active Measures Campaigns and Interference in the 2016 U.S. Election, Volume 2: Russia's Use of Social Media," October 8 2019, https://www.intelligence.senate.gov/sites/default/files/documents/Report_Volume2.pdf

40. U.S. Department of Justice, Special Counsel's Office, *Report on the Investigation*, vol. I, p. 149.

41. Glenn Paskin, "The 1990 Playboy Interview with Donald Trump," *Playboy*, March 1990, https://www.playboy.com/read/playboy-interview-donald-trump-1990.

42. Speech: Donald Trump in Raleigh, NC, July 5, 2016, https://fact-ba.se/transcript/donald-trump-speech-raleigh-nc-july-5-2016.

43. Transcript of Donald Trump's December 30 speech in Hilton Head, SC, January 20, 2016, https://www.kansascity.com/news/local/news-columns-blogs/the-buzz/article55604115.html.

44. United Nations, *Report of the Commission of Inquiry on Human Rights in The Democratic People's Republic of Korea*, February 7, 2014, https://documents-dds-ny.un.org/doc/UNDOC/GEN/G14/108/66/PDF/G1410866.pdf?OpenElement.

45. Colin Campbell, "Trump: You've Got to Give That 'Maniac' in North Korea Some Credit," *Business Insider*, January 9, 2016, https://www.businessinsider.com/donald-trump-north-korea-kim-jong-un-2016-1.

46. Donald J. Trump, Twitter post, January 2, 2018, https://twitter.com/realDonaldTrump/status/948355557022420992.

47. John Wagner, "'He's a Tough Guy': Trump Downplays the Human Rights Record of Kim Jong Un," *Washington Post*, June 14, 2018, https://www.washingtonpost.com/politics/hes-a-tough-guy-trump-downplays-the-human-rights-record-of-kim-jong-un/2018/06/14/90ed487e-6fbb-11e8-bf86-a2351b5ece99_story.html.

48. Philip Rucker, "Trump Praises Kim's Authoritarian Rule, Says 'I Want My People to Do the Same,'" *Washington Post*, June 15, 2018, https://www.washingtonpost.com/pb/politics/trump-praises-kims-authoritarian-rule-says-i-want-my-people-to-do-the-same/2018/06/15/cea20aa2-70a5-11e8-bf86-a2351b5ece99_story.html.

49. Donald J. Trump, Remarks at a "Make America Great Again" Rally in Wheeling, WV, September 29, 2018, online by Gerhard Peters and John T. Woolley, The American Presidency Project, https://www.presidency.ucsb.edu/documents/remarks-make-america-great-again-rally-wheeling-west-virginia.

50. Alex Ward, "Read the Full Transcript of Trump's North Korea Summit Press Conference in Vietnam," Vox, February 28, 2019, https://www.vox.com/2019/2/28/18241334/trump-north-korea-press-conference-full-text.

51. David A. Graham, "Trump Sides with North Korea against the CIA," *The Atlantic*, June 11, 2019, https://www.theatlantic.com/ideas/archive/2019/06/trump-kim-no-north-korea-spying-under-my-auspices/591457.

52. Phelim Kine, "Killing and Lies: Philippine President Duterte's 'War on Drugs' Exposed," Human Rights Watch, March 9, 2017, https://www.hrw.org/news/2017/03/09/killing-and-lies-philippine-president-dutertes-war-drugs-exposed.

53. "Transcript of Call between President Trump and Philippine President Duterte," *Washington Post*, May 24, 2017, http://apps.washingtonpost.com/g/documents/politics/transcript-of-call-between-president-trump-and-philippine-president-duterte/2446.

54. Mynardo Macaraig and Karl Malakunas, "Outrage after Duterte Justifies Philippine Journalists' Murders," AFP, June 1, 2016, https://www.yahoo.com/news/philippines-duterte-endorses-killing-corrupt-journalists-155911848.html.

55. Remarks by President Trump and President Duterte of the Philippines before Bilateral Meeting, Manila, Philippines, November 13, 2017, https://www.whitehouse.gov/briefings-statements/remarks-president-trump-president-duterte-philippines-bilateral-meeting-manila-philippines.

56. Donald J. Trump, Remarks Prior to a Meeting with President Abdelfattah Said Elsisi of Egypt, April 3, 2017, online by Gerhard Peters and John T. Woolley, The American Presidency Project, https://www.presidency.ucsb.edu/node/326548

57. Nancy A. Youssef, Vivian Salama, and Michael C. Bender, "Trump, Awaiting Egyptian Counterpart at Summit, Called Out for 'My Favorite Dictator,'" *Wall Street Journal*, September 13, 2019, https://www.wsj.com/articles/trump-awaiting-egyptian-counterpart-at-summit-called-out-for-my-favorite-dictator-11568403645.

58. Donald J. Trump, Remarks Prior to a Meeting with President Recep Tayyip Erdogan of Turkey and an Exchange with Reporters in New York City, September 21, 2017, online by Gerhard Peters and John T. Woolley, The American Presidency Project, https://www.presidency.ucsb.edu/node/331313.

59. Remarks by President Trump upon Arrival of Air Force One, Fort Worth, Texas, October 17, 2019, https://www.whitehouse.gov/briefings-statements/remarks-president-trump-upon-arrival-air-force-one-fort-worth-tx/.

60. Donald J. Trump, Twitter post, October 18, 2019, https://twitter.com/realDonaldTrump/status/1185219641972539392?s=20.

61. Josh Dawsey, "In Post Interview, Trump Calls Saudi Crown Prince Mohammed a 'Strong Person' Who 'Truly Loves His Country,'" *Washing-*

ton Post, https://www.washingtonpost.com/politics/in-post-interview-trump-calls-saudi-crown-prince-mohammed-a-strong-person-who-truly-loves-his-country/2018/10/20/1eda48c0-d4d5-11e8-b2d2-f397227b43f0_story.html.

62. Statement from President Donald J. Trump on Standing with Saudi Arabia, November 20, 2018, https://www.whitehouse.gov/briefings-statements/statement-president-donald-j-trump-standing-saudi-arabia.

63. "Highlights: Key Quotes from the Reuters Interview with Trump," Reuters, December 11, 2018, https://www.reuters.com/article/us-usa-trump-highlights/highlights-key-quotes-from-the-reuters-interview-with-trump-idUSKBN1OB075.

64. Manu Raju and Ted Barrett, "Senate Set to Rebuke White House's Handling of Saudi Arabia after Khashoggi Murder," CNN, December 6, 2018, https://www.cnn.com/2018/12/06/politics/congress-khashoggi-yemen-saudi-arabia-reaction/index.html.

65. Luke Baker, "With Trump Sitting Nearby, Macron Calls Nationalism a Betrayal," Reuters, November 11, 2018, https://www.reuters.com/article/us-ww1-centenary-macron-nationalism/with-trump-sitting-nearby-macron-calls-nationalism-a-betrayal-idUSKCN1NG0IH.

66. Speech: Donald Trump in Mobile, Alabama, August 21, 2015, https://factba.se/transcript/donald-trump-speech-mobile-al-august-21-2015.

67. David A. Fahrenthold and Jonathan O'Connell, "'I Like Them Very Much:' Trump Has Long-Standing Business Ties with Saudis, Who Have Boosted His Hotels since He Took Office," *Washington Post*, October 11, 2018, https://www.washingtonpost.com/politics/i-like-them-very-much-trump-has-long-standing-business-ties-with-saudis-who-have-boosted-his-hotels-since-he-took-office/2018/10/11/0870df24-cd67-11e8-a360-85875bac0b1f_story.html.

68. David A. Fahrenthold and Jonathan O'Connell, "Saudi-Funded Lobbyist Paid for 500 Rooms at Trump's Hotel after 2016 Election," *Washington Post*, December 5, 2018, https://www.washingtonpost.com/politics/saudi-funded-lobbyist-paid-for-500-rooms-at-trumps-hotel-after-2016-election/2018/12/05/29603a64-f417-11e8-bc79-68604ed88993_story.html.

69. David A. Fahrenthold, Jonathan O'Connell, and Morgan Krakow, "At Trump's Big-City Hotels, Business Dropped as His Political Star Rose, Internal Documents Show," *Washington Post*, https://

www.washingtonpost.com/politics/at-trumps-big-city-hotels-business-dropped-as-his-political-star-rose-internal-documents-show/2018/10/03/bd26b1d6-b6d4-11e8-a7b5-adaaa5b2a57f_story.html.

70. Shelby Hanssen and Ken Dilanian, "Reps of 22 Foreign Governments Have Spent Money at Trump Properties," NBC News, June 12, 2019, https://www.nbcnews.com/politics/donald-trump/reps-22-foreign-governments-have-spent-money-trump-properties-n1015806.

71. Antonio Development, "Trump Tower Philippines," http://antonio-development.com/trump-tower.html.

72. Richard C. Paddock et al., "Potential Conflicts around the Globe for Trump, the Businessman President," *New York Times*, November 26, 2016, https://www.nytimes.com/2016/11/26/us/politics/donald-trump-international-business.html.

73. The Trump Organization, "Trump Towers: Istanbul, Turkey," https://www.trump.com/residential-real-estate-portfolio/trump-towers-istanbul-turkey.

74. Ivanka Trump, Twitter post, April 20, 2012, https://twitter.com/IvankaTrump/status/193337302066540545.

75. Ashley Dejean, "Donald Trump Has a Conflict of Interest in Turkey. Just Ask Donald Trump," *Mother Jones*, April 18, 2017, https://www.motherjones.com/politics/2017/04/trump-turkey-erdogan-conflict-interest.

76. Joshua Partlow, David A. Fahrenthold, and Taylor Luck, "A Wealthy Iraqi Sheikh Who Urges a Hard-Line U.S. Approach to Iran Spent 26 Nights at Trump's D.C. Hotel," *Washington Post*, June 6, 2019, https://www.washingtonpost.com/politics/a-wealthy-iraqi-sheikh-who-urges-a-hard-line-us-approach-to-iran-spent-26-nights-at-trumps-dc-hotel/2019/06/06/3ea74c5e-7bf9-11e9-a66c-d36e482aa873_story.html.

77. The Constitutional Accountability Center provides relevant documents and a useful timeline at https://www.theusconstitution.org/litigation/trump-and-foreign-emoluments-clause.

78. Alexander Hamilton, *Federalist 73*, https://avalon.law.yale.edu/18th_century/fed73.asp.

79. Damian Paletta, "Trump's 'Take the Oil' Plan Would Violate Geneva Conventions, Experts Say," *Wall Street Journal*, September 8, 2016, https://blogs.wsj.com/washwire/2016/09/08/trumps-take-the-oil-plan-would-violate-geneva-conventions-experts-say/.

80. Donald J. Trump, Twitter post, December 21, 2011, https://twitter.com/realDonaldTrump/status/149554857991352320.

81. Donald J. Trump, Twitter post, January 23, 2013, https://twitter.com/realDonaldTrump/status/294161251137884160.

82. Donald J. Trump, Remarks at the Central Intelligence Agency in Langley, Virginia, January 21, 2017, online by Gerhard Peters and John T. Woolley, The American Presidency Project, https://www.presidency.ucsb.edu/documents/remarks-the-central-intelligence-agency-langley-virginia-2.

83. Jonathan Swan and Alayna Treene, "Trump to Iraqi PM: How about That Oil?" Axios, November 25, 2018, https://www.axios.com/trump-to-iraqi-pm-how-about-that-oil-1a31cbfa-f20c-4767-8d18-d518ed9a6543.html.

84. Donald J. Trump, Twitter post, June 4, 2017, https://twitter.com/realDonaldTrump/status/871328428963901440.

85. Donald J. Trump, Twitter post, June 2, 2017, https://twitter.com/realDonaldTrump/status/1135453895277203458.

86. Remarks by President Trump at the Conservative Political Action Conference, February 24, 2017, https://www.whitehouse.gov/briefings-statements/remarks-president-trump-conservative-political-action-conference.

87. Josh Dawsey, Damian Paletta, and Erica Werner, "In Fundraising Speech, Trump Says He Made Up Trade Claim in Meeting with Justin Trudeau," *Washington Post*, March 15, 2018, https://www.washingtonpost.com/news/post-politics/wp/2018/03/14/in-fundraising-speech-trump-says-he-made-up-facts-in-meeting-with-justin-trudeau.

88. Zoya Sheftalovich, "Donald Trump: 'Belgium Is a Beautiful City,'" *Politico*, June 16, 2016, https://www.politico.eu/article/donald-trump-belgium-is-a-beautiful-city-hellhole-us-presidential-election-2016-america.

89. Remarks by President Trump to Troops at Al Asad Air Base, Al Anbar Province, Iraq, December 26, 2018, https://www.whitehouse.gov/briefings-statements/remarks-president-trump-troops-al-asad-air-base-al-anbar-province-iraq.

90. Donald J. Trump, Twitter post, May 25, 2019, https://twitter.com/realDonaldTrump/status/1132459370816708608.

91. Donald J. Trump, Twitter post, May 25, 2019, https://twitter.com/realDonaldTrump/status/1132506111884636160.

92. Brooke Singman, "Fox News Exclusive: Trump Says Mueller Made a 'Fool' of Himself," Fox News, June 6, 2019, https://www.foxnews.com/politics/fox-news-exclusive-trump-says-mueller-made-a-fool-of-himself.

93. Jason Schwartz, "Trump's 'Fake News' Mantra a Hit with Despots," *Politico*, December 8, 2017, https://www.politico.com/story/2017/12/08/trump-fake-news-despots-287129.

94. "Video: PM Orbán Calls Index, Leading Hungarian Portal, A 'Fake News' Factory," XpatLoop, June 8, 2018, https://www.xpatloop.com/channels/2018/06/video-pm-orban-calls-index-the-leading-hungarian-portal-a-fake-news-factory.html.

95. Zoltan Simon, "Trump Compared Orban to a Twin Brother, Ambassador Says," Bloomberg, May 15, 2019, https://www.bloomberg.com/news/articles/2019-05-15/trump-compared-orban-to-a-twin-brother-envoy-tells-444-hu.

96. Julie Ray, "Image of U.S. Leadership Now Poorer Than China's," Gallup, February 28, 2019, https://news.gallup.com/poll/247037/image-leadership-poorer-china.aspx.

97. Richard Wike et al., "Trump's International Ratings Remain Low, Especially among Key Allies," Pew Research Center, October 1, 2018, https://www.pewresearch.org/global/2018/10/01/trumps-international-ratings-remain-low-especially-among-key-allies.

98. Eric Parajon, Susan Peterson, Ryan Powers, and Michael J. Tierney, "Snap Poll: What Experts Make of Trump's Foreign Policy," *Foreign Policy*, December 7, 2018, https://foreignpolicy.com/2018/12/07/snap-poll-experts-trump-foreign-policy.

99. Dina Smeltz et al., "America Engaged," Chicago Council on Global Affairs, October 2, 2018, https://www.thechicagocouncil.org/publication/america-engaged.

100. Jordan Fabian, "UN Audience Laughs When Trump Boasts of Achievements," *The Hill*, September 25, 2018, https://thehill.com/homenews/administration/408260-un-audience-laughs-when-trump-boasts-of-achievements.

101. Memorandum of Telephone Conversation with President Zelenskyy of Ukraine, July 25, 2019, https://www.whitehouse.gov/wp-content/uploads/2019/09/Unclassified09.2019.pdf

102. Jim Zarroli, "Trump Used to Disparage an Anti-Bribery Law; Will He Enforce It Now?" National Public Radio, November 8, 2017, https://www.npr.org/templates/transcript/transcript.php?storyId=561059555.

103. Remarks by President Trump Before Marine One Departure, October 4, 2019, https://www.whitehouse.gov/briefings-statements/remarks-president-trump-marine-one-departure-68/.

104. Deposition of William B. Taylor, House Permanent Select Committee on Intelligence, October 22, 2019, https://docs.house.gov/meetings/IG/IG00/CPRT-116-IG00-D008.pdf.

105. Sabra Ayres and Sergei L. Loiko, "Trump Froze Military Aid—As Ukrainian Soldiers Perished in Battle," *Los Angeles Times*, October 16, 2019, https://www.latimes.com/world-nation/story/2019-10-16/as-ukraine-waited-for-u-s-assistance-death-toll-on-eastern-front-line-grew.

106. Remarks by President Trump and President Zelensky of Ukraine before Bilateral Meeting | New York, September 25, 2019, https://www.whitehouse.gov/briefings-statements/remarks-president-trump-president-zelensky-ukraine-bilateral-meeting-new-york-ny/.

107. Press Briefing by Acting Chief of Staff Mick Mulvaney, October 17, 2019, https://www.whitehouse.gov/briefings-statements/press-briefing-acting-chief-staff-mick-mulvaney/.

6. OUR LIVES, OUR FORTUNES,
AND OUR SACRED HONOR

1. James Madison, *Federalist 51*, https://avalon.law.yale.edu/18th_century/fed51.asp.

2. George Washington, Farewell Address, September 19, 1796, online by Gerhard Peters and John T. Woolley, The American Presidency Project, https://www.presidency.ucsb.edu/documents/farewell-address.

3. From John Adams to Massachusetts Militia, October 11, 1798, https://founders.archives.gov/documents/Adams/99-02-02-3102.

4. James Madison, Virginia Ratifying Convention, June 20, 1788, http://press-pubs.uchicago.edu/founders/documents/v1ch13s36.html.

5. James Madison, *Federalist 55*, https://avalon.law.yale.edu/18th_century/fed55.asp.

6. James Q. Wilson, *The Moral Sense* (New York: Free Press, 1993).

7. Robert A. Heinlein, "Our Noble, Essential Decency," 1952, https://thisibelieve.org/essay/16630.

8. Alexander Hamilton, *Federalist 68*, https://avalon.law.yale.edu/18th_century/fed68.asp.

9. From George Washington to Catharine Sawbridge Macaulay Graham, January 9, 1790, https://founders.archives.gov/documents/Washington/05-04-02-0363.

10. Eliana Johnson and Daniel Lippman, "Trump's 'Truly Bizarre' Visit to Mt. Vernon," *Politico*, April 10, 2019, https://www.politico.com/story/2019/04/10/donald-trump-mount-vernon-george-washington-1264073.

11. Khizr Khan, speech to Democratic National Convention, Philadelphia, July 28, 2016, https://abcnews.go.com/Politics/full-text-khizr-khans-speech-2016-democratic-national/story?id=41043609.

12. Chris Cillizza, "Donald Trump's ABC Interview May Be His Best/Worst Yet," *Washington Post*, August 1, 2016, https://www.washingtonpost.com/news/the-fix/wp/2016/08/01/donald-trumps-abc-interview-may-be-his-bestworst-yet.

13. House Oversight, *Hearing with Michael Cohen*, 19.

14. Steve Reilly, "USA Today Exclusive: Hundreds Allege Donald Trump Doesn't Pay His Bills," *USA Today*, June 9, 2016, https://www.usatoday.com/story/news/politics/elections/2016/06/09/donald-trump-unpaid-bills-republican-president-laswuits/85297274.

15. Russ Buettner and Charles V. Bagli, "How Donald Trump Bankrupted His Atlantic City Casinos, but Still Earned Millions," *New York Times*, June 11, 2016, https://www.nytimes.com/2016/06/12/nyregion/donald-trump-atlantic-city.html.

16. "Annotated Transcript: The Aug. 6 GOP Debate," *Washington Post*, August 6, 2015, https://www.washingtonpost.com/news/post-politics/wp/2015/08/06/annotated-transcript-the-aug-6-gop-debate.

17. Reuben Kramer and Christian Hetrick, "Donald Trump in Atlantic City: Jackpot or crackpot?" *The Press of Atlantic City*, February 10, 2016, https://www.pressofatlanticcity.com/news/donald-trump-in-atlantic-city-jackpot-or-crackpot/article_7ae16c2c-3d14-11e5-aa3b-5b415c6c45e9.html.

18. Timothy Bella, "'And Now It's the Tallest': Trump, in Otherwise Somber Interview on 9/11, Couldn't Help Touting One of His Buildings," *Washington Post*, September 11, 2018, https://www.washingtonpost.com/news/morning-mix/wp/2018/09/11/and-now-its-the-tallest-trump-in-otherwise-somber-9-11-interview-couldnt-help-touting-one-of-his-buildings.

19. Philip Bump, "On 9/11, Trump Pointed Out He Now Had the Tallest Building in Lower Manhattan. He Didn't," *Washington Post*, Septem-

ber 11, 2018, https://www.washingtonpost.com/politics/2018/09/11/trump-pointed-out-that-he-now-had-tallest-building-lower-manhattan-he-didnt.

20. Ross Buettner, "Feds Gave Donald a Quick Bundle," *New York Daily News*, January 29, 2006, https://www.nydailynews.com/archives/news/feds-gave-donald-quick-bundle-titans-9-11-funds-set-small-biz-article-1.558429.

21. Cameron Joseph, "Donald Trump's Claim He Got $150G in Post-9/11 State Funds for Small Businesses Because He Helped People in Need Is Unfounded, Docs Show," *New York Daily News*, September 10, 2016, https://www.nydailynews.com/news/politics/exclusive-trump-didn-post-9-11-funds-helping-people-article-1.2786879.

22. David Boaz, "Donald Trump's Eminent Domain Love Nearly Cost a Widow Her House," *The Guardian*, August 19, 2015, https://www.theguardian.com/commentisfree/2015/aug/19/donald-trumps-eminent-domain-nearly-cost-widow-house.

23. Larry Kudlow, "*Kelo* Was Un-American," *National Review*, July 28, 2006, https://www.nationalreview.com/kudlows-money-politics/kelo-was-un-american-larry-kudlow.

24. Nick Penzenstadler, "Elderly Trump University Plaintiffs Die Waiting for Checks," *USA Today*, May 26, 2017, https://www.usatoday.com/story/news/2017/05/26/elderly-trump-university-plaintiffs-die-waiting-checks/102193734.

25. Commission on Presidential Debates, September 26, 2016, Debate Transcript, https://debates.org/voter-education/debate-transcripts/september-26-2016-debate-transcript/.

26. House Oversight, *Hearing with Michael Cohen*, 14.

27. David Barstow, Susanne Craig, and Russ Buettner, "Trump Engaged in Suspect Tax Schemes as He Reaped Riches from His Father," *New York Times*, October 2, 2018, https://www.nytimes.com/interactive/2018/10/02/us/politics/donald-trump-tax-schemes-fred-trump.html.

28. US Attorney's Office for the Southern District of New York, sentencing memorandum in *United States of America v. Michael Cohen*.

29. Russ Buettner and Susanne Craig, "As the Trumps Dodged Taxes, Their Tenants Paid a Price," *New York Times*, December 15, 2018, https://www.nytimes.com/2018/12/15/us/politics/trump-tenants-taxes.html.

30. "Presidential Profiteering: Trump's Conflicts Got Worse in Year Two," Citizens for Responsibility and Ethics in Washington, January 17,

2019, https://www.citizensforethics.org/presidential-profiteering-trumps-conflicts-got-worse.

31. Reid Wilson, "Republicans Spend More Than $4 Million at Trump Properties," *The Hill*, May 24, 2019, https://thehill.com/homenews/campaign/445307-republicans-spend-more-than-4-million-at-trump-properties.

32. Brad Heath, "Trump Picks Golf Club, Mar-a-Lago Members as Ambassadors," *USA Today*, February 8, 2019, https://www.usatoday.com/story/news/investigations/2019/02/08/donald-trump-picks-ambassadors-golf-club-mar-lago-members/2748260002.

33. Richard Luscombe, "'Pay-for-Access to Trump Club': Mar-a-Lago Faces Renewed Ethics Concerns," *The Guardian*, March 16, 2019, https://www.theguardian.com/us-news/2019/mar/16/mar-a-lago-trump-season-end-controversy-ethics-concerns.

34. Representative Mark A. Takano, letter to Secretary Robert Wilkie, February 8, 2019, https://www.documentcloud.org/documents/5732493-2019-02-08-Letter-Fr-Chairman-Takano-to-VA-Sec.html.

35. Remarks by President Trump and Prime Minister Varadkar of Ireland before Bilateral Meeting, Shannon, Ireland, June 5, 2019, https://www.whitehouse.gov/briefings-statements/remarks-president-trump-prime-minister-varadkar-ireland-bilateral-meeting-shannon-ireland.

36. Alexander Hamilton, *Federalist 72*, https://avalon.law.yale.edu/18th_century/fed72.asp.

37. Michael D. Shear and Eileen Sullivan, "'Horseface,' 'Lowlife,' 'Fat, Ugly': How the President Demeans Women," *New York Times*, October 16, 2018, https://www.nytimes.com/2018/10/16/us/politics/trump-women-insults.html.

38. "Trump on Accuser: She Would Not Be My First Choice." CNN, October 14, 2016, https://www.cnn.com/videos/politics/2016/10/14/donald-trump-on-accuser-she-not-my-first-choice-sot.cnn.

39. Jordan Fabian and Saagar Enjeti, "Trump Vehemently Denies E. Jean Carroll Allegation, Says 'She's Not My Type,'" *The Hill*, June 24, 2019, https://thehill.com/homenews/administration/450116-trump-vehemently-denies-e-jean-carroll-allegation-shes-not-my-type.

40. Marlow Stern, "The Time Donald Trump Turned Away in Disgust While a Man Was Bleeding to Death in Front of Him," *The Daily Beast*, September 28, 2017, https://www.thedailybeast.com/the-time-donald-trump-turned-away-in-disgust-while-a-man-bled-to-death-in-front-of-him.

41. Gabriel Sherman, "Final Days," *New York*, October 29, 2016, http://nymag.com/intelligencer/2016/10/trump-campaign-final-days.html.

42. Brian Kilmeade, "President Donald Trump on Tax Reform: We're the Highest Taxed Nation in the World, We Need the Tax Cuts," Fox Radio News, October 17, 2017, https://radio.foxnews.com/2017/10/17/president-donald-trump-on-tax-reform-were-the-highest-tax-nation-in-the-world-we-need-the-tax-cuts.

43. John M. Donnelly, "Pentagon Document Contradicts Trump's Gold Star Claims," *Roll Call*, October 20, 2017, https://www.rollcall.com/news/politics/after-trump-claim-white-house-still-lacked-casualty-list.

44. Betsy Klein, "Trump's Note Card for Parkland Shooting Discussion: 'I Hear You,'" CNN, February 21, 2018, https://www.cnn.com/2018/02/21/politics/trump-parkland-notecard/index.html.

45. Charities Aid Foundation, *CAF World Giving Index 2018*, October 2018, https://www.cafonline.org/docs/default-source/about-us-publications/caf_wgi2018_report_webnopw_2379a_261018.pdf.

46. Marc Fisher, "'Grab That Record': How Trump's High School Transcript Was Hidden," *Washington Post*, March 5, 2019, https://www.washingtonpost.com/politics/grab-that-record-how-trumps-high-school-transcript-was-hidden/2019/03/05/8815b7b8-3c61-11e9-aaae-69364b2ed137_story.html.

47. David A. Farenthold, "Trump Boasts about His Philanthropy. But His Giving Falls Short of His Words," October 29, 2016, *Washington Post*, https://www.washingtonpost.com/politics/trump-boasts-of-his-philanthropy-but-his-giving-falls-short-of-his-words/2016/10/29/b3c03106-9ac7-11e6-a0ed-ab0774c1eaa5_story.html.

48. David A. Fahrenthold and Rosalind S. Helderman, "Missing from Trump's List of Charitable Giving: His Own Personal Cash." *Washington Post*, April 10, 2016, https://www.washingtonpost.com/politics/a-portrait-of-trump-the-donor-free-rounds-of-golf-but-no-personal-cash/2016/04/10/373b9b92-fb40-11e5-9140-e61d062438bb_story.html.

49. Farenthold, "Trump Boasts about His Philanthropy."

50. David A. Farenthold, "This Is the Portrait of Donald Trump That His Charity Bought for $20,000," *Washington Post*, November 1, 2016, https://www.washingtonpost.com/news/post-politics/wp/2016/11/01/this-is-the-portrait-of-himself-that-donald-trump-bought-with-20000-from-his-charity.

51. "A.G. Underwood Announces Stipulation Dissolving Trump Foundation under Judicial Supervision, with AG Review of Recipient Charities," December 18, 2018, https://ag.ny.gov/press-release/ag-underwood-announces-stipulation-dissolving-trump-foundation-under-judicial.

52. Dan Alexander, "How Donald Trump Shifted Kids-Cancer Charity Money into His Business," *Forbes*, June 6, 2017, https://www.forbes.com/sites/danalexander/2017/06/06/how-donald-trump-shifted-kids-cancer-charity-money-into-his-business.

53. David A. Farenthold, "Trump Boasts about His Philanthropy. But His Giving Falls Short of His Words," *Washington Post*, October 29, 2016, https://www.washingtonpost.com/politics/trump-boasts-of-his-philanthropy-but-his-giving-falls-short-of-his-words/2016/10/29/b3c03106-9ac7-11e6-a0ed-ab0774c1eaa5_story.html.

54. Remarks by President Trump in Briefing on Hurricane Maria Relief Efforts, October 3, 2017, https://www.whitehouse.gov/briefings-statements/remarks-president-trump-briefing-hurricane-maria-relief-efforts.

55. Peter Baker, "As a New Hurricane Roars In, Trump Quarrels over the Last One," *New York Times*, September 13, 2018, https://www.nytimes.com/2018/09/13/us/politics/trump-denies-puerto-rico-death-roll.html.

56. Donald J. Trump, Twitter post, April 2, 2019, https://twitter.com/realDonaldTrump/status/1113041708730802176.

57. Donald J. Trump, Twitter post, April 2, 2019, https://twitter.com/realdonaldtrump/status/1113044765405315073.

58. "Sessions Says He Hopes Child Separation Policy Will Serve as a Deterrent," Axios, June 18, 2018, https://www.axios.com/sessions-says-he-hopes-child-separation-policy-will-serve-as-a-deterrent-e1b7d3b2-60ef-4099-a3d2-2c3ce986dca3.html.

59. John Burnett, "Transcript: White House Chief of Staff John Kelly's Interview with NPR," National Public Radio, May 11, 2018, https://www.npr.org/2018/05/11/610116389/transcript-white-house-chief-of-staff-john-kellys-interview-with-npr.

60. Remarks by President Trump at a Meeting with the National Space Council and Signing of Space Policy Directive-3, June 18, 2018, https://www.whitehouse.gov/briefings-statements/remarks-president-trump-meeting-national-space-council-signing-space-policy-directive-3.

61. Hamilton, *Federalist 72*.

62. Aaron Blake, "Trump Says 'Nobody Disobeys My Orders.' Here Are 15 Recorded Instances of Exactly That," *Washington Post*, April 22, 2019, https://www.washingtonpost.com/politics/2019/04/22/trump-says-nobody-disobeys-my-orders-heres-how-wrong-he-is.

63. Dennis F. Thompson, "Constitutional Character: Virtues and Vices in Presidential Leadership," *Presidential Studies Quarterly* 40 (March 2010): 23–37.

64. Itay Hod, "Note to Rudy Giuliani: Trump Appeared in 3 Playboy Videos," *The Wrap*, June 7, 2018, https://www.thewrap.com/note-rudy-giuliani-trump-appeared-3-soft-core-porn-videos.

65. "Transcript: Donald Trump's Taped Comments about Women," October 8, 2016, https://www.nytimes.com/2016/10/08/us/donald-trump-tape-transcript.html.

66. Alyssa Fisher, "Ivanka Talks about Her Father Admitting He Was in Massive Debt in Old Clip," *Forward*, May 9, 2019, https://forward.com/fast-forward/424037/ivanka-trump-president-trump-samantha-bee-debt.

67. David Enrich, "Deutsche Bank Staff Saw Suspicious Activity in Trump and Kushner Accounts," *New York Times*, May 19, 2019, https://www.nytimes.com/2019/05/19/business/deutsche-bank-trump-kushner.html.

68. National Counterintelligence and Security Center, "Fiscal Year 2017 Annual Report on Security Clearance Determinations," August 27, 2018, p. 10, at https://www.dni.gov/files/NCSC/documents/features/20180827-security-clearance-determinations.pdf.

69. Donald J. Trump, Twitter post, August 12, 2016, https://twitter.com/realDonaldTrump/status/764147591114137600.

70. Byron York, "Donald Trump's Most Casually Broken Promise," *Washington Examiner*, March 5, 2018, https://www.washingtonexaminer.com/byron-york-donald-trumps-most-casually-broken-promise.

71. "Donald Trump Visited the Golf Course for the 198th Time as President," Golf News Net, June 16, 2019, https://thegolfnewsnet.com/golfnewsnetteam/2019/06/16/donald-trump-visited-the-golf-course-for-the-198th-time-as-president-115134.

72. Harriett Sinclair, "Trump Has Visited Golf Clubs on 237 Days of His Presidency," *Newsweek*, November 8, 2019, https://www.newsweek.com/trump-has-visited-golf-clubs-237-days-his-presidencythats-23-percent-days-hes-been-office-1470392.

73. Alexi McCammond and Jonathan Swan, "Scoop: Insider Leaks Trump's 'Executive Time'-Filled Private Schedules," Axios, February 3, 2019, https://www.axios.com/donald-trump-private-schedules-leak-executive-time-34e67fbb-3af6-48df-aefb-52e02c334255.html.

74. Elyse Perlmutter-Gumbiner, Ken Dilanian, and Courtney Kube, "On Trump's Calendar, Just 17 Intelligence Briefings in 85 Days," NBC News, February 6, 2019, https://www.nbcnews.com/politics/national-security/trump-s-calendar-just-17-intelligence-briefings-85-days-n967386.

75. Donald J. Trump, Twitter post, January 30, 2019, https://twitter.com/realDonaldTrump/status/1090609577006112769.

76. Perlmutter-Gumbiner, "On Trump's Calendar."

77. This discussion follows the outline of Thompson, "Constitutional Character."

78. Donald J. Trump, Twitter post, June 15, 2019, https://twitter.com/realDonaldTrump/status/1140065300186128384.

79. David E. Sanger and Nicole Perlroth, "U.S. Escalates Online Attacks on Russia's Power Grid," *New York Times*, June 15, 2019, https://www.nytimes.com/2019/06/15/us/politics/trump-cyber-russia-grid.html.

80. Remarks by President Trump before Marine One Departure, June 18, 2019, https://www.whitehouse.gov/briefings-statements/remarks-president-trump-marine-one-departure-48.

81. John F. Kennedy, "The President's News Conference, April 21, 1961," online by Gerhard Peters and John T. Woolley, The American Presidency Project, https://www.presidency.ucsb.edu/documents/the-presidents-news-conference-213 .

82. Fox News: Interview with *Fox & Friends* and Donald Trump, February 27, 2017, https://factba.se/transcript/donald-trump-interview-fox-friends-february-27-2017.

83. NBC News, *Meet the Press* transcript, June 23, 2019, https://www.nbcnews.com/meet-the-press/meet-press-6-23-n1020766.

84. Remarks by President Trump before Marine One Departure, January 10, 2019, https://www.whitehouse.gov/briefings-statements/remarks-president-trump-marine-one-departure-30.

85. Donald J. Trump, Remarks at the National Scout Jamboree in Glen Jean, West Virginia, July 24, 2017, online by Gerhard Peters and John T. Woolley, The American Presidency Project, https://www.presidency.ucsb.edu/documents/remarks-the-national-scout-jamboree-glen-jean-west-virginia.

86. Remarks by President Trump and Vice President Pence Announcing the Missile Defense Review, January 17, 2019, https://www.whitehouse.gov/briefings-statements/remarks-president-trump-vice-president-pence-announcing-missile-defense-review.

87. Laura Meckler, "McCain Asks Supporters to Show Obama Respect," *Wall Street Journal*, October 12, 2008, https://www.wsj.com/articles/SB122368132195924869.

88. Donald J. Trump, Twitter post, May 30, 2012, https://twitter.com/realdonaldtrump/status/207917815779430401.

89. Ben Schreckinger, "Trump Attacks McCain: 'I Like People Who Weren't Captured,'" *Politico*, July 19, 2015, https://www.politico.com/story/2015/07/trump-attacks-mccain-i-like-people-who-werent-captured-120317.

90. Lindsey Graham, Twitter post, July 18, 2015, https://twitter.com/LindseyGrahamSC/status/622455743917215744.

91. Lindsey Graham, Twitter post, July 18, 2015, https://twitter.com/LindseyGrahamSC/status/622457428676886528.

92. Donald J. Trump, Twitter post, March 16, 2019, https://twitter.com/realDonaldTrump/status/1107020360803909632.

93. Donald J. Trump, Twitter post, March 17, 2019, https://twitter.com/realDonaldTrump/status/1107260609974943745.

94. "Trump Talks the Fed, McCain in Exclusive Interview with Maria Bartiromo," Fox Business, March 22, 2019, https://youtu.be/1Bwa5ffuTSs.

95. Lyndon B. Johnson, Address to the Nation Following the Attack on Senator Kennedy, June 5, 1968, online by Gerhard Peters and John T. Woolley, The American Presidency Project https://www.presidency.ucsb.edu/documents/address-the-nation-following-the-attack-senator-kennedy.

96. Lesley Stahl, "John McCain: The Fighter," CBS News, September 24, 2017, https://www.cbsnews.com/news/john-mccain-fights-back-60-minutes.

97. Alexander Hamilton, *Federalist 76*, https://avalon.law.yale.edu/18th_century/fed76.asp.

98. Jonathan Swan, Juliet Bartz, Alayna Treene, and Orion Rummler, "Exclusive: Leaked Trump Vetting Docs," Axios, June 24, 2019, https://www.axios.com/leaked-donald-trump-vetting-docs-hbo-6ce3cd26-1eb9-4da8-b15e-47b56020aef7.html.

99. Jeanna Smialek, "Trump Redoubles Attacks on Fed Chair, Saying 'I Made Him,'" *New York Times*, June 26, 2019, https://www.nytimes.com/2019/06/26/business/jerome-powell-donald-trump.html.

100. Lynne Patton, Facebook Post, May 22, 2019, https://www.facebook.com/photo.php?fbid=10157427430547904&set=a.10150210631677904&type=3&theater.

101. Lynne Patton, Twitter post, May 26, 2019, https://twitter.com/LynnePatton/status/1132800358269444097.

102. Brett Samuels, "Kellyanne Conway Dismisses Hatch Act Violation: 'Let Me Know When the Jail Sentence Starts,'" *The Hill*, May 29, 2019, https://thehill.com/homenews/administration/445914-kellyanne-conway-dismisses-hatch-act-violation-let-me-know-when-the.

103. US Office of Special Counsel, cover letter, "Report of Prohibited Political Activity under the Hatch Act," June 13, 2019, https://assets.documentcloud.org/documents/6152218/Report-to-the-President-Re-Kellyanne-Conway.pdf.

104. Michelle Ye Hee Lee, Lisa Rein, and Josh Dawsey, "Federal Watchdog Agency Recommends Removal of Kellyanne Conway from Federal Office for Violating the Hatch Act," *Washington Post*, June 13, 2019, https://www.washingtonpost.com/politics/office-of-special-counsel-recommends-removal-of-kellyanne-conway-from-federal-office-for-violating-the-hatch-act/2019/06/13/0786ae2e-8df4-11e9-8f69-a2795fca3343_story.html.

105. Michael Gerson, "An Administration without a Conscience," *Washington Post*, July 13, 2017, https://www.washingtonpost.com/opinions/in-trumps-world-innocence-is-proved-by-guilt/2017/07/13/07e69a82-67ea-11e7-8eb5-cbccc2e7bfbf_story.html.

7. NEW GUARDS FOR THEIR FUTURE SECURITY

1. "Import Duties," IGM Forum, October 4, 2016, http://www.igmchicago.org/surveys/import-duties.

2. Michael R. Pompeo, "Remarks at the Claremont Institute 40th Anniversary Gala: 'A Foreign Policy from the Founding,'" May 11, 2019, https://www.state.gov/remarks-at-the-claremont-institute-40th-anniversary-gala-a-foreign-policy-from-the-founding.

3. David Farenthold, Josh Dawsey, Jonathan O'Connell, and Michelle Ye Hee Lee, "When Trump Visits His Clubs, Government Agencies and Republicans Pay to Be Where He Is," *Washington Post*, June 20, 2019, https://www.washingtonpost.com/politics/when-trump-visits-his-clubs-government-agencies-and-republicans-pay-to-be-where-he-is/2019/06/20/a4c13c36-8ed0-11e9-adf3-f70f78c156e8_story.html.

4. Trump and Schwartz, *The Art of the Deal*, 1.

5. Asawin Suebsaeng and Lachlan Markay, "Trump on Coming Debt Crisis: 'I Won't Be Here' When It Blows Up," *The Daily Beast*, December 5, 2018, https://www.thedailybeast.com/trump-on-coming-debt-crisis-i-wont-be-here-when-it-blows-up.

6. Washington, Farewell Address.

7. George Bush, Address on Administration Goals before a Joint Session of Congress, February 9, 1989, online by Gerhard Peters and John T. Woolley, The American Presidency Project, https://www.presidency.ucsb.edu/documents/address-administration-goals-before-joint-session-congress.

8. US Department of Justice, Special Counsel's Office, *Report on the Investigation*, 72.

9. Brad Parscale, Twitter post, April 20, 2019, https://twitter.com/parscale/status/1123212317376811009.

10. "MTV/AP-NORC Youth Political Pulse, March 2018: Young Americans' Political Outlook and Perspectives on the Trump Presidency," March 30, 2018, http://www.apnorc.org/PDFs/MTV%20Wave%201/MTV_AP-NORC%20Youth%20Political%20Poll%201%20Topline_FINAL.pdf.

11. Carroll Doherty, Jocelyn Kiley, and Olivia O'Hea, "Wide Gender Gap, Growing Educational Divide in Voters' Party Identification," Pew Research Center, March 20, 2018, https://www.people-press.org/2018/03/20/wide-gender-gap-growing-educational-divide-in-voters-party-identification.

12. Kim Parker, Nikki Graf, and Ruth Igielnik, "Generation Z Looks a Lot Like Millennials on Key Social and Political Issues," Pew Research Center, January 17, 2019, https://www.pewsocialtrends.org/2019/01/17/generation-z-looks-a-lot-like-millennials-on-key-social-and-political-issues.

13. Eliot Cohen, "The Republican Party Abandons Conservatism," *The Atlantic*, September 30, 2018, https://www.theatlantic.com/ideas/archive/2018/09/republican-party-conservative/571747.

14. Chris Massie, "Maine Gov. Paul LePage: Maybe the Country Needs Trump to Show 'Authoritarian Power.'" CNN, October 11, 2016, https://www.cnn.com/2016/10/11/politics/paul-lepage-authoritarian-power/index.html.

15. Ipsos, "Politicians Seen as Some of the Worst Things about America, and Most Americans Aren't Proud of America Right Now," June 27, 2018, https://www.ipsos.com/sites/default/files/ct/news/documents/2018-06/usa_today_patriotism_topline_062818.pdf

16. Amy B. Wang, "Some Trump Supporters Thought NPR Tweeted 'Propaganda.' It Was the Declaration of Independence," *Washington Post*, July 5, 2017, https://www.washingtonpost.com/news/the-fix/wp/2017/07/05/some-trump-supporters-thought-npr-tweeted-propaganda-it-was-the-declaration-of-independence.

17. Omarosa Manigault Newman, *Unhinged: An Insider's Account of the Trump White House* (New York: Gallery, 2018), 196.

18. David Lewicki, Twitter post, January 29, 2019, https://twitter.com/dlewicki/status/1090228039345147904.

19. Donald J. Trump, Twitter post, November 11, 2012, https://twitter.com/realDonaldTrump/status/267626951097868289.

20. Donald J. Trump, Twitter post, May 3, 2013, https://twitter.com/realDonaldTrump/status/330339116359225344.

21. Sarah Rodriguez, "Falwell Speaks: Interview Addresses Trump Endorsement," Liberty Champion, March 8, 2016, https://www.liberty.edu/champion/2016/03/falwell-speaks.

22. Franklin Graham, "Clinton's Sins Aren't Private," *Wall Street Journal*, August 27, 1998, https://www.wsj.com/articles/SB904162265981632000.

23. Russell Moore, Twitter post, June 24, 2019, https://twitter.com/drmoore/status/1143418475723055106.

24. Jerry Falwell, Twitter post, June 25, 2019, https://twitter.com/JerryFalwellJr/status/1143613031450103813.

25. Aliza Nadi and Ken Dilanian, "In Closed-Door Meeting, Trump Told Christian Leaders He Got Rid of a Law. He Didn't," NBC News, August 28, 2018, https://www.nbcnews.com/politics/elections/trump-told-christian-leaders-he-got-rid-law-he-didn-n904471.

26. Remarks by President Trump at the Faith and Freedom Coalition "Road to Majority" 2019 Conference, June 26, 2019, https://www.whitehouse.gov/briefings-statements/remarks-president-trump-faith-freedom-coalition-road-majority-2019-conference.

27. Mark Galli, "The Biggest Loser in the Alabama Election," *Christianity Today*, December 12, 2017, https://www.christianitytoday.com/ct/2017/december-web-only/roy-moore-doug-jones-alabama-editorial.html.

28. Sarah Pulliam Bailey, "Dozens of Evangelical Leaders Meet to Discuss How Trump Era Has Unleashed 'Grotesque Caricature' of Their Faith," *Washington Post*, April 16, 2018, https://www.washingtonpost.com/news/acts-of-faith/wp/2018/04/12/when-you-google-evangelicals-you-get-trump-high-profile-evangelicals-will-meet-privately-to-discuss-their-future.

29. Megan Brenan, "Religion Considered Important to 72% of Americans," Gallup, December 24, 2018, https://news.gallup.com/poll/245651/religion-considered-important-americans.aspx.

30. Mark Silk, "Why More and More Americans Think Religion Is Irrelevant," Religion News, December 31, 2018, https://religionnews.com/2018/12/31/why-more-and-more-americans-think-religion-is-irrelevant.

31. Alexis deTocqueville, *Democracy in America*, ed. George Lawrence, trans. J. P. Mayer (New York: Harper Perennial, 2000), 297–98.

32. Richard Danzig et al., "A Preface to Strategy: The Foundations of American National Security," Johns Hopkins Applied Physics Laboratory, December 11, 2018, https://www.jhuapl.edu/Content/documents/PrefaceToStrategy.pdf. See also: Will Marshall, "Donald Trump Has Zero Faith in the Power of American Ideas," *The Hill*, January 28, 2019, https://thehill.com/opinion/white-house/427258-donald-trump-has-zero-faith-in-the-power-of-american-ideas.

33. Steven Erlanger, "'Fake News,' Trump's Obsession, Is Now a Cudgel for Strongmen," *New York Times*, December 12, 2017, https://www.nytimes.com/2017/12/12/world/europe/trump-fake-news-dictators.html.

34. Remarks by President Trump and President Duda of the Republic of Poland Before Bilateral Meeting, June 12, 2019, https://www.whitehouse.gov/briefings-statements/remarks-president-trump-president-duda-republic-poland-bilateral-meeting-2.

35. Remarks by President Trump and Crown Prince Mohammad Bin Salman of the Kingdom of Saudi Arabia Before Working Breakfast, Osa-

ka, Japan, June 28, 2019, https://www.whitehouse.gov/briefings-statements/remarks-president-trump-crown-prince-mohammad-bin-salman-kingdom-saudi-arabia-working-breakfast-osaka-japan.

36. Remarks by President Trump in Press Conference, Osaka, Japan, June 29, 2019, https://www.whitehouse.gov/briefings-statements/remarks-president-trump-press-conference-osaka-japan.

37. Julian Borger, "Trump Jokes to Putin They Should 'Get Rid' of Journalists," *The Guardian*, June 28, 2019, https://www.theguardian.com/us-news/2019/jun/28/smirking-trump-jokes-to-putin-dont-meddle-in-us-election-g20.

38. Connor Mannion, "Putin, With Whom Trump Joked about 'Fake News,' Has Seen 26 Journalists Murdered during His Reign," Mediaite, June 28, 2019, https://www.mediaite.com/trump/putin-with-whom-trump-joked-about-fake-news-has-seen-26-journalists-murdered-during-his-reign.

39. Remarks by President Trump and President Putin of the Russian Federation before Bilateral Meeting, Osaka, Japan, June 28, 2019, https://www.whitehouse.gov/briefings-statements/remarks-president-trump-president-putin-russian-federation-bilateral-meeting-osaka-japan.

40. Remarks by President Trump in Press Conference, Osaka.

41. Remarks by President Trump and Chairman Kim Jong Un of the Democratic People's Republic of Korea in 1:1 Meeting, June 30, 2019, https://www.whitehouse.gov/briefings-statements/remarks-president-trump-chairman-kim-jong-un-democratic-peoples-republic-korea-11-meeting.

42. Remarks by President Trump to US Service Members, June 30, 2019, https://www.whitehouse.gov/briefings-statements/remarks-president-trump-u-s-service-members.

43. Megan Trimble, "America Perceived Less Trustworthy in Trump Era," *US News and World Report*, January 23, 2019, https://www.usnews.com/news/best-countries/articles/2019-01-23/america-falls-in-trustworthy-countries-ranking-under-trump.

44. John Gramlich and Kat Devlin, "More People around the World See U.S. Power and Influence as a 'Major Threat' to Their Country," Pew Research Center, February 14, 2019, https://www.pewresearch.org/fact-tank/2019/02/14/more-people-around-the-world-see-u-s-power-and-influence-as-a-major-threat-to-their-country.

45. Marc Bennetts, "Western Liberalism Is Obsolete, Warns Putin, Ahead of May Meeting," *The Guardian*, June 28, 2019, https://www.theguardian.com/world/2019/jun/27/putin-skripal-attack-should-not-affect-uk-russia-relations.

46. Vladimir Isachenkov, "Putin Says Liberalism 'Eating Itself,' Migrant Influx Wrong," Associated Press, June 29, 2019, https://www.washingtonpost.com/entertainment/music/putin-says-liberalism-eating-itself-migrant-influx-wrong/2019/06/29/15084dfc-9ad1-11e9-9a16-dc551ea5a43b_story.html.

47. Remarks by President Trump in Press Conference, Osaka.

48. James Madison, *Federalist 51*, https://avalon.law.yale.edu/18th_century/fed51.asp.

49. Mike DeBonis and Ellen Nakashima, "Democrats to Launch Fresh Push to Counter Foreign Interference in Elections," *Washington Post*, June 13, 2019, https://www.washingtonpost.com/world/national-security/democrats-to-launch-fresh-push-to-counter-foreign-interference-in-elections/2019/06/13/40d46b7c-7b42-11e9-8bb7-0fc796cf2ec0_story.html.

50. Dan Clark, "Trump Was Outspent by His Closest Primary Opponents," PolitiFact, July 1, 2016, https://www.politifact.com/new-york/statements/2016/jul/01/michael-caputo/trump-was-outspent-his-closest-primary-opponents.

51. Niv Sultan, "Election 2016: Trump's Free Media Helped Keep Cost Down, but Fewer Donors Provided More of the Cash," Open Secrets, April 13, 2017, https://www.opensecrets.org/news/2017/04/election-2016-trump-fewer-donors-provided-more-of-the-cash.

52. Newt Gingrich, "A Dictatorial President Obama versus the American People's Congress," Gingrich 360, November 14, 2014, https://www.gingrich360.com/2014/11/a-dictatorial-president-obama-versus-the-american-peoples-congress.

53. Kevin McCarthy, "Congress Stands Athwart Obama's Imperial Presidency," *National Review*, March 17, 2016, https://www.nationalreview.com/2016/03/obama-congress-constitution-supreme-court-immigration-lawsuit/.

54. James Madison, "Notes on the Debates in the Federal Convention," July 20, 1787, https://avalon.law.yale.edu/18th_century/debates_720.asp

55. Neha Prakash, "Donald Trump Freaks Out on Twitter after Obama Wins Election," Mashable, November 6, 2012, https://mashable.com/2012/11/06/trump-reacts-to-election.

56. Donald J. Trump, Twitter post, November 6, 2012, https://twitter.com/realDonaldTrump/status/266034630820507648.

57. Donald J. Trump, Twitter post, November 6, 2012, https://twitter.com/realDonaldTrump/status/266035509162303492.

58. Donald J. Trump, Twitter post, November 6, 2012, https://twitter.com/realDonaldTrump/status/266034957875544064.

59. "Trump: If I Were President Khan's Son Wouldn't Have Died; Election in November Will Be Rigged," Fox News, August 1, 2016, https://www.foxnews.com/transcript/trump-if-i-were-president-khans-son-wouldnt-have-died-election-in-november-will-be-rigged.

60. David Becker, "Updating Voter Registration," Pew Research Center, February 28, 2012, https://www.pewtrusts.org/en/research-and-analysis/articles/2012/02/28/david-becker-upgrading-voter-registration.

61. Commission on Presidential Debates, October 19, 2016, Debate Transcript, https://www.debates.org/voter-education/debate-transcripts/october-19-2016-debate-transcript.

62. Matt Ford, "Did Donald Trump Jr. Cross the Line with Wiki-Leaks?" *The Atlantic*, November 14, 2017, https://www.theatlantic.com/politics/archive/2017/11/donald-trump-jr-wikileaks/545894.

63. Donald J. Trump, Twitter post, February 9, 2019, https://twitter.com/realDonaldTrump/status/1094242164857556992.

64. Dylan Scott, "Michael Cohen's Parting Shot: I Fear What Happens If Trump Loses in 2020," Vox, February 27, 2019, https://www.vox.com/policy-and-politics/2019/2/27/18243686/michael-cohen-testimony-closing-statement.

65. Alexander Hamilton, "Enclosure: [Objections and Answers Respecting the Administration]," August 18, 1792, https://founders.archives.gov/documents/Hamilton/01-12-02-0184-0002.

INDEX

ABOUT THE AUTHOR

John J. Pitney Jr. writes for USA Today, The National Review, Claremont Review of Books, and other publications and is frequently interviewed by the Los Angeles Times, National Public Radio, and many other media outlets. He teaches political science at Claremont McKenna College and resides in Claremont, California.